Introduction to Existentialism

Also available at Bloomsbury

*Medieval Philosophy: A Multicultural Reader*, ed. Bruce Foltz
*Phenomenology: An Introduction*, Michael Lewis

# Introduction to Existentialism

From Kierkegaard to *The Seventh Seal*

Robert L. Wicks

BLOOMSBURY ACADEMIC
LONDON • NEW YORK • OXFORD • NEW DELHI • SYDNEY

BLOOMSBURY ACADEMIC
Bloomsbury Publishing Plc
50 Bedford Square, London, WC1B 3DP, UK
1385 Broadway, New York, NY 10018, USA

BLOOMSBURY, BLOOMSBURY ACADEMIC and the Diana logo are trademarks
of Bloomsbury Publishing Plc

First published in Great Britain 2020

Copyright © Robert L. Wicks, 2020

Robert L. Wicks has asserted his right under the Copyright, Designs and Patents Act, 1988, to be identified as Author of this work.

For legal purposes the Acknowledgments on p. viii constitute an extension of this copyright page.

Cover design by Alice Marwick
Photographs © Elia Clerici, Hannah Eckman and Johny Greig

All rights reserved. No part of this publication may be reproduced or transmitted in any form or by any means, electronic or mechanical, including photocopying, recording, or any information storage or retrieval system, without prior permission in writing from the publishers.

Bloomsbury Publishing Plc does not have any control over, or responsibility for, any third-party websites referred to or in this book. All internet addresses given in this book were correct at the time of going to press. The author and publisher regret any inconvenience caused if addresses have changed or sites have ceased to exist, but can accept no responsibility for any such changes.

A catalogue record for this book is available from the British Library.

A catalog record for this book is available from the Library of Congress.

ISBN: HB: 978-1-4411-8893-9
PB: 978-1-4411-9234-9
ePDF: 978-1-4742-7252-0
eBook: 978-1-4742-7253-7

Typeset by Deanta Global Publishing Services, Chennai, India

To find out more about our authors and books visit www.bloomsbury.com and sign up for our newsletters.

# Contents

| | |
|---|---|
| Preface | vi |
| Acknowledgments | viii |
| 1 Introduction: An Earthly and Earthy Outlook | 1 |

Part One  Six Traditional Existentialist Thinkers

| | |
|---|---|
| 2 Søren Kierkegaard (1813–55) | 13 |
| 3 Friedrich Nietzsche (1844–1900) | 34 |
| 4 Martin Heidegger (1889–1976) | 57 |
| 5 Jean-Paul Sartre (1905–80) | 79 |
| 6 Albert Camus (1913–60) | 98 |
| 7 Simone de Beauvoir (1908–86) | 115 |

Part Two  Existentialism in Religion, Culture, Psychology, and Film

| | |
|---|---|
| 8 Christian Existentialism | 131 |
| 9 Jewish Existentialism | 144 |
| 10 American Existentialism | 157 |
| 11 Existentialist Psychology | 171 |
| 12 Existentialism in the Cinema | 184 |
| 13 Conclusion: Why Existentialism Today?—The Need for Realistic, Humane, and Responsible Leadership | 209 |
| Bibliography | 215 |
| Index | 220 |

# Preface

This book divides into two parts. The first half presents the thought of six philosophers who have been traditionally described as leading exponents of existentialist thought; the second presents existentialism more thematically, as influenced by Christianity and Judaism, as it first appeared influentially in America, and as it has impacted upon psychology as well as the cinema. The treatment has been selective due to constraints of space, but I have tried to provide solidly representative thinkers in the various spheres when there were many from which to choose. The chapter on Christian existentialism highlights Paul Tillich and Gabriel Marcel; the chapter on Jewish existentialism features Franz Rosenzweig and Martin Buber. The chapter on existentialist psychology focuses on Viktor Frankl and R. D. Laing, with Rollo May and Ludwig Binswanger as the formative thinkers. The chapter on existentialism in the cinema discusses some films that have been canonically associated with existentialism such as *The Seventh Seal* and *Ikiru*, in addition to others, including two by Woody Allen, that impressed me as having strong and illustrative existentialist resonance.

Interpretations of the philosophers represented are always affected by the background assumptions and experience of the interpreters. My own orientation is historically centered and guided by a hermeneutical ideal that is impossible to realize, namely, to try to understand the philosophers as they understood themselves, in their own time period, with their particular interests. In this respect I have tried to be faithful to the philosophers involved, although my own judgment of what is essential to their thought, and what is not, has inevitably entered into the exposition.

Some of the philosophers who are discussed never heard of a philosophical movement called "existentialism"—Kierkegaard and Nietzsche, for instance—and some disavowed the label at one time or another, sometimes emphatically, such as Albert Camus and Martin Heidegger. This was usually to distance and distinguish themselves from Jean-Paul Sartre's presentation of existentialism. I refer to them all as "existentialist" philosophers in recognition of the basic contents of their philosophical outlooks and their historical reception, rather than in view of the more local controversies in which they were engaged.

# Acknowledgments

The foundation of this book extends back several decades to when I was graduate student at the University of Wisconsin-Madison, working as a teaching assistant for a course in existentialism taught by one of my respected instructors, and now good friend, Ivan Soll. Some years after that, when I began teaching at the University of Auckland in New Zealand, one of my courses—a course that I taught for a number of years, and still do occasionally—was on twentieth-century French philosophy. I owe a great deal to Ivan for initially exposing me to existentialism, as well as to my many students in Auckland over the years who inspired me to think about the existentialist philosophers in greater depth than I might otherwise have. My studies in Zen Buddhism also contributed to the perspective from which I write, having shown me a further and alternative way to have a down-to-earth outlook and to be down to earth.

More recently, I owe thanks to a group of friends and fellow-scholars that especially include John Bishop, Vladimir Krstic, Geoffrey Roche, Matheson Russell, Paul Taillon, Paul Warren, and Daniel Wilson, with whom I've had productive conversations about the philosophical figures and themes described in this book. An anonymous reviewer of an earlier version of the manuscript was extremely helpful in showing me how to improve the expository accuracy, to whom I am thankful. Finally, my appreciation goes to the person who assisted and persevered with me in the editorial realm—Frankie Mace—whose patience, understanding, and helpfulness allowed me to complete the book in a longer time period than either of us had originally anticipated.

I dedicate this book lovingly to the memory of my father, my brother, and my nephew, Charles Edward Wicks III, along with the fathers of my best friends when growing up, Al and Rich, whose moral integrity, kindness, intelligence, and professionalism served impeccably as role models to me when I was young, Myron M. Nagelberg, and Marvin J. Levy.

# 1

# Introduction: An Earthly and Earthy Outlook

The fundamental orientation of the existentialist outlook—"being-down-to-earth"—is easy to appreciate. If an existentialist discusses God in a positive way, then he or she will conceive of God as an earthly presence, rather than as a being in a heavenly beyond. If the subject of discussion is the human being, then there will be little interest in the immortality of the soul as a serious proposition. The focus will rather be on how it feels to be a human being facing inevitable death. In the same earthly spirit, abstractions such as "the perfect circle," "ideal justice," or "pure love" that presumably reside on another otherworldly dimension will be replaced by detailed characterizations of actual things, human relationships and feelings, in this or that place and time.

Instead of invoking broad generalizations such as "the human being," which refer to people facelessly, collectively, and universalistically, an existentially oriented interest tends to focus on specific individuals who happen to wear these clothes today, who breathe now at a certain rate, and who presently have particular beliefs and desires in mind. This mentality accordingly recoils at abstractive, cartoonlike, one-dimensional caricatures of full-blooded, complex people, as when a newspaper labels a certain man a "murderer" or "thief" and obscures his personal history as someone's son, husband, father, uncle, next-door neighbor, and coworker.

Although the existentialist outlook is realistic, it is relatively recent in its philosophical formulation, emerging saliently as a culturally influential force only after the scientific revolution of the seventeenth and eighteenth centuries. Previously inspirational was an opposing perspective—one that remains strong and popular—namely, an abstractive, scientific outlook that intentionally disregards, or tries to discern beneath and beyond, the immediate perceptual details of what appears before us. Its goal is to comprehend for the sake of prediction and control of nature the stable, underlying principles that govern the diversity of worldly change. Let us consider that alternative perspective for a moment.

Thinking in terms of the law of gravitation is a prime example. Suppose we are in a stadium filled with cheering people, each of whom has a distinct appearance, previous history, hopes, fears, and plans. A scientific mind, perhaps of an engineer, would be disposed to consider, for example, the combined effect of the weight of the people upon the building's material supports as they jump up and down. With the same attitude, one might survey an entire landscape with trees, houses, people, animals, farm equipment, and such, reflecting upon how these aesthetically interesting perceptual differences tend to obscure, rather than reveal, the gravitational forces that ground them all.

The scientific mind aims to capture the essences of the things in the world, inanimate and animate, by attending especially to their mathematically describable properties that fit exactly into the shapes of formulas. What objects have in common, what is constant between them as the kinds of things they are, and what stably underlies the diversity of appearances are central.

Whereas one ordinarily might perceive as separate phenomena the ocean, the clouds, and the steam rising from someone's hot cup of tea on an autumn afternoon, the scientific mind discerns the same chemical compound, water, in its various forms. Whereas one ordinarily might acknowledge the presence of many religions in the world, or many philosophies, or many arts, the scientific mind—and we can refer to this also as the Enlightenment mind or even as the classically philosophic mind, for we have the same mentality in Socrates and Plato—would ignore differences in ritual, doctrine, or practice for the sake of discerning what all religions, philosophies, or arts have in common.

With respect to religion, it is frequently thought that the ethical core—the familiar rule of which is that we should treat each other with love and respect—is what religion is essentially about. According to this abstractive style of mind, differences in historical details and ritual expression become tangential, beside the essential and universal point.

Although during the seventeenth and eighteenth centuries, scientists and mathematicians were sometimes regarded with suspicion by religious authorities as proponents of atheism, the intellectual atmosphere and prevailing philosophies were nonetheless steeped in religious language and religiously oriented philosophical questions. In the philosophies of René Descartes (1596–1650), Nicholas Malebranche (1638–1715), Gottfried Wilhelm Leibniz (1646–1716), Baruch Spinoza (1632–77), and George Berkeley (1685–1753), to name some major representatives, the concept of God remains crucial as it consolidates and integrates their outlooks to resolve problems that would otherwise receive no solution.

For the most part, the philosophies of that era are impossible to understand without attending carefully to the positions taken on God's existence. Even Immanuel Kant (1724–1804), writing at the end of this Enlightenment period in the late 1700s, despite his skepticism toward traditional proofs of God's existence, wholly advocates a moral argument for God's existence. Without it, he is at a loss to explain how the highest good can be realized.

The nineteenth-century European philosophers from whose thought issued a more existentialist mentality framed their views within a religiously defined atmosphere as well. Complementing his emphasis upon concrete, realistic thinking, G. W. F. Hegel (1770–1831) is also sometimes described as one of the greatest theologians of the time. With his notable humanism and materialism, Ludwig Feuerbach (1804–72) also expressed himself in distinctively religious language. Søren Kierkegaard (1813–55)—our first theorist—spent his life struggling with what it means to become a genuine Christian. Friedrich Nietzsche (1844–1900)—a philosopher whose thought we will discuss in light of Kierkegaard's—proclaimed himself emphatically to be an anti-Christian, certainly inverting, but also heavily depending upon, the problems and verbiage of Judeo-Christian spirituality. His most well-known book *Thus Spoke Zarathustra* (1883–85) inverts, mimics, and parodies biblical passages and themes throughout.

Such nineteenth-century thinkers developed views that aim to provide a meaning to human life within a religious and cultural context that has been infiltrated by nihilistic despair. Although the sheer fact of widespread human suffering is sufficient to question whether there are benevolent, meaning-lending forces that underlie the natural world, the intensified, down-to-earth historical awareness that characterized the beginnings of the nineteenth century—an awareness that rendered increasingly implausible, hypotheses of a just and rewarding world beyond—underscored the need to establish a more earthly beachhead for human meaning.

## 1.1 The divided religious consciousness

Hegel's characterization of the inner tensions and frustrations of the religious consciousness—he refers to it as the "unhappy consciousness"—in his *Phenomenology of Spirit* (1807) does well to reveal the existential condition that thinkers such as Kierkegaard and Nietzsche—not to mention Fyodor Dostoevsky (1821–81), Leo Tolstoy (1828–1910), and Arthur Schopenhauer (1788–1860)—were experiencing, and were trying to resolve in their writings. In his portrayal of the unhappy consciousness, the religiously oriented consciousness seeks meaning—seeks its true self—by uniting with God through a series of methods, only to suffer continual frustration in its inescapable finitude. The upshot of its journey is to descend into a condition of meaninglessness—one that within existentialist thought looms definitively in the background of the human condition: no matter how the unhappy consciousness seeks unification with God, human finitude stares back frustratingly, unhappily, and seemingly inescapably.

The unhappy consciousness works through a series of ways to relate to God, all of which occur universally. One can worship God as an inscrutable and infinitely distant being beyond, hoping for a mysterious dispensation of strength and moral favor through prayer and the careful observance of ritual. An example is the orientation toward God found in the Hebrew scriptures, as well as some of Kierkegaard's final sermons. One can alternatively worship God in an objectified physical form separate from oneself, in the appearance of a divine savior, prophet, emperor, king, holy site, or relic. Included here is Jesus as an earthly materialization of God, along with the veneration of Jerusalem as a holy city and destination for religious pilgrimage. Similarly, one can work on the earth itself, imagined to be a quasi-divine physical body created by God, devoting oneself to it and nurturing it. Generations of monks who have lovingly and selflessly tended monastery fields exemplify this approach to divinity.

Although the shared hope is to experience the salvation of God's spirit infusing itself throughout one's being, in each of these relationships God remains external and alien. Even in the next step, when one assumes that the human being harbors God within itself as a dimension of its true substance, Hegel notes that the difficulty in uniting with God—a struggle now conceived of as that of achieving metaphysical harmony with oneself—painfully persists.

At this more intimate level it is appreciated that human beings' very capacity to imagine the infinite reveals a transcendent dimension within themselves. We might appear to be smaller than specks of dust from the standpoint of a distant star, but we nonetheless apprehend both imaginatively and with astounding mathematical detail the infinite expanse of space and time with its billions of galaxies, within which that star is situated. We can also turn our gaze in the opposite direction and appreciate equally the immeasurably tiny world of subatomic particles that is again endlessly explorable. As they fill our imagination, the infinitely large and infinitely small are both within the range of our comprehension. This is a staggering, almost divine, capacity for what can appear to be a mere speck in the cosmic expanse.

A person's self-conception is consequently conflicted, like oil and water, or worse yet, like the inseparable north and south poles of a magnet. One seems to be both body and mind, finite and infinite, determined and free, and if one extrapolates, mortal and immortal. Kierkegaard conveys this by saying "if there were nothing eternal in a human being, the person would simply be unable to despair" (Kierkegaard 1989: 51). Also recognizing the difficulty of reconciling this array of dualisms, Kierkegaard refers to the ultimate synthesis and realization of our true self as a distant goal:

> A human being is a synthesis of the infinite and the finite, of the temporal and the eternal, of freedom and necessity. In short, a synthesis. A synthesis is a relation between two terms. Looked at in this way, a human being is not yet a self. (Kierkegaard 1989: 43)

Hegel describes how the religious consciousness, frustrated in its attempt to achieve unity, suffers acutely from this dualistic condition:

> This *unhappy, inwardly disrupted* consciousness, since its essentially contradictory nature is for it a *single* consciousness, must for ever have present in the one consciousness the other also; and thus it is driven out of each in turn in the very moment when it imagines it has successfully attained to a peaceful unity with the other. (Hegel 1977: 126, unless otherwise noted, the emphasis is as in the original quotations in all indented quotes.)

Hegel refers here to the inner turmoil of a religious ascetic, but his observation is relevant to all people who seek God. After experiencing a profound insight into the divine nature of things, physical demands return one to the ordinary, instinctually driven field of activity. After some further time in the mundane environment and with the resurgence of the longing to unite with God, one revisits the more inspired otherworldly state of mind, feeling once again satisfied and ecstatic, but only until one starts to fall back again into the commonplace. A constant swinging back and forth of this kind is sufficiently engaging, forceful, and frustrating, to define the experiential structure of a lifetime.

With respect to our interest in existentialism, Hegel identifies the rock-bottom point of the religious consciousness' quest to unify with God as a condition filled with feelings of utter despair. It arises like this: after identifying first with the divine, universal, and meaningful aspect of itself, only to be driven back repeatedly into an awareness of itself as a worldly, trivial individual, the religious consciousness experiences a moment of reflection that leads it to disengage itself from, and consequently abandon, the entire project of trying to identify substantially with either aspect of itself. It forsakes its physical individuality along with its spiritual universality, recognizing itself to be merely the insubstantial, empty transition point between two struggling and incongruent poles.

With this loss of substance, the religious consciousness experiences the proverbial dark night of the soul. It feels like nothing, hopelessly akin to the imaginary line that demarcates without any substance, two patches of color, just as the letters on this page stand demarcated against their background by a line with no thickness, or mere differential.

As a consequence of its intensifying and prolonged frustration, the unhappy consciousness finds itself in limbo, hanging in emptiness between the physical world and God. Having forsaken its identity as either a material body or immaterial soul, suspended between the two and lacking any real sense of self, the religious consciousness regards itself as a nonentity.

It is a testament to Hegel's genius that he discerned how this dark night of the soul entails its own sunlight and salvation. Consider, at first, how the religious consciousness struggles with the incongruence between mind and body, trying to achieve some unity of its opposing aspects. This internal conflict may be described alternatively as spirit as opposed to flesh, universal as opposed to individual, permanence as opposed to flux, reality as opposed to illusion, truth as opposed to deception, freedom as opposed to determinism, eternal as opposed to temporal, infinite as opposed to finite, and God as opposed to human. By disengaging from both sides of the opposition, however defined, and identifying simply with the relation that stands between them, the religious consciousness retreats and dislocates to an intermediary position.

The original situation's fundamental form—one of dualistic opposition—thus undergoes a transformation. Whereas the religious consciousness initially conceives of its predicament in *binary*, "either/or" terms—either God or human, mind or body—a *three-termed* structure emerges to cast new light on the religious consciousness' experience. There is God, there is the human being, and there is the intermediary position between the two, suspended and in itself empty, but connecting the two nonetheless. As empty as it may be, Hegel observes that this intermediary role is none other than the structural equivalent of the role assumed by a priest, Jesus-figure, religious leader, or prophet, whose social position is to convey the word of God to people and to speak to God for the people.

Upon finding itself in this intermediary position, and dimly, if only subconsciously, realizing that it has become the bare form of a priest, the religious consciousness apprehends that salvation is within reach. It still lacks content as nothing more than a transitional point, but a renewed sense of self begins to crystallize, along with a confidence that starts to surpass its fading despair.

As Hegel sees it, the next logical step is for the religious consciousness to fill its empty self with some spiritual substance, having grown unexpectedly into a priestly shape appropriate for its needs. This involves a worldly search for masterful figures who can act as spiritual advisors and educators, whose substance the religious consciousness can absorb to become a real priest, thus giving content to its empty form.

Hegel's analysis rings true to some extent. It is common knowledge that after having suffered through utter destitution and despair, many people "find God" and are "saved," and moreover, often proceed to assume the role of a religious teacher in their communities to guide others. What, however, do Kierkegaard and Nietzsche say about priests? Their comments make us wonder about who, exactly, one is supposed to enlist as an enlightening spiritual advisor subsequent to a dark night of the soul and what the result of our religious quest would be in a less philosophically abstract, more existentially valid context:

> In a little country, scarcely three poets are born to each generation, but priests are plentiful, many more than get appointments. The poet is said to have a call; in the minds of most people (and that means Christians) to be

a priest it is enough to have passed an examination. And yet, a true priest is an even greater rarity than a true poet, and the word "call" has originally a religious sense. (Kierkegaard 1989: 134–35)

As is well known, the priests are the most evil enemies—but why? Because they are the most impotent. It is because of their impotence that in them hatred grows to monstrous and uncanny proportions, to the most spiritual and poisonous kind of hatred. The truly great haters in world history have always been priests; likewise the most ingenious haters: other kinds of spirit hardly come into consideration when compared with the spirit of priestly vengefulness. (Nietzsche 1969: 33)

## 1.2 The disengagement of freedom from rationality

We can ask here at the outset why the problem of "finding oneself," "becoming authentic," or "establishing a meaningful life for oneself in the face of primal contradictions" appears as a central theme in existentialist thought. Why was the issue *not* as pressing in earlier theorists? Exemplary is the structure of Kant's outlook, where the troubling and searching problem of finding oneself does not significantly arise in his discussion of human meaning and destiny. Authenticity and the reconciliation of basic philosophical tensions, such as that between freedom and determinism, are built into his theory as the immediate upshot of realizing effectively what we humans unavoidably are.

Kant maintains classically that humans are essentially rational animals, governed by logical forms and the idea of reason. On his view, we inevitably structure our experience in a logical way. When it comes to our self-conception and our self-respect, we recognize our rational side as superior, dignified, and unconditional, and within moral contexts, how it precipitates an inner demand for everyone to behave consistently.

Since Kant equates our moral awareness with our self-respect as rational beings and our consequent esteem for consistent behavior, acting morally becomes straightforwardly a matter of realizing our rational potential by being true to ourselves. We always remain free to do otherwise, of course, but our sense of respect for ourselves as dignified rational beings guides and shapes our freedom. It is always possible to make irrational choices, but it goes against the grain of what we essentially are. The inherent resistance to be irrational, moreover, gives a solid meaning to the human condition: our ultimate purpose is to realize our rational substance in a perfect moral community.

There are many ways to conceive of human beings, though, one of which is to regard humans not as essentially rational but as essentially free. Our freedom can be located at our core, absolute and fully divorced from rationality, and once we conceive of ourselves in this way, a new world of responsibility comes into view. Life is no longer a classical matter of realizing our rationality. Human meaning is now determined by our will, and it depends squarely upon the choices we make. Instead of asking "Who am I?" in view of a fixed essence or potentiality we are disposed to realize, the question becomes "What shall I make of myself?" as if facing a blank canvas.

Kierkegaard is often referred to as the "father of existentialism," but we should also recognize Arthur Schopenhauer, who published *The World as Will and Representation* in 1818, when Kierkegaard was only three years old. Among the major philosophers of his time, most of whom were still equating reality with rationality, Schopenhauer was the first to argue at length that ultimate reality is irrational, characterizing it as a meaningless and timeless primal impulse that is best called "Will." As manifestations of irrational Will, human beings are filled with endless and insatiable desire, which ordinarily produces feelings of conflict and frustration to the last breath.

Unlike Kierkegaard and later existentialists, Schopenhauer did not elevate individual human choice to supremacy, but by disengaging freedom from rationality and by transporting the sheer force of will into the core of reality itself, he opened the door to the idea that human choice, free from rationality, is the prime determinant of human meaning. It is revealing to hear Dostoevsky give a Schopenauerian voice, existentially augmented, to his main character in his 1864 novella *Notes from the Underground* (i.e., notes from the cellar):

> You see, gentlemen, reason is an excellent thing, there's no disputing that, but reason is nothing but reason and satisfies only the rational side of man's nature, while will is a manifestation of the whole life, that is, of the whole human life including reason and all the impulses. And although our life, in this manifestation of it, is often worthless, yet it is life and not simply extracting square roots. (Dostoevsky 1956: 73)

In his quest for truth, Schopenhauer furthermore emphasizes the importance of identifying with the inner experience and inner character of everything, as opposed to attending in an alienated fashion to the merely external, scientific, objective presentations of that inner reality. Appreciating how people and animals suffer, how viciousness permeates life, and how deeper instinctual forces underlie human behavior, Schopenhauer tried to coincide imaginatively with the inner being of things, similar to how Freud sympathetically examined the structure of the unconscious. This concentration upon the internal and psychological, as opposed to the external and scientific, is another of Schopenhauer's contributions to the existentialist tradition.

As initially mentioned, an existentialist orientation intends to be down to earth. One can be down to earth, however, in the manner of an atheist and a materialist, and have little appreciation for the internal, private psychological states that people experience, perhaps going so far as to exclude them altogether from an understanding of what it means to be human. Schopenhauer's contrasting emphasis upon the inner being of the world foreshadows how in the existentialist tradition the psychological experience of making, as well as avoiding, real choices—ones that give meaning to our lives—becomes central. As we shall see, the experience typically involves dread, anxiety, and suffering in the face of responsibility.

Part One

# Six Traditional Existentialist Thinkers

2

# Søren Kierkegaard (1813–55)

## 2.1 Kierkegaard's existentiality

As an existentialist thinker, Kierkegaard is renowned for his persistent criticisms of Hegel, who made it his lifelong effort to construct a perfectly comprehensive philosophical system. Assuming its unrealistic quality from the start, Kierkegaard refers derisively to Hegel's grand philosophy as "the System," holding it up for everyone's recognition as a false ideal. Notwithstanding Hegel's genius, there is a sense in which Kierkegaard's judgment is correct: the world's perceptual details resist a seamless capture and systematization in a humanly constructed network of abstract concepts, and Kierkegaard makes the most of this fact.

With the same pragmatic and critical disposition toward philosophy, Marx remarked with a similar dissatisfaction that "philosophers have only *interpreted* the world, in various ways; the point, however, is to *change* it" (Marx 1978: 145). Comparing well to Marx, Kierkegaard aims for something beyond a philosophical interpretation of the world. He seeks a direct, truth-filled experience of what it means to be an existing human being.

Kierkegaard consequently has little sympathy for Hegel's expansive metaphysical aspirations and philosophical claims to have attained absolute knowledge. With his strong existential orientation toward the world, impressed by the sheer presence—some call it the "this-ness"—of things, abstract systems of philosophy appear to Kierkegaard as unconvincing expressions of truth. The presence of things slips through their philosophizing's finest abstractions, just as tiny fish swim through a fishnet's holes.

Not only do philosophical systems fall short of capturing the immediate reality of things as they appear in sense perception, the systems are limited in their ability to convey the subjective richness of human experience and, hence, to present the full truth of that experience. As one's outlook becomes increasingly concrete, the detailed inner experiences of individuals call out for inclusion in any attempt to understand the human condition, as well as what would count as a meaningful life. Once, however, a person's feelings within some determinate context come into play—for instance, finding out that one is terminally ill, as we can read in Tolstoy's *The Death of Ivan Ilyich* (1886)—philosophical systems that intend to secure truth appear to be out of touch.

Hence arises a strong motivation to enhance traditional philosophical modes of expression with literary modes, supposing that the latter's more nuanced and multifaceted descriptions of human experience might realistically move us closer to a truthful awareness of ourselves. It is no accident that existentialist thinkers such as Sartre and Camus also wrote novels, that Dostoevsky is a leading existentialist writer, that both Nietzsche and Heidegger were advocates of poetry, and that Kierkegaard's prose is spiced with entertaining anecdotes, fictional characters, and literary excursions. When their down-to-earth mentality eventually runs up against the limits of literalistic, generalized, and abstract philosophical expression, they are led to supplement it with other ways of writing—ones that more effectively include the details of lived experience in reference to both sensory perception and personal feelings. The disposition toward an increasingly concrete outlook challenges the effectiveness of philosophy itself.

Although Hegel was committed to expressing philosophical ideas in literalistic terms, it is unfortunate that he is not sufficiently appreciated in relation to his predecessors as a champion of a more down-to-earth outlook. He himself criticized philosophers such as Kant, Fichte, and Schelling for philosophizing in a manner that was too abstract, one-sided, formalistic, and insufficiently historical for capturing the full truth. It is ironic that Kierkegaard aims the same kind of criticism at Hegel, as appropriate as it is within the later context of the 1840s.

Hegel's *Phenomenology of Spirit* (1807) exemplifies his own groundbreaking attempt to achieve a more concrete outlook. The book ambitiously arranges in a developmental order almost every possible perspective in the theory of knowledge, ranging from the most superficially sensory and immediate orientations toward the world, to the most inclusively cultural and reflective, constructing thereby an ascending and ever-encompassing spiral of comprehension that carries us to the point of realizing what true knowing ought to be. Admittedly, Hegel's characterizations of each form of knowledge vary in their detail and depth, but no one before had ever outlined the different ways to know the world as comprehensively, sequentially, and systematically. Most examinations of human knowledge written before the publication of Hegel's *Phenomenology* appear contrastingly thin and one dimensional.

Within its literalistic register, the *Phenomenology* achieves a more multidimensional expression of truth as an upshot of its dialectically structured method. Inspired by the elementary structure of self-consciousness and noticing how a wide range of phenomena—especially those related to human beings, considered both individually and socially—develop accordingly through a process of opposition and reconciliation, Hegel applies this dynamic structure in the construction of his theory of knowledge and philosophical system as a whole. With a sweeping overview of people and human history, he perceives that conflict tends toward peace, isolation toward sociality, oppression toward freedom, unconsciousness toward self-awareness, simplicity toward complexity, and narrow-mindedness toward increased sophistication, usually through a painful and laborious process of opposition and reconciliation. His method leaves no view completely negated and is impressively comprehensive in this regard.

Inspired by Hegel's example, Kierkegaard is also acutely aware of the deep tensions in human experience, but he observes realistically that no finite being will ever comprehend all of reality in full systematic detail, Hegel included. This is only possible for God. To make his point, he recalls the remarks of Gotthold Ephraim Lessing (1729–81) that urge us to appreciate that with respect to attaining absolute knowledge, we humans can at best strive persistently for truth, and nothing more. Lessing states that if God held all truth in his right hand and the everlasting pursuit of truth in his left, with the condition that one could be everlastingly mistaken, and asked him to choose one hand or the other, he would still choose the left, for the absolute truth, Lessing reverently concedes, is reserved only for God.

Matching his agreement with Lessing, Kierkegaard favors the more humanly aware Socrates in contrast to the otherworldly Plato. According to Kierkegaard, Socrates appreciated insightfully that the truth resides within ourselves—to find the truth we must introspect with intense self-penetration—and that it will always appear to us as an irresolvable puzzle. Socrates's famous insistence of his ignorance, of how he knows that he does not know, marks and acknowledges this finitude.

Socrates's humility in the face of the cosmos, Kierkegaard maintains, sets him above most other people who take their relationship to truth as easy and for granted. In their unreflective confidence and failure to realize how incomprehensible everything is, he believes that these individuals fail to appreciate their human position and condition. To the contrary, being aware of one's ignorance like Socrates—that is, situating oneself at the opposite end of the epistemological spectrum from Hegel or Plato—is the epitome of an honest, down-to-earth mentality:

> The Socratic ignorance, which Socrates held fast with the entire passion of his inwardness, was thus an expression for the principle that the eternal truth is related to an existing individual, and that this truth must therefore be a paradox for him as long as he exists; and yet it is possible that there was more truth in the Socratic ignorance as it was in him, than in the entire objective truth of the [Hegelian] System, which flirts with what the times demand and accommodates itself to the *Privatdocents*. (Kierkegaard 1941: 180–81)

The paradox and absurdity to which Kierkegaard refers is that the eternal truth has come into being in time. In Christian terms—the ones in which he tends to speak—the paradox and absurdity is that God, an infinite being regarded as the creator and master of the universe, became a finite human being who was born, grew up, and suffered the same fate and fatality as any other perishable individual. For Kierkegaard, contemplating absurdities such as these plays a central role in experiencing the intense inwardness that he calls "truth as subjectivity."

At present, we need notice only that despite his condemnations of Hegel, who often seems to be his arch-enemy, Kierkegaard shares Hegel's philosophical disposition to discern patterns of opposition and conceptual tension, here expressed in reference to the conflict between the eternal and the historical. In Kierkegaard's writings, however, these oppositions frequently assume the form of "double-bind" structures or dilemmas, where two paths are marked out, and where each leads to a frustrating dead end. Typically, he does not blend, reconcile, or resolve the two opposing sides into a harmonious synthesis as does Hegel. Kierkegaard rather leaves the tension-ridden situation exactly as it is, opting instead to break away from the "either/or" dilemma by introducing an entirely different approach from another angle, after playing out each option.

We should note here how Hegel's influence enters into Kierkegaard's writing style. Like many of Hegel's passages, the following excerpt from one of Kierkegaard's later and hallmark books *The Sickness Unto Death*—a segment of which we cited in the Introduction—is particularly dense and difficult to decipher. It is indeed so dense that its immediate incomprehensibility could lead one to wonder whether Kierkegaard is poking fun at Hegel. It seems, though, that Kierkegaard speaks seriously when he begins his book with the following:

> The human being is spirit. But what is spirit? Spirit is the self. But what is the self? The self is a relation which relates to itself, or that in the relation which is its relating to itself. The self is not the relation but the relation's relating to itself. A human being is a synthesis of the infinite and the finite, of the temporal and the eternal, of freedom and necessity. In short a synthesis. A synthesis is a relation between two terms. Looked at in this way, a human being is not yet a self. (Kierkegaard 1989: 43)

One can interpret this passage as saying that we are self-conscious beings who have not yet achieved—and, as it is implicitly suggested, will never achieve—full self-consciousness to become a true "self," which is indeed the endpoint of Hegel's philosophical system. Part of the reason for our perpetual incompleteness is that we are paradoxical beings who harbor within ourselves a set of fundamental and seemingly irreconcilable metaphysical tensions. As Hegel describes this conflicted condition, and as we discussed earlier, we are— as far Fas Kierkegaard can see—inescapably "unhappy consciousnesses." This is Kierkegaard's existential point about the human condition, of which we will speak more. For the present, we should note simply the Hegelian writing style and influence in the above passage.

It remains that Kierkegaard's sensitivity to being a presently existing individual surpasses Hegel's. Perhaps unsurprisingly, such a feeling of finitude precipitates a comparable *aesthetic* appreciation of the incomprehensibly rich details of sensory experience. Consider an excerpt from Jean-Paul Sartre's novel *Nausea* (1938) which displays well the tension Kierkegaard perceives between the tangible reality of existing things and Hegel's attempt to comprehend the world in a system of concepts or "world of explanations"—one that Kierkegaard regards as unrealistic and unattainable:

> The world of explanations and reasons is not the world of existence. A circle is not absurd, it is clearly explained by the rotation of a straight segment

around one of its extremities. But neither does a circle exist. This root, on the other hand, existed in such a way that I could not explain it. Knotty, inert, nameless, it fascinated me, filled my eyes, brought me back unceasingly to its own existence. In vain to repeat: "this is a root"—it didn't work any more. I saw clearly that you could not pass from its function as a root, as a breathing pump, to *that*, to this hard and compact skin of a sea lion, to this oily, callous, headstrong look. (Sartre 1964: 129)

The existentialist orientation toward the world expressed above is reflected in Kierkegaard's characterization of the "aesthetic" lifestyle. He does not stop with the aesthetic lifestyle, as we shall see, but retains this down-to-earth orientation in his journey inward to the depths of his subjectivity.

## 2.2 The task of finding oneself

In a soul-searching journal entry dated August 1, 1835, written when he was twenty-two years old, Kierkegaard expresses his frustration with his academic studies, having failed to discover in them sufficient spiritual stimulation. He asks himself what good it would do to command the history of philosophy in all of its details, with the ability to cite the advantages and flaws of each system of thought, or what good it would do to know the objective truth, or the meaning of Christianity, if it had no bearing on himself and his life. *Finding himself* is his main concern. External matters, worldly and academic, appear secondary.

Kierkegaard frames his query in religious terms, as he asks himself how he can discover what *God* wants him to do, almost as if he were seeking a personal relationship with God. More objectively speaking, his question amounts to asking what he, Søren Kierkegaard, is fundamentally and *absolutely* all about. To answer this question, he seeks the "principle of my life" and "the idea for which I can live and die."

To reveal one's character and underlying motivations, it is indeed useful to ask what the sacrifice of one's life is worth. Would one die to save a mosquito's life? Would one die to save a cat or a dog? To save a complete stranger, or a murderer? To save one's immediate family? To save someone else's child? To save an artistic masterpiece from destruction? Would one die to preserve one's honor, or for one's chosen profession, or for one's country or religion?

Would one die to uphold justice, equality, freedom, democracy, or reason itself, as Socrates supposedly did? Would one die for no one? Would one die for nothing, pointlessly? If the universe is inherently meaningless, do we have no choice but to live and die ultimately, for nothing?

When devoting a lifetime to some career, one also "has died" for that career, for when one actually dies, one will have used up most of one's time on earth in relation to that career, representing it and furthering it. The question, then, is not only whether right now I might sacrifice my life to save a person nearby who is in distress or to preserve a cherished style of social order under immediate threat from invaders. The question concerns how I am to spend my life, or how I am to live. It is about what lifestyle I should choose, perhaps in the face of oblivion.

Although it may sound reasonable and unquestionably plain for Kierkegaard's soul searching to seek "the" principle of his life and "the" idea for which he can live and die, his quest assumes that there *is* some single principle or idea waiting for him to uncover. Much is philosophically implicit in this assumption. It introduces the view, for instance, that there is some single, well-defined, and well-directed potentiality that each person ought primarily to realize, where, upon realizing that ideal point where potentiality and actuality coincide, we would become our true selves.

This particular style of self-understanding has the virtue of generating a high intensity of personal meaning. The assumption of a sole task, idea, or principle that one ought to realize directs all of Kierkegaard's personal meaning into this singularity, however it happens to be defined, and helps him thereby to experience an enhanced meaning for his life. Such a way of securing personal meaning contrasts with how people can remain dabblingly indecisive, wavering and spreading their attention across a number of activities and interests, none of which predominates in significance. Instead, Kierkegaard conceives of a maximally meaningful life as involving a passionate, focused devotion to a single task, idea, or principle. Once that purpose is defined, the next question will be whether one has the willpower to realize it.

Nietzsche also adheres to this single-purpose approach to giving one's life meaning, framing the idea aesthetically in terms of "style." He advises that we should "give style" to our character, once we have discovered who we are:

> *One thing is needful.*—To "give style" to one's character—a great and rare art! It is practiced by those who survey all the strengths and weaknesses of their

nature and then fit them into an artistic plan until every one of them appears as art and reason and even weaknesses delight the eye. Here a large mass of second nature has been added; there a piece of original nature has been removed—both times through long practice and daily work at it. Here the ugly that could not be removed is concealed; there it has been reinterpreted and made sublime. Much that is vague and resisted shaping has been saved and exploited for distant views; it is meant to beckon toward the far and immeasurable. In the end, when the work is finished, it becomes evident how the constraint of a single taste governed and formed everything large and small. Whether this taste was good or bad is less important than one might suppose, if only it were a single taste! (Nietzsche 1974: 232)

Nietzsche expresses the enhancement of personal meaning as artistic self-formation in accord with a single taste, assuming throughout as a matter of self-expression, that it is preferable to have a determined focus and concentration. Like Kierkegaard, he sees no benefit in being tossed about by changing circumstances, and advocates exercising one's freedom to maintain artistic control over one's life. Nietzsche's prescription, as we can see, nonetheless remains formalistic: he focuses upon style and appearances rather than substance and does not here emphasize the kind or quality of character that such an ideally integrated and pleasing manner would present.

In Kierkegaard, since everything depends upon a person's quality of character and choice of lifestyle, he finds it essential to compare and contrast the values of alternative, highly focused, single-minded lifestyles. His interests coalesce into the comparison, contrast, and fundamental choice between three basic lifestyles, corresponding to the philosophical distinction between the realms of sensation, rationality, and what is incomprehensively beyond the distinction between sensation and intellect. They are, namely, the "aesthetic," "ethical," and "religious" lifestyles.

## 2.3 Alternative lifestyles and the search for meaning

As noted, Hegel's *Phenomenology* surveys a wide array of perspectives that human knowledge can take, organizing them in an ascending sequence of increasing complexity to arrive at absolute knowledge. Although Kierkegaard abandons the idea of absolute knowledge in an objective sense, he follows

Hegel's practice of examining, comparing, and contrasting alternative perspectives, finding it existentially revealing to attend to the aesthetic, ethical, and religious lifestyles, which he explores thoroughly in their complexity and richness. Devoting entire books to each outlook, Kierkegaard regards each as if it were a prism, holding it up in the air, turning it variously in the light, all in an effort to reveal the nuances of meaning contained and reflected therein.

His first published book, *Either/Or* (1843), a two-volume work, describes the first two lifestyles in sequence. Volume one presents the aesthetic lifestyle through a collection of writings by a character named "A"; volume two, the ethical, through writings by a character named Judge William. The published works thereafter, most notably, *Fear and Trembling* (1843), *Philosophical Fragments* (1844), *Concluding Unscientific Postscript* (1846), and *The Sickness Unto Death* (1849), explore the religious lifestyle through an assortment of angles, characters, and stories, such as the story of Abraham and Isaac.

Although Kierkegaard's writing style has its straightforwardly philosophical moments, it is typically more literary, composed with a cast of fictional characters, stories, anecdotes, and sermons. Almost all of his books were published under a series of pseudonyms, challenging his readers to decide which of the works indicate Kierkegaard's true position. The religious lifestyle takes precedence in his thought, but he aims to have us decide for ourselves whether the aesthetic, ethical, or religious outlook is preferable.

The word "aesthetic" derives from the Greek word, *aestheta* (αίσθητά), which refers to the ordinary objects of sense experience. These objects contrast with those that can be grasped through the intellect alone, immaterial and invisible to sense, called *noeta* (νοητά). The distinction can be marked by the difference between a circle drawn perceivably on a piece of paper and the ideal circle that we can conceive as its underlying plan, as expressed in a conceptual definition. Following the word's etymology, an "aesthetic" lifestyle would, in one way or another, be immersed in sensory experience. It is a down-to-earth lifestyle as such, whose initial attractiveness to Kierkegaard, and indeed, to any existentialist, immediately presents itself. We will see Camus advocate a version of this lifestyle, for instance.

If one steps behind the veil of sensory appearances to enter intellectually into another, non-sensory dimension, the first stop for many philosophers is the realm of rationality—one that can serve as the basis of morality, as it did for Kant. Within this rationalistic perspective, it is possible to formulate unconditional rules and regulations for ordinary life, as embodied in the Ten Commandments: "Thou shalt respect other people, thou shalt not lie, and thou shalt not steal or kill." Such a reason-based, moralistic attitude defines the "ethical" lifestyle that Kierkegaard describes through Judge William, who addresses his writings to "A" with the hope of convincing him to revise and redirect his path in life.

Insofar as it purports to be objectively formulable and unconditional, the rationalistic moral realm resonates with publicly universal conceptual structures and uniform moral demands. We can go further inward, however, in line with a conception of the self that detaches our rationality from our freedom, to recognize pure freedom at the core of our being. According to this self-conception, *making choices* emerges as the essential human activity. As completely free, but nonetheless finite, beings, our freedom comes with a price: serious choices and the assumption of responsibility tend to generate anxiety. This is the groundless realm of the religious lifestyle, where, without any rational compass to follow, we are entirely on our own, often in fear and trembling.

Kierkegaard characterizes each lifestyle through fictional constructions that allow him to idealize, focus, and intensify the presentations. He formulates the lifestyles as single-minded viewpoints, all-consuming for their advocates, and difficult, if not unrealistic for anyone to embody wholeheartedly, exclusively and constantly. Each represents a way of giving meaning to one's life in terms of a single, focused passion, whether it is the dedication to sensory pleasures, rationality, or the inwardness of pure freedom. He thus presents us with distillations and essentializations of alternative lifestyles that reveal how certain tendencies inherent in us all would appear, if they were to be realized with extraordinarily focused willpower and passion.

## The aesthetic lifestyle

The world of ordinary perception and daily life—a world of constant change—has been the object of philosophical suspicion and criticism for millennia. Plato, for example, regarded the sensory world as a world that never quite "is," for it is always only "becoming" and is thereby not completely true. For him the truth must be permanent, and with this realization, he had little choice but to seek truth on an unchanging dimension beyond space and time.

After having found it there, he regarded the sensory world as the merely moving shadow of that reality.

Sensation and perception may have been philosophically subordinated to intellect and conception for ages, but upon shifting our orientation to become more down to earth and existentially centered, the sensory realm acquires a new value as the importance of otherworldly dimensions proportionately fades. Within these parameters, Kierkegaard begins his quest for meaning with the aesthetic lifestyle, which is directed squarely and hedonistically toward the external world and the sensory pleasures it supplies.

Although the aesthetic lifestyle has a sensory orientation, Kierkegaard does not construe "sensation" or the "aesthetic" exclusively as a gluttonous and indiscriminate quest for raw sensory pleasures. He has a more subtle conception that includes the sophisticated appreciation of fine art and music, as well as pleasures stemming from the artistic manipulation of one's surroundings. All share the aim of creating meaning for oneself squarely within the register of sensory experience.

To begin, one might seek satisfaction in the aesthetic appreciation of sensory surfaces, as when setting aside considerations of past and future and attending with an open and non-preoccupied mind to the inexhaustible arrays of colors, sounds, and textures as they presently appear. Alternatively, one could continually shift one's surroundings in a self-conscious way, as in a lifestyle of constant travel, moving from one exotic place to another in an effort to keep life interesting. A third aesthetic approach would be to fill one's life with especially intense, unique, or notably organically unified experiences, as when experiencing a new love, or when apprehending a sequence of events as if they were unfolding into a meaningful story of their own intrinsic accord, or when apprehending them as if they were a kind of musical performance.

The diversity of these experiences notwithstanding, Kierkegaard is discouraged by the transitoriness and superficiality of such efforts to create meaning for oneself through sensation, as he observes how the experiences lack constancy and inwardness of emotion. Searching further within the aesthetic lifestyle for experiences with greater significance, he considers yet another approach that appears more promising: here, one plays with the surrounding world, manipulating its elements artistically, often using other people as one would use paint on a canvas.

A simple, and relatively passive, way to manipulate and play with one's surroundings is to reinterpret them in a more exciting way. For example, the aesthete named "A" tells the story of an annoying person who he was obliged to meet periodically. This person bored A terribly with his philosophical lecturing—bored him, that is, until A discovered he could appreciate aesthetically how the person would sweat profusely during his long-winded expositions. The subsequent meetings consequently became more interesting to A, and so much so, that A began enthusiastically to look forward to the meetings merely to watch the sweat accumulate and drip in a glistening bead from the person's nose. Nothing was "done" except reinterpret the given situation in a new aesthetic, self-entertaining light.

A related, but more active aesthetic approach is to manipulate people to create for oneself artistically, a kind of theatrical play that one manages unbeknownst to the individuals involved. Kierkegaard portrays this lifestyle through a cold and calculating seducer, who, for the sake of entertainment and a feeling of power, plans and follows through with the seduction of an unsuspecting and trusting woman. As a seduction per se, the seducer's behavior is morally objectionable, but one can also more generally question the morality of manipulating people for one's self-entertainment. As with the other examples of aesthetic lifestyle, Kierkegaard regards a life of manipulating others as an empty and unfriendly one, insofar as the seducer's egoism and consequent social distance from the people he uses, leaves him without any genuine social relationships.

Inspired by an understanding of art history from Hegel's lectures on aesthetics, Kierkegaard also considers the appreciation of fine art and music as another way to live aesthetically. According to Hegel, artistic expression in human culture proceeds historically through a series of shifting relationships between an artwork's form and its content. He maintains that during early times—in Assyria, India, and Egypt, for instance—human beings' self-conception was not highly developed or articulated. Humans appreciated themselves as living beings opposed to inanimate beings, but did not regard their humanness as a feature that distinguished them sharply from the rest of the animal and plant kingdom. Upon this assumption, Hegel interprets the art in these cultures as expressing the fertility, energy, and productivity of the general idea of life itself, noting the artistic occurrence of many-armed figures, the worship of animals, and a wild and wide-ranging assemblage of themes.

Here, during the "symbolic" period of art, the diversity of artistic "form" exceeds the generic, relatively thin and abstract, "content" of the artworks.

With the emergence of Greek civilization, Hegel identifies an awareness that is more humanly specific and self-centered: more cognizant of their self-consciousness and rationality, the Greeks regarded human beings as distinct and superior to all other animals. From this more distinctive self-awareness emerged an artistic culture that took a greater interest in the human being per se. We consequently see in ancient Greece idealized sculptures and idealized drama that emphasize the human form and intense social interactions.

Since this human-centered age was nonetheless only at its beginning, "art"—which Hegel conceives as the sensuous expression of a culture's highest aims or the sensuous expression of "the divine"—was the perfect medium to convey the Greek self-conception. Their self-awareness was not as generic as that of the pre-Greek civilizations, but neither was it as inwardly directed, or as "subjective," as what would appear during the Roman and medieval periods. In ancient Greece, the attitude was rationalistic, externally oriented, and well grounded in the reality of the spatiotemporal world. Within this context, Hegel maintains that "art" reached its perfection, for in the best and paradigmatic Greek works of art—to be found in their sculpture and theatre—the external form and the expressed content attained a perfect blend.

The artistic balance and beauty of Greek culture historically tips with Christianity's emergence and its more intense focus on subjective feelings. In contrast to the previous "classical" period, the Christian period is "romantic," wherein artistic expression becomes increasingly incapable of expressing intense inward emotion. Hegel states famously that the purity of art—that is, art "as art"—"dies" with the decline of classical Greek culture, for although art's spiritual depth intensifies with the advent of Christianity, the artistic balance between form and content is disturbed with the infusion of more complicated emotional depth into the works. The content now exceeds the form and we witness the "death of art." Religion, expressed typically through mental imagery more suited to express emotional depth, thus takes over historically from art as the main vehicle to express the deepest interests of society. Within the sphere of artistic media, sculpture gives way to the romantic arts of painting, music, and literature, just as architecture gives way to sculpture in the transition from the symbolic to the classical period.

This shift from artistic expression to religious expression, accompanied by the recognition of the artistic perspective's inadequacy for expressing deep feeling, is one of the main ideas that Kierkegaard directly adopts from Hegel's aesthetics. Kierkegaard agrees with Hegel that when one reaches a certain intensity and depth of feeling, artistic expression—as in tragedy—along with any kind of aesthetically oriented lifestyle becomes inadequate. He accordingly writes: "This is the real reason why one has always been ashamed to call the life of Christ a tragedy, because one instinctively feels that aesthetic categories do not exhaust the matter" (Kierkegaard 1959: 148).

At one point, Kierkegaard has "A" admit that the aesthetic lifestyle is empty, and that something more is needed:

> If I were offered all the glories of the world, or all its pain, the one would move me as little as the other. . . . Aye, if I might behold a constancy that could withstand every trial, an enthusiasm that endured everything, a faith that could remove mountains, a thought that could unite the finite and the infinite. But my soul's poisonous doubt is all-consuming. My soul is like the Dead Sea, over which no bird can fly; when it has flown midway, then it sinks down to death and destruction. (Kierkegaard 1959: 36)

## The ethical lifestyle

The search for "a constancy that could withstand every trial" eventually leads away from the constant play of sensory pleasures, since the hopelessness of finding meaning by immersing oneself in a superficial, wavering world soon becomes evident. A more promising course presents itself in the effort to coalesce one's sense of self though firm commitments. Such is the essence of Judge William's advice to "A": to be committed and be responsible is paramount.

The Judge's focus is practical in his dedication to marriage, family, duty, work, respectable social roles, and contributions to civic life. Unlike the aesthete, the grounding of his ethical lifestyle has a manifestly otherworldly orientation insofar as the Judge seeks "the absolute," "eternal validity," and a transformation into the "paradigmatic man" or "universal man"—all of which, on the face of things, defy the external, physical world of constant change (Kierkegaard 1944: 265–66).

Kierkegaard's characterization of the ethical attitude accordingly has a Kantian, universalistic flavor, as Judge William advocates the unconditional respect for rules, the absolute importance of duty, and the consciousness of one's eternal nature as related to the immortality of the soul. The Judge explains to the aesthete that there is a rational order of things into which every person has a place and that the ethical task is to subordinate individuality for the sake of expressing the "universal-human" in one's life.

This Kantian moral atmosphere is expressed, tempered, and modified by Kierkegaard's own interests and intellectual orientation, which is distinctively more practical and worldly. Judge William does not explicitly ground his life-purpose upon timeless and intangible abstractions; with a measure of hope, he aims concretely to achieve a measure of constancy within, rather than outside of, the constantly changing world. Although Kant's moral theory inspires Kierkegaard's characterization of the Judge's dedication to standard social norms, the Judge does not have a developed philosophical awareness of Kant's philosophy. He refers to himself as a plain and practical man.

There is a specific aspect of Kant's moral theory worth noting that bears closely on the Judge's practical interest in becoming a solid, respectable, human being and member of society. This is Kant's view that each person has a timeless, unchanging character—an "intelligible" character—that is the person's ultimate and timeless reality. The Judge speaks of unconditional duties, but the bulk of his advice to the aesthete concerns the importance of finding and living in accordance with a unified sense of self. To the Judge, the aesthete's problem is that a lack of constant personality is rendering the aesthete whimsical, arbitrary, and lacking the willpower to remain predictable and committed, and thereby to have a meaningful life.

The aesthete's whimsicality and lack of commitment are presented as the natural result of identifying too much with the external, changing world. The ethical outlook accordingly turns away from this world, and in its search for an alternative it turns in two opposing directions, namely, outwards toward transcendent otherworldly realities and inwards toward increasingly deeper subjectivity. Throughout Kierkegaard's rendition of the combat between the aesthete and Judge William, a tension-ridden existential component persists: Judge William resists the external world's changeableness while aiming to live concretely within that world. This presents the problem of how to remain down to earth while denying the validity of the aesthete's plunge into sensory change and sensory pleasure.

Judge William's discussion about how to find oneself amid a changing world consequently introduces some existentially themed aspects, in particular, the "inward turning" aspects that later figure centrally in what Kierkegaard will characterize as the religious stage. When he was writing *Either/Or*, this religious stage had not yet clearly emerged for him, and it only became thematized clearly in the book quickly to follow, *Fear and Trembling*. The second volume of *Either/Or*—some parts of which were written before the first volume—presents an amalgam of "ethical" and "religious" aspects and is a transitional work in this respect. Let us consider some of these aspects, which concern the idea of finding oneself.

Judge William distinguishes between the ethical outlook and the aesthetic outlook by attending to what it means genuinely to "make a choice." The Judge claims that as driven by whim, sensuality, change, and arbitrariness, the aesthete's actions are always immediate, relatively unreflective, and certainly uncommitted. The aesthete never makes any real choices, but is more like an instinct-driven animal. Since the very idea of making choices and taking responsibility is itself foreign to the aesthete, the Judge associates making choices with the ethical outlook per se.

Emphasizing the importance of making choices in the formation of one's personality, the Judge states that it does not matter what one chooses, as long as one remains committed to the choice. The primary importance resides not in the "what," but in the "how," for the overriding concern is to establish some constancy and predictability in one's personality and life, as opposed to whimsicality and emptiness. The discussion then gravitates into considering the state of consciousness involved in making a serious—and at the extreme, an "absolute"—choice of any kind, as opposed to prescribing the contents of choices, notwithstanding the Judge's particular prescriptions and interests in being married, and in remaining socially stable and civically responsible.

The Judge argues in *Either/Or* that there is only one absolute choice: either one chooses morality or one chooses non-morality. "Either" one recognizes the distinction between good and evil "or" one acknowledges a thoroughly neutral world. In contemporary life, the latter is exemplified in pragmatic politics, when it is asserted that considerations of right and wrong do not fundamentally determine policy decisions, but rather power and gaining advantage over one's actual and potential adversaries. To reverse a popular saying: it is not how one plays the game that matters; it is whether one wins or loses.

On the side of morality, the Judge argues that shifting one's commitments and allegiances in view of changing contingencies—for example, today, our enemy is this group, but tomorrow that same group can be our friend, although the day after it can be our enemy again—amounts to not choosing at all, and hence betrays in its opportunism a lack of moral awareness from the start. Once a person resolves genuinely to choose, a moral awareness has already dawned (Kierkegaard 1944: 173). The problem then—and here we have a classical existentialist theme coming to light—is that of taking responsibility for one's actions and for oneself.

Judge William adds that the great thing is to be oneself, and that choosing oneself bestows personal dignity. Such a choice, which allows one to become conscious of oneself in one's eternal validity, is, for the Judge, the most significant thing in the world. The very act of choosing acquires an absolute status here, as the Judge refers to our inner being as "freedom." He adds cautiously, however, that choosing oneself takes courage, because being oneself in an absolute sense requires a disconnection from the contingencies of past history, habits, and conditioning. The benefit of attaining such a self-conception is having reached a level of fundamentality, for the choice to be what one is subsequently determines everything else that one does (Kierkegaard 1944: 227).

As a small example of choice and the freedom contained therein, Judge William refers to the gambler whose lust for gambling could be extinguished, if only the gambler would choose to wait, and not gamble for an hour, when the compulsion hit (Kierkegaard 1944: 235). These emphases on the absoluteness of freedom, the personality-defining fundamental choice, and even the example of the gambler that appear in the second volume of *Either/Or* will appear once again in Jean-Paul Sartre's existentialist philosophy.

## The religious lifestyle

In *Fear and Trembling*, published in October 1843, Kierkegaard resolves some of the expository blurriness in the second volume of *Either/Or* by distinguishing the universalistic, objective, ethical attitude from a more personal, subjective, faith-based, religious one. His ongoing motivation is to come up with a solid and reliable down-to-earth attitude in the face of change, if not some way to touch paradoxically upon, or even embody, "the absolute" within such a transient worldly situation and finitude of his consciousness.

Now writing under the name of Johannes *de silentio* (John, the silent one), Kierkegaard reiterates that the ethical is "the universal" and, as such, is higher than human individuality and personal interests. In the ethical perspective, given its Kantian formulation, the unique individual is subordinated to universal rules and is expected to set aside his or her particular personality. The absolute moral command, or categorical imperative, is that lying is wrong in general; Michael should not lie and neither should Mary, who is in the same circumstances, for neither Michael nor Mary is special. Here, in a universalistic ethical perspective, the uniqueness of the individual is a secondary consideration in view of higher purposes and higher regularities. To its disadvantage and incompleteness, *Either/Or* offers only an "absolute" choice between the aesthetic lifestyle and the ethical lifestyle, posited as two opposing, exclusive, and exhaustive alternatives.

For Kierkegaard's ends, however, neither option in *Either/Or* is satisfactory. The aesthetic lifestyle, despite the elegant, art-critical sophistications it can embody, is essentially uncommitted, whimsical, and empty, and the ethical lifestyle, despite its greater consistency and respectable social solidity, is too universalistic, impersonal, and blunt to capture the subjective nuances of a person's individuality. The ethical lifestyle neglects subjective inwardness and remains emotionally superficial in its external focus upon respect for duty, rules, and civic life.

With the completion of *Either/Or*, Kierkegaard had thereby landed himself in a double-bind of his own creation, where neither the aesthetic nor the ethical attitude, which he had taken such pains to elaborate, was providing the constancy and down-to-earth recognition of the personal depths of feeling and uncertainty that were central to his existence. Kierkegaard was grasping for an "absolute," but the ethical outlook could provide this only in the form of an "eternal validity" framed in exclusively universalistic, individual-dissolving terms.

To access a more personally absolute aspect of himself, to discover what God wanted of him, Kierkegaard found a model in the story of Abraham and Isaac. Abraham loved his son with all of his heart, and from an ethical standpoint, his dedication to maintaining and fostering Isaac's welfare was of the highest moral caliber and entailed the highest moral responsibility. From a moral perspective, Abraham was committed above all to taking care of Isaac without qualification, hesitation, or reflection. Nothing morally could ever stand in the way of interrupting Abraham's duty to his son, and in this respect their relationship was morally absolute.

Within this steadfast moral context, Abraham hears a command from God to sacrifice his son. The directive makes no sense to Abraham, for it contradicts the general Mosaic commandment not to kill. Indeed, Abraham finds himself facing a devastating double-bind: either he kills Isaac, respects God's command, and violates the absolute moral relationship he has with his son, or he saves Isaac, disrespects God's command, and violates the absolute personal relationship he has with the highest spiritual and cosmic authority. Worse yet, if Abraham is only imagining that he hears God's command, then only the ethical outlook remains and Abraham becomes a murderer upon respecting what he believes to be God's word. Torn apart emotionally, Abraham nonetheless chooses to regard the command as a test of faith from the highest authority, and proceeds with some laborious travel to make the sacrifice of his son in accord with what he perceives to be God's will.

Assuming the reality of God's command, Abraham realizes that the moral outlook is unable to provide any guidance, for it impossibly requires that he respects God's command and also not kill his son. The psychological tension involved is sufficient to drive a person insane, and is enough to turn a person's attention inward, onto the very pressure involved in making a no-win, momentous choice. Following his belief that God is personally testing him, Abraham decides to make the sacrifice, shaken to his very core, filled with fear and trembling. Miraculously, Isaac is saved, and is returned to Abraham by God, who supplies an animal to be sacrificed in Isaac's place at the last moment.

On "the strength of the absurd," Isaac is returned to Abraham in moral consistency, who Kierkegaard describes as a knight of unwavering and optimistic faith. Throughout his ordeal, Abraham maintains his faith in the face of utter resignation, moral contradiction, and certain doom, believing that somehow, despite the terribly hopeless situation he was in, and despite what he had chosen murderously to do, Isaac would be returned to him.

Inspired by the Abraham and Isaac story and possibly by one of the Brothers Grimm fairy tales entitled "The Faithful Servant," which has a similar narrative, Kierkegaard arrives at a new standpoint that differs from either the whimsical aesthetic or the rule-bound ethical. Going beyond the universality of the ethical outlook and its binding authority of rules and regulations, Abraham is said to have a personal, one-on-one, absolute relationship to God, or "absolute relation to the absolute." God's command to Abraham is an exclusively personal matter, unrelated and incomprehensible to anyone else—so Abraham stays silent, presumably finding it pointless to talk to anyone about his experience— and insofar as the command has a divine origin, the command's contents supersede, suspend, and neutralize all other considerations, including moral ones, in a "teleological suspension of the ethical."

This leads us to ask how Abraham finds himself "absolutely" in his encounter with God, for this matter of self-discovery is the broader purpose of Kierkegaard's having drawn our attention to the biblical story. One way to understand this is to appreciate how one's self-concept is determined by other people. A person is called a "musician," "chauffeur," "mayor," "waiter," "criminal," "faithful son," "hunter," "priest," "anthropologist," "soldier," "secretary," "student," and so on, typically because others have said so, or have confirmed so. In the eyes of "the Other," a person's self-definition is solidified. This, at least, is the principle that Kierkegaard recognizes in his discussions of finding oneself, for he tries to find himself by imaging the look of an absolute being who can define him absolutely in its gaze. A revealing excerpt is from *The Sickness Unto Death*, written later in his life:

> A herdsman who (if this is possible) is a self directly before cattle is a very low self; similarly a master who is a self directly before slaves, indeed really he is not a self—for in both cases there is no standard of measurement. The child, who up to then has had only its parents' standard, becomes a self through acquiring, as an adult, the State as its standard. But what an infinite accent is laid upon the self when it acquires God as its standard! The standard for the self is as always: that directly in the face of which it is a self. (Kierkegaard 1989: 111)

Abraham's encounter with God thus raises for our general consideration the dynamics and meaning of being in a private relationship with what one believes is an absolute power or absolute authority. This is nothing more, though, than to be acutely aware of the human condition. It is to be aware of one's particular existence as a finite, perishable, human being in the midst of an infinitely extensive universe whose source and purpose remains unclear, and whose ultimate reality one constantly faces. Insofar we live in the midst of terrible, anxiety-producing dilemmas that require major decisions, the story of Abraham illuminates what it means to be free. Kierkegaard realizes that every one of us is in this situation without release, as we contemplate the meaning of our lives and the meaning of our death, and need perpetually and consequently to choose a personal orientation toward the cosmos. In ordinary circumstances, at each moment, and in a similar way, we constantly face the possibility and the choice to alter the course of our lives.

Rarely do we contemplate such choices at length or in any depth, so entrenched in habit and communal regularities as we typically and normally are. One could, however, decide today to quit one's job for another, to leave one's family to join a monastery, to commit suicide, to commit murder, to dedicate one's life entirely and selflessly to others, to change from a theist to an atheist, or vice versa, with the effect of dissolving entirely one's present situation and style of interpreting the world.

If the constant presence of such options were to be recognized and taken seriously, the tension, anxiety, and uncertainty involved might very well compare to Abraham's. Kierkegaard's existentialism is fundamentally about personal matters, and in particular, about deciding how to face the inscrutable universe as a finite, self-conscious, and physical being. It is about how to live, serious decisions, the inability to explain oneself to others, moral questionability, along with the suffering, struggle, and sometimes despair, that one experiences in making hard decisions, which in the end become nothing more than leaps of faith. Kierkegaard finds that to endure these difficult choices and to remain sane, down to earth, and realistic thereafter, one must find something absolute in oneself, and perhaps most importantly, that the very practice of making such difficult choices brings that absolute dimension of oneself into awareness.

# 3

# Friedrich Nietzsche (1844–1900)

## 3.1 Truth, health, and the quest for meaning

Friedrich Nietzsche is a philosopher of health. With great health comes great strength. With great health also comes creativity, self-confidence, the ability to turn adversity to one's advantage, a sense of meaningfulness, a love of life, and perhaps even a feeling of invincibility, as illusory as that may be. "Be healthy," one could say, is Nietzsche's categorical imperative and absolute command.

If we recall Nietzsche's own physiological condition, it is not surprising that health is his preeminent value. He suffered physically throughout his life, struggling at times to overcome weeks of debilitation where he was bedridden with migraines, vomiting, and nervous exhaustion. His career as a professor of classical philology at the University of Basel lasted only a decade, from 1869 to 1879, at his ages of twenty-four to thirty-four, ending with his early retirement from the university on the grounds of ill-health. Remaining intellectually active for only another decade thereafter, his mental faculties collapsed in January 1889 when he was forty-four years old, after which point he remained an invalid until his death on August 25, 1900. When Nietzsche was in his prime, one can only imagine the joy he experienced on those days when his mind was crystal clear, his body was working normally, and he was fit to appreciate the beauty and richness that life offers. His philosophy highlights the intrinsic value of such outstanding experiences.

Under certain circumstances health can become so important, that truth—especially truth of an absolute or metaphysical sort, as abstract and distant as it can appear to be—becomes insignificant. Someone could be so ill and thirsty for recuperation, that speculating about the nature of ultimate reality would present itself as a secondary matter at best. As a coherent philosophical position in its own right, though, the defense of supreme health at the expense of truth requires some qualification. In its crudest form, one cannot assert truthfully that health should always override truth, without acknowledging the truth of that very assertion, and the implied priority of truth over health.

Nietzsche occasionally falls victim to such contradictions, but there is a way—which is also an existential way—to understand his emphasis upon health over truth more consistently. This is to consider carefully some of his truth-antagonistic assertions against the background of Kant's skeptical conclusions in the *Critique of Pure Reason*, with which he was familiar.

Kant argues that metaphysical knowledge is impossible for us, because—to use Nietzschean wording—we are "human, all-too-human." We are finite beings and cannot avoid apprehending ultimate reality in our limited human way, namely, as Kant specifies at some length, through the forms of space and time, as well as through a set of fundamental logical concepts, all argued to be inherent within us and unshakeable. These forms and logical concepts, so thoroughly reliable, define the basic contours of human experience, as they construct and precipitate a world filled with publicly observable and measurable relationships, particularly scientific ones, which are always true for us, but not true in the ultimate scheme of things. Natural science is not metaphysics, for the spatiotemporal world does not represent reality as it is in itself. Our very humanity prevents us from going behind the daily scenes to know the absolute truth, or how things are in themselves.

Kant's *Critique of Pure Reason* concludes that if our goal is to establish definitive, conclusive, logical proofs about the nature of metaphysical realities, then we are grasping at illusions: the hard philosophical fact is that we cannot know whether we are free, whether we each have an immortal soul, or whether there is a God. He consequently urges us to concentrate on more practical matters, which for him are matters of moral decision and action.

With notable consolation, Kant adds that if our moral awareness is real, then we must suppose nonetheless that we are free. If we are to do everything we ought, then we must suppose that each of us will have the time to do so, and will thereby persist immaterially beyond our present lives. To receive the happiness we will accordingly deserve, if we do exclusively what we ought to do, we must postulate the existence of God as an all-powerful, all-knowing, and all-good being who can make that happiness come true for everyone. What Kant emphatically denies us with his rigorous, philosophical, and scientific hand, he provides to us hopefully and faithfully with his softer, moral, and implicitly religious hand. Nietzsche appreciates this aspect of Kant, albeit irreverently:

> *Kant's joke.*—In a way that would dumfound the common man, Kant wanted to prove that the common man was right: that was the secret joke of his soul. He wrote against the scholars in support of popular prejudice, but for scholars and not for the people. (Nietzsche 1974: 205–06)

Insofar as he concurs with Kant, Nietzsche acknowledges that what we ordinarily call "truth" is true only for us humans. Kant refers to such truth—the truth that there is an infinite space filled with galaxies, water in our oceans, sands on the beaches, and dust on the floor—as "empirical truth" merely. Nietzsche agrees that metaphysics is a fruitless enterprise, which for Kant promises only uncertainty conjoined with arbitrary and endless dispute. The difference is that Nietzsche draws a more radical conclusion from Kant's informed and almost existential advice to redirect our primary attention to practical concerns, here on earth.

Throughout his writings, Nietzsche expresses this Kantian sentiment with a tone more tenaciously dismissive of otherworldly pursuits. In an 1873 essay titled "On Truth and Lies in a Nonmoral Sense," he maintains that virtually everything to which we refer ordinarily as "truths" is nothing more than an army of metaphors which we have lost track of as metaphors, which, through the buildup of ignorance over time, appears to us falsely as a set of facts (Nietzsche 1979: 84). Over a decade later, in an 1886 self-criticism of his earlier work *The Birth of Tragedy* (1872), he urges us to laugh and to throw metaphysical speculation to the devil (Nietzsche 1967: 26). In the midst of an 1888 presentation of how the timelessly true world of Platonic ideas has slowly become implausible over the centuries, he reiterates Kant's position that ultimate reality is unknowable (Nietzsche 1954b: 485–86). Hammering the last nail into the coffin, he adds that since ultimate reality is unknowable, and hence pragmatically useless, we should not bother ourselves to worry about it (Nietzsche 1986: 15–16).

As strong as his attitudes may be, Nietzsche does not inconsistently reject all truth in these instances. He abandons the project that Kant labeled "dogmatism," namely, of trying in a traditional philosophical manner to determine the absolute or metaphysical truth. Nietzsche sees no practical value in ascertaining the nature of "truth with a capital 'T,'" one could say.

If we understand "God" as representative and expressive of this idea of absolute truth, it is easy to appreciate one of Nietzsche's most well-known themes, namely, his advocacy of the "death of God." Such a divine fatality dramatically and existentially implies that we need to redirect our attention to more earthly matters. The most pressing earthly matter for Nietzsche is not morality, as Kant was convinced, or metaphysical truth, as we see in traditional philosophy, but maintaining and enhancing our health, especially because it can give a meaning to suffering. If we are living beings, and if we appreciate directly that we are on earth right here and now, then we ought to aim to be as healthy as possible.

## 3.2 Early Nietzsche: *The Birth of Tragedy*

Nietzsche's early outlook as presented in *The Birth of Tragedy* was influenced significantly by Schopenhauer's *The World as Will and Representation* (1818)—a work that impressed itself upon Nietzsche at the age of twenty-one. In addition to his natural attraction to Schopenhauer's honesty and intellectual strength, Schopenhauer's formulation of the existential problem of suffering provided a lens through which Nietzsche subsequently interpreted the therapeutic effects of Greek tragedy. Prior to Nietzsche's encounter with Schopenhauer's philosophy, Schopenhauer was himself struck by the overwhelming presence of suffering in the world.

At first hearing, Schopenhauer's estimation of the world's basic condition might sound strange or excessively downbeat. If we imagine beautiful sunsets in the tranquil countryside, quaint seaside villages, warm breezes, chirping birds, and happy children in the playground, the world hardly appears to contain the intense suffering to which Schopenhauer points. The world appears rather to be fundamentally peaceful. If we view the world from the "inside," however, Schopenhauer believes that a different picture emerges.

As a paradigmatic image, contrast the lion's pleasure in eating the flesh of a freshly killed antelope with the agony the antelope suffers when being torn apart by the lion's teeth and claws. Then multiply this asymmetrical relationship of pleasure and pain across the animal kingdom in millions of instances. Add to this, the suffering and frustration that human beings experience and have experienced throughout their existence—we need only sum up the pain of everyone across the centuries who was tortured or who has suffered heavy psychological losses. The result is an unimaginable accumulation of suffering.

This global vision of suffering sentient beings underlies Schopenhauer's philosophy as he identifies with what it is like to be the consciousness of all sentient beings at once, finding himself horribly transported into an ocean of pain in the world's inner being. In addition, he finds that the immeasurable suffering of any innocent child or infant is unjustifiable and can never be compensated. If the world were genuinely good, and were the product of a benevolent being, he is convinced that such suffering would have never seen the light of existence.

On the basis of this simple compassion, global empathy, and universalistic consciousness, Schopenhauer formulates a metaphysics that accounts for this immense suffering. If each of us looks deeply and honestly into ourselves, he believes we will discover ultimately an utterly meaningless, irrational, and aimless impulse at the core. When this primordial impulse manifests itself as the individuals that constitute the ordinary world, it appears as a vicious, morally repulsive entity that feasts constantly upon itself in a war of all against all, always hungry, never completely satisfied, and endlessly suffering in its forms of individuality. Schopenhauer finds the appropriate name for this ultimate driving force to be "Will," and he speaks accordingly of the world "as Will."

This conception of the world raises the key question of the meaning of suffering—a question central to both Schopenhauer's and Nietzsche's philosophy. Within Schopenhauer's framework, suffering arises from the nature of reality as Will, as it is manifested through the division-introducing, articulating lens of our human way of knowing the world, which, as Kant stated, creates the appearance of individuals dispersed throughout space and time. Life as we ordinarily know it thus reveals itself to be a meaningless enterprise as people struggle through their years, continually desiring and repeatedly frustrated, always anticipating in the depressing background, the ever-approaching moment of death—the point where our consciousness and everything we know will absolutely disappear. The only remaining salvation for Schopenhauer is presently to tone down our desires, detach ourselves from the world of life, and direct our attention transcendently toward a more tranquil and relieving dimension where our individuality fades and our sense of timeless universality intensifies, through aesthetic experience, compassion, or mystical experience.

Struck hard by Schopenhauer's philosophical rendition of how suffering permeates the world's inner being, Nietzsche came to realize as a professor of classical studies that the ancient Greeks had discovered and embodied a healthy way to address this situation. As he learned from their myths, they were similarly plagued by the debilitating threat of meaninglessness—a kind of existential nausea—in the face of suffering (Nietzsche 1967: 41–44). Having found the Greeks nonetheless to be one of the healthiest societies in human history, it became clear that if he could understand the nature of the Greek's supreme health and ability to overcome hopelessness, he would have preciously in hand a response to Schopenhauer's life-negating outlook and a solution to the problem of human meaning and to the nihilism inherent in his own era.

If we paint with a broad-stroked brush, an underlying inspiration for Nietzsche's writings can be seen to issue from his two complementary accounts of the ancient Greek's source of health and subsequent success in overcoming the meaninglessness of existence. Nietzsche's early work of the 1870s expands upon the proposition that meaninglessness can be overcome through a universalistic love of life itself, as conveyed through the performances of Greek tragedy. His later work of the 1880s enlarges his early insight that meaninglessness can be overcome through a Greek attitude of intense and sporting one-upmanship, or pain-embracing, enthusiastic competitiveness known as *agon*—an idea which is the seed of his doctrine of the will to power.

Nietzsche's therapeutic appreciation of Greek tragedy rests squarely upon how tragedies were performed in the springtime. The context was the annual festival of Dionysus—a god, who, expressive of the springtime season and its accompanying enlivening feelings, represented fertility, rebirth, and rejuvenation. Inspired by Dionysus's mythological meaning, Nietzsche identified with this life-giving deity throughout his writings, first pitting Dionysus against Socrates, aiming to resist Socrates's total commitment to logic and pure reasoning as a force that should dominate over life and instinct. In Nietzsche's later work, turning his attention to the Christianity's detrimental cultural effects, he upheld Dionysus over Jesus, "the Crucified," who by Nietzsche's lights stood contrastingly and enfeeblingly for a more Schopenhauerian, unhealthy, life-negating, pain-avoiding attitude.

In conjunction with Dionysus, the theatrical chorus played a key role in Greek tragic theatre as well: it reinforced the vivifying feelings of the springtime season, supplying a musical foundation against which the play's tragic events unfolded. Nietzsche agreed with Schopenhauer's aesthetics that music is the art that best expresses the driving, willful energies of the world. For him, the Schopenhauerian interpretation of music's significance did well to explain the function of the tragic chorus, which he regarded as the underlying and eternal voice of life itself.

When we combine the springtime season and the tragic chorus to constitute the supportive and surrounding cushion for the play's tragic events, a consoling attitude arises toward those events, as violent, incestuously terrifying, and awful as they are. Tempering the horror, the tragic performance offers peace: everything is untroubling in the end, for the springtime feeling and musical chorus reassuringly confirm that despite the most dreadful circumstances, we remain inextricably part of the enthusiastic energy of life itself:

> And this is the immediate effect of the Dionysian tragedy, that the state and society and, quite generally, the gulfs between man and man give way to an overwhelming feeling of unity leading back to the very heart of nature. The metaphysical comfort—with which, I am suggesting even now, every true tragedy leaves us—that life is at the bottom of things, despite all the changes of appearances, indestructibly powerful and pleasurable. This comfort appears in incarnate clarity in the chorus of satyrs, a chorus of natural beings who live ineradicably, as it were, behind all civilization and remain eternally the same, despite the changes of generations and of the history of nations. (Nietzsche 1967: 59)

> Dionysian art, too, wishes to convince us of the eternal joy of existence: only we are to seek this joy not in phenomena, but behind them. We are to recognize that all that comes into being must be ready for a sorrowful end; we are forced to look into the terrors of the individual existence—yet we are not to become rigid with fear: a metaphysical comfort tears us momentarily from the bustle of the changing figures. We are really for a brief moment primordial being itself, feeling its raging desire for existence and joy in existence; the struggle, the pain, the destruction of phenomena, now appear necessary to us, in view of the excess of countless forms of existence which force and push one another into life, in view of the exuberant fertility of the

universal will. We are pierced by the maddening stings of these pains just when we have become, as it were, one with the infinite primordial joy in existence, and when we anticipate, in Dionysian ecstasy, the indestructibility and eternity of this joy. In spite of fear and pity, we are the happy living beings, not as individuals, but as the one living being, with whose creative joy we are united. (Nietzsche 1967: 104–05)

Nietzsche dons the philosophical robes of eternal springtime as he urges us to exhibit constantly the upbeat, feral, creative, and inexhaustible spirit of life that the tragic theatrical experience and Dionysus convey. Here, an eternalistic dimension of his prescription comes forward as a therapeutic force—a dimension that persists throughout Nietzsche's writings, most notably in his supreme doctrine of the eternal recurrence, as we shall see.

The original title of Nietzsche's 1872 book was *The Birth of Tragedy from the Spirit of Music*. In 1886, he published a second edition of the work, retitled *The Birth of Tragedy, Or: Hellenism and Pessimism*, wherein he offered a prefatory and incisive "self-criticism" of his earlier philosophical self. By this time, now fourteen years later, Nietzsche's outlook had become more consistently down to earth as his philosophizing realistically captured more concrete detail in reference to both history and perceptual experience. He also became less interested in securing or defining any comforts or tranquilizers that would alleviate the depressing force of pain and suffering, preferring instead an outlook which harbors the strength to affirm pain in a healthy way without any anesthetic.

Despite the criticisms he directed toward his earlier work, *The Birth of Tragedy* conveys in its emphasis upon life, and by implication, health, a more existentially oriented perspective than Schopenhauer's. In a conceptually subtle, but significant departure from Schopenhauer, Nietzsche's emphasis upon life and health softens the metaphysical concern with the nature of the world as Will and anticipates his characterization of ordinary truth as an accumulation of dead metaphors, and hence as metaphysically untrue, that he expressed only a year later. Even in his early writings, Nietzsche's preoccupation with health tempers how he assimilates Schopenhauer's description of the spatiotemporal world as permeated permanently with suffering.

Nietzsche departs from Schopenhauer's otherworldliness from the start, but he importantly adopts Schopenhauer's philosophical style of attending to the inner being of the subject at hand. In *The Birth of Tragedy*, the main subject is "life itself," universalistically considered, into which Nietzsche submerges himself and experiences sublimely as an overwhelming surge of power, pleasure, joy, struggle, and deep desire. The suffering is there, but it is surpassed by an ecstatic, invigorating, and inspiring thrill, far beyond the sphere of ordinary moral evaluation. To feel the surging energies of life itself is to feel supremely healthy and powerful, and this is Nietzsche's goal. The solution to the problem of human suffering is to fall in love with life, immersing oneself thereby in life's inexhaustibly vivifying energy.

Nietzsche's overriding concern with health is evident in his fundamental motivation for composing *The Birth of Tragedy*. Superficially considered, this is a work by a young scholar who needed to prove himself to his colleagues. He received his doctorate without having written a dissertation, was offered a professorship at the young age of twenty-four, was acclaimed to possess an extraordinary mind, and was the subject of high academic expectations. Under such conditions, one might have expected Nietzsche to have composed a stiff, technical, and scholarly work, relatively uninteresting to a wider audience, designed to appeal to a handful of dais-sitting pundits who wielded political power in the world of classical scholarship, expecting thereby to guarantee for himself a secure place in academia.

Rather than bend to conventional academic expectations, Nietzsche wrote with a higher purpose in view: he ambitiously composed a manifesto intended to help heal spiritually, his surrounding, seemingly unhealthy and nihilistic culture. Finding the world around him debilitated, increasingly industrialized and dehumanized, and worse yet, succumbing to an ethic of complacent, pleasure-seeking comfort, it is as if he traveled back to ancient Greek culture, grabbed hold of the treasure that made the Greeks healthy and great, and brought it back to his own times to distribute therapeutically to his contemporaries. To rejuvenate Germany is main goal of *The Birth of Tragedy*:

> Out of the Dionysian root of the German spirit a power has arisen which, having nothing in common with the primitive conditions of Socratic culture, can neither be explained nor excused by it, but which is rather felt by this culture as something terribly inexplicable and overwhelmingly hostile— *German music* as we must understand it, particularly in its vast solar orbit from Bach, to Beethoven, from Beethoven to Wagner. (Nietzsche 1967: 119)

> Now at last, upon returning to the primitive source of its being, it may venture to stride along boldly and freely before the eyes of all nations

without being attached to the lead strings of a Romanic civilization; if only it can learn constantly from one people—the Greeks, from whom to be able to learn at all is itself a high honor and a rare distinction. (Nietzsche 1967: 121)

Nietzsche's interest in health underlies his critical reference to "Socratic culture," which for him represents the forces of rationalism and logic gone pathologically out of control. For most philosophers in the Western tradition, Socrates is a patron saint, respected for his courageous, challenging, and discrediting conversations with socially powerful and influential Athenian individuals, who, as a result, chose to sacrifice his life to uphold reason. He stands for many as a great, strong-willed human being who epitomized the philosophical ideal of relentless logic, reflection, and incisively fearless inquiry in the pursuit of truth.

Contrary to popular opinion and inverting the traditional estimation, Nietzsche, unlike Kierkegaard, remains unimpressed by Socrates's interest in truth and reason at all costs. Reluctant to elevate truth to the highest value, he judges Socrates in reference to the healthiness of his perspective, and the judgment is negative. He regards Socrates as a decadent insofar as the excessive reason he espoused and displayed has the detrimental effect of stifling life-energies.

Nietzsche's critique of Socrates anticipates Sigmund Freud's observation in *Civilization and Its Discontents* (1930) that the development of civilization requires everyone to suppress their instinctual energies, leading potentially to psychopathological behavior. Nietzsche discerned similar psychological and physiological oppression in the rise of science and the consequent social regimentation, narrowing of outlooks, and dampening of creativity that followed in its wake. Socrates, Nietzsche maintains, is the fountainhead of this downward trend, appearing on the historical scene unsurprisingly when the ancient Greek civilization began its decline.

## 3.3 Later Nietzsche: Philosophizing from the perspective of life

As Nietzsche matured, his interest in formulating a prescription to heal his ailing culture assumed a more considered form. It was inevitable that

Christianity—the prevailing religion of his European culture, as well as the religion of his personal upbringing as the son and grandson of Lutheran pastors—moved into his philosophical crosshairs. To appreciate Nietzsche's discontent with Christianity, Kant is again instructive, for his moral theory is consistently Christian in its combination of traditional moral values and otherworldliness.

As noted, Kant maintains that we cannot know the absolute truth because the structure of our mind obscures that truth in our very act of trying to know it. We construct a world in space and time, of objects that stand in causal relationships to each other, and this presentation does not represent things as they are in themselves. Scientifically attractive in its affirmation that within this spatiotemporal world, mechanistic explanation thoroughly holds, the price of upholding the integrity of scientific inquiry is the denial of metaphysical knowledge.

With respect to morality, Kant's mechanistic interpretation of the spatiotemporal world implies that freedom must be grounded elsewhere, on a dimension independent of space and time. Insofar as Kant locates God on this transcendent dimension, and insofar as his moral theory lends philosophical legitimacy to dictates that resemble the Ten Commandments, it nicely integrates three subjects that Nietzsche finds unhealthy, namely, traditional moral values, otherworldliness, and God.

Generally speaking, when searching for meaning in one's life, there are four alternative spheres in which to secure it. One can seek meaning on another dimension, as when investing one's faith in God and eternal salvation in heaven. One can extract meaning from the past, as when looking back nostalgically at the ancient Greeks or early tribal cultures as inspirations for an improved present-day life. One can derive meaning from anticipations of a better future, as when working to realize a perfect, exploitation-free, communal society to come. One can also find meaning in the world as it exists right now. The last option is the most existential.

As we have seen, Nietzsche self-consciously spurns otherworldly efforts to secure meaning. His reaching back to the ancient Greeks for inspiration indicates that he is not adverse to extracting meaning from the past, although he eventually realizes that the Greek civilization is long gone. His doctrine of the superhuman, which we will consider, is distinctively future-oriented, as he urges us to find meaning in the great task of preparing the way for this powerful being. Finally and most characteristically, he tries to find meaning in the present as it exists, acknowledging, if not embracing, how it is often permeated with suffering.

In reference to the therapeutic problem at hand, Nietzsche identifies the prevailing Christian culture as the immediate and truly major obstacle in the way of achieving greater health, power, and meaning. The bulk of his attention thus gravitates to a critique of Christianity, which assumes a variety of forms. This critique clears the ground for his more positive, life-affirming doctrines.

Revealing the seedier sources of presently honored values is a salient feature of Nietzsche's argumentative style. In *The Gay Science*, he asks whether our proverbial love for our neighbor is actually a lust for more possessions (Nietzsche 1974: 88). In *On the Genealogy of Morals*, among other values, he describes the origin of obedience as the submission to those whom one hates, and the origin of patience and virtue as the inability to avenge oneself (Nietzsche 1969: 47). Inverting traditional morality, he also suggests that hatred and robbery are not evil, but beneficial in the preservation of the species (Nietzsche 1974: 73). He advances these subversive analyses to make the broader point that our present-day valuations are socially constructed and artificial. As such, they stand to be swept away in favor of healthier values.

Nietzsche's discussion of different moralities is part and parcel of his critique of Christianity. The morality in which we presently live and are standardly taught—one which impresses upon us the importance of treating others with respect, not injuring other people, instituting justice and equality, speaking the truth, and acting compassionately—he judges as grounded in weakness and resentment. He is convinced that the strongest people neither respect nor live according to this kind of morality, as they naturally dominate and exploit others. His position is that those who are the exploited ones—the servants, serfs, and slaves—pragmatically developed the present morality to alleviate the pain inflicted upon them by the stronger, dominating classes: by converting the vicious master to Christianity, one can stop the crack of that master's whip.

For Nietzsche, a particularly enfeebling embodiment of this "slave morality" is utilitarianism, which advises explicitly that we should minimize pain and maximize pleasure, since happiness, it believes, is none other than pleasure. Appreciating to the contrary how suffering can help a person grow to become strong, Nietzsche regards the institution of the utilitarian morality as spelling the complacent and toothless end of humanity—a more physiologically and psychologically weakening doctrine he finds difficult to imagine.

With the death of God follows the practical abandonment of all perspectives that claim to be absolute. Nietzsche consequently does not recognize any "God's eye view" that we could ever adopt, but admits more realistically only a set of finite perspectives, one of the most fundamental and indispensable of which is the perspective of life—the perspective from which he philosophizes, from which he advocates health as the leading value, and within which we live. Contrary to the values of slave morality, he identifies more closely with the more life-affirming master morality of the aristocratic and warrior classes.

Master morality is a morality of self-glorification, where, with an overflowing feeling of power, one gives commands, rules over others, and rules over oneself. Nietzsche mentions as an example the attitudes of the ancient Greek nobility toward themselves vis-à-vis the noncitizens and foreigners. Here, duties extend only to one's peers, and one feels more important than the bulk of humanity. An athletic and aggressive aspect is also featured:

> The knightly-aristocratic value judgments presupposed a powerful physicality, a flourishing, abundant, even overflowing health, together with that which serves to preserve it: was, adventure, hunting, dancing, war games, and in general all that involves vigorous, free, joyful activity. (Nietzsche 1969: 33)

Aristotle's characterization of the magnanimous or great-souled person (*megalopsychos*) is also instructive and illustrative. This is a person of considerable material wealth who thinks in grand terms, who is concerned mainly with honor and dishonor, who, having a proper distance on the world, is not emotionally shaken by either overwhelming success or overwhelming failure, and who is courageous when reasonably called upon, unflinchingly to the point of sacrificing his life if necessary. The great-souled person exudes nobility, but—and this is important to add—he is not a habitual risk-seeker, amazing pioneer, or dancer with death. As so temperate and rational, he serves significantly as a healthy inspiration to Nietzsche, but not entirely. Exhibiting health at an even higher register is Nietzsche's daredevilish superhuman.

## 3.4 Nietzsche's mythologies

If we accept that Nietzsche philosophizes principally from the perspective of life, and that this is only one of many possible perspectives, none of which provide the absolute truth or "God's eye" perspective, then it is inappropriate to describe him as a traditional metaphysician who aims to articulate unconditionally how the world is in itself. His interest is rather in cultivating supreme health, and his philosophizing intends to be culturally therapeutic. From this standpoint, the well-known Nietzschean doctrines of the superhuman, the will to power, and eternal recurrence are best interpreted in a medicinal light, not as expressions of a Nietzschean metaphysics, but as new perspectives that can serve as antidotes to the existing and culturally prevailing outlooks of Christianity and traditional morality.

Like a person who reads through a restaurant menu, choosing items that would constitute a healthy dinner, Nietzsche reads through the history of philosophy, searching for healthy outlooks to live by. Not encountering any that perfectly suit his conception of health, while nonetheless inspired by aspects of some, he formulates some improved recipes of his own. We can refer to them as his therapeutic mythologies.

Nietzsche recognizes that all doctrines are provisional and pragmatic. Observing that "we still live in the age of tragedy, the age of moralities and religions," he appreciates that to advance humanity beyond its presently unhealthy state, he needs to frame his discourse in a manner consistent with his audience's standpoint and degree of receptivity (Nietzsche 1974: 74). He thus supplies in new religious clothing, doctrines and tablets of values to replace the outworn and unhealthy ones, despite how he foresees a time further ahead when religiosity itself will evaporate and disappear.

Within this pragmatic and prescriptive perspective, we can hear the voice of Zarathustra who says:

> Behold, I teach you the superhuman. The superhuman is the meaning of the earth. Let your will say: the superhuman *shall be* the meaning of the earth! I beseech you, my brothers, *remain faithful to the earth*, and do not believe those who speak of otherworldly hopes! (Nietzsche 1954a: 13)

Nietzsche's Zarathustra communicates with biblical-sounding phrasings, like a prophet or religious leader. We need not take his words and doctrines as absolute truths, but as inspirations to promote health, now and in the future. The message in the above passage is simple: it is imperative to develop a more existential, down-to-earth outlook, and reject views which motivate people through promises of reward or the threat of punishment in a world beyond. If one is seeking something to live for—some grand, meaning-giving task—then one can help clear the way for future days and generations when the culture is healthier and when stronger beings will manage the earth.

Embodying Nietzsche's conception of supreme health is the heroic image of the superhuman, or the being that is "over and above the human." The image of this towering *Übermensch* is challenging, not least because it resists assimilation into traditional moral values. As embodying and expressing the perspective of life itself, this superior being displays the characteristics of life in their utmost purity and intensity. We speak here of a dangerous, nonmoral perspective that is aggressive, exploitative, injurious to others, expansive, selfish, self-determining, free, creative, accustomed to pain, ingenious in its ability to overcome obstacles, daredevilish, dominating, aristocratic, immune to psychological depression or debilitation, rebellious, fearless, and fundamentally victorious. This powerful superhuman—Nietzsche's ideal of a this-worldly sort—is both morally terrifying and terrifically sublime.

If one admits that the spatiotemporal world provides no absolute truth, and if one accordingly abandons the traditional philosophical quest for absolute truth, then an objective examination of the ordinary world, and of the life within it, will provide truths relative to that world—truths that are no less true within that world, simply because they are relative to that world.

Consider Euclidean geometry, for instance, within which it is true that the interior angles of a triangle equal 180 degrees. Within non-Euclidean geometry, the proposition does not hold true. The existence of non-Euclidean geometry nonetheless does not undermine the truth about the interior angles of a triangle within Euclidean geometry. In a parallel way, when Nietzsche pronounces that he has put his ear to the heartbeat of life and has discovered that life is the will to power, we can recognize this pronouncement as a potentially objective truth about life.

Nietzsche's doctrine of the will to power is health promoting insofar as it offers a vision consistent with his empirical observations of how life operates. A helpful way to conceive of the will to power is to imagine the set of individuals in the world as a set of shining suns of various sizes and intensities, each of which is glowing, expanding, and exuding energy. The relatively larger suns inevitably outshine and overpower the relatively smaller suns. The suns of equal size and power tend to group together, as they reciprocally hold the expansive energies of the others at bay.

The latter condition, where we have a network of individuals of equal power, mutually balancing each other, establishes the basis for the development of friendships, laws, equality, justice, peacefulness, and stability, along with other expressions of rationality. The situation can be relatively long-lived, although it is inherently unstable and transient. With time, some suns grow in power and some decrease in power, thus causing a change in their previously established interrelationships. If a wealthy person is suddenly devastated financially, then the person's powerful friends may become scarce. If a great scholar or great athlete suddenly suffers a loss of capacities, then his or her status in scholarly or athletic activities will accordingly change.

There is no morality inherent in these transformations. They are matters of power relations undergoing rearrangement. By adopting this liberating view that life, and perhaps the entire world, is governed by the will to power, acts of aggression and hatefulness will produce less guilt, injury will be regarded as part of the natural course of things, risking one's life to attain more power will make more sense, and there will be less concern with discovering an underlying metaphysical meaning to existence. Creating one's own meaning in an atmosphere suffused with health will become one's vocation and intrinsic value.

In an often-cited excerpt from his notebooks, Nietzsche describes the will to power as what the world is "to him" (Nietzsche 1968: 549–50). With this personalized phrasing, he offers an interpretation of the world, rather than an absolute account of it. To him, the world is a fixed quantity of energy, mechanically recirculating, "eternally flooding back, with tremendous years of recurrence." It is a sea of forces that transforms itself continually, and which is going nowhere beyond that set of transformations—ones that move from the simple to the complex, and from the complex to the simple, forever, with nothing further beneath or beyond.

Nietzsche penned this account of the will to power in 1885, four years after he first envisaged his supreme doctrine of eternal recurrence in the Swiss mountain hamlet of Sils Maria, and two years after he first gave explicit voice to the thought of the will to power in 1883, in *Thus Spoke Zarathustra*.

He intends the doctrines to go hand in hand to express a healthier interpretation of the world. In his 1888 notebooks, he reiterates the substance of his 1885 notebook account of the will to power mentioned above, using it to formulate a pseudo-cosmological rationale for eternal recurrence (Nietzsche 1968: 549).

Specifically, Nietzsche speculates that the energy in the cosmos is a perfectly fixed quantity, and that with infinite time, the series of transforming energy states must eventually arrive at a reiteration of one of the earlier states, thus beginning a mechanical replay of the entire series in exact duplication. With infinite time, an endless sequence of repeat performances would result.

This interpretation of the universe contains only the fixed quantity of energy and its repetitive content. The difference between the excerpts on the will to power and the eternal recurrence is that in the latter, Nietzsche renders his earlier reference to the "eternally flooding back, with tremendous years of recurrence" more articulate by conceptualizing the world as a set of discrete and mechanically related events within in an infinite time. By implication, the doctrine of eternal recurrence similarly expresses how the world appears "to him" as he philosophizes from the perspective of life.

More important than Nietzsche's interpretive assimilation of eternal recurrence and the will to power is how he employs the doctrine of eternal recurrence existentially to assess the pain-accommodating strength of one's character. It serves as a test to determine how at home one is in the world of suffering, and hence, how resistant to depression and nihilism one is. For Nietzsche, the crucial question in each and every thing is "Do you desire this once more and innumerable times more?" (Nietzsche 1974: 273–74)

One can ask the question in reference to one's own life, as one considers the prospect of living through it over and over again. One can also ask it in reference to the entire world, as one considers the endless recurrence of wars and suffering. If everything is interconnected, it is impossible consistently to will the recurrence of one's own life, without willing the recurrence of the rest of world history.

Nietzsche's doctrine of eternal recurrence is a matter of imagination, not a matter of truth, for it does not make complete sense upon extended philosophical reflection. We would in fact not remember anything from recurrence to recurrence, so there is no reason to care about reiteration. Moreover, if each recurrence is completely identical, then there can be no series of recurrences that follow one another, since the complete identity between any two would entail their collapse into a singularity.

The doctrine serves instead as a test of health insofar as it is possible to ask imaginatively in relation to every action—including the most morally repugnant and unbearable—whether one would want affirmatively to inscribe its contents into eternity, not just once, but repeatedly. If there is sufficient strength to affirm wholeheartedly the horrible things in life, then one will have interpretively, virtually magically, turned lead into gold, and a hell into a heaven, rendering the suffering-filled world that was so morally repugnant to Schopenhauer, into the best of all possible worlds. Such is the therapeutic function of Nietzsche's mythologies, which he designs and advances to replace Christian mythology.

## 3.5 Nietzsche in existential perspective

Nietzsche, and existentialist thought in general, intends to be as down to earth as possible. We can ask consequently how realistic Nietzsche's views actually are. As noted, he asserts in *Thus Spoke Zarathustra* that the superhuman is the "meaning of the earth" adding shortly thereafter that the superhuman is the "meaning of human existence." Both expressions imply that we should live for a future when earthly conditions will be highly improved.

As we know from political history, the postulation of grand tasks and single, overriding goals effectively provides meaning for people, but these single-minded projective hopes also divert our attention from what is happening here and now. Moreover, these single, overriding goals often prove to be illusory and the success of grand tasks remains uncertain. This applies not only to Nietzsche's superhuman, but to all views which secure meaning by lifting us out of the present moment to attend to some anticipated future that is usually distant, challenging, and attained through demanding struggle.

On a smaller, but no less relevant scale, consider the psychological tendency to ignore the rich perceptual details of one's surroundings when pangs of hunger or any other strong desire motivate one to find satisfaction. In general, projections into the future draw our attention away from the present. Nietzsche's superhuman is intended to be realized on earth, but its anticipated realization at some presently untouchable future can now seem almost as unreal as a world located on another dimension.

This leads us to question the present-day applicability of Nietzsche's health-promoting doctrines which have been drawn substantially from a society long gone, namely, ancient Greece. Aristotle's ideal of the great-souled person significantly motivates Nietzsche's conception of the superhuman. Greek tragedy underlies Nietzsche's ideal of a healthy attitude toward life. Greek one-upmanship and competitiveness motivate his conception of the will to power. The premier Nietzschean figure of Dionysus, who stands against both Socrates and Jesus, stems also from ancient Greece, as does Nietzsche's conception of master morality. When reflecting upon these sources, our attention shifts from the present-day reality to a nostalgic past, now out of reach, at least insofar as we try to extract meaning from the Greeks to project and enrich our present situation.

Among his life-affirming doctrines, that of eternal recurrence perhaps comes closest to cultivating positively and realistically the most explicit and consistent attention to the rich perceptual details of the here and now:

> *The greatest weight.*—What, if some day or night a demon were to steal after you into your loneliest loneliness and say to you: "This life as you now live it and have lived it, you will have to live once more and innumerable times more; and there will be nothing new in it, but every pain and every joy and every thought and sigh and everything unutterably small or great in your life will have to return to you, all in the same succession and sequence—even this spider and this moonlight between the trees, and even this moment and I myself. The eternal hourglass of existence is turned upside down again and again, and you with it, speck of dust!" (Nietzsche 1974: 273–74)

The doctrine is immediately grounded in our immediate, first-person perception of the present moment with all of its inexhaustible detail. Despite this concreteness, it requires us also to assume a distanced and eternalistic perspective that weakens its existentiality: we must adopt a detached and objectifying mountaintop outlook from which to look down upon our own and everyone else's situation, perceiving them as mere specks of dust. From this distant perspective, so far removed, we all stand as debris in a bottle, repeatedly shaken by a cosmic, but uncaring, hand.

This distanced perspective is not peculiar to the doctrine of eternal recurrence. It is an essential feature of Nietzsche's philosophizing which complements, contrasts, and puts into perspective itself his interest in attending to the inner being of the subject at hand. In his early writings, for instance, we encounter the same, disengaged position:

> Once upon a time, in some out of the way corner of that universe which is dispersed into numberless twinkling solar systems, there was a star upon which clever beasts invented knowing. That was the most arrogant and mendacious minute of "world history," but nevertheless, it was only a minute. After nature had drawn a few breaths, the star cooled and congealed, and the clever beasts had to die. (Nietzsche 1979: 79)

Associated with this faraway perspective is the eternalistic dimension of the doctrine of eternal recurrence, which simultaneously covers the future, the past, and the present. As in the doctrine of the superhuman, Nietzsche draws our attention to the future. Compatibly with his appeal to the ancient Greeks, he also draws our attention to the past. Although eternal recurrence completely and existentially solidifies the future and the past into the present moment, without introducing any anticipatory hopes or reminiscing nostalgia, Nietzsche presents the reiterative quality of this solidified "past-present-future" with a metaphysical aura that is almost religious in tone. Just as he expressed love for life itself in *The Birth of Tragedy*, he expresses love for eternity in connection with eternal recurrence, sexualizing all existence romantically, as he was disposed to do:

> Never yet have I found the woman from whom I wanted children, unless it be this woman whom I love: for I love you, O eternity. *For I love you, O eternity!* (Nietzsche 1954a: 228–31)

In *The Birth of Tragedy*, Nietzsche presents his conception of life with the same sexual charge, reflecting thereby the psychological and physiological truth of how our instinct to reproduce life is among the most dominating and overpowering. *The Birth of Tragedy*'s presentation is highly sublimated and idealized as he describes how the ancient Greek's love of life manifested itself as the experience of perpetually apprehending an ideal love-image, namely, Helen of Troy's supremely beautiful face:

> And so the spectator may stand quite bewildered before this fantastic excess of life, asking himself by virtue of what magic potion these high-spirited men could have found life so enjoyable that, wherever they turned, their

eyes beheld the smile of Helen, the ideal picture of their own existence, "floating in sweet sensuality." (Nietzsche 1967: 41)

Despite its attractiveness, the romantic, religious, and quasi-metaphysical atmosphere that pervades Nietzsche's doctrine of eternal recurrence turns our attention away from the present moment and "this spider and this moonlight between the trees," at least insofar as the present moment could be more realistically appreciated in its raw, existential, contingent, and momentarily unique reality. Admittedly, the doctrine immerses and locks us into a material world that is filled with suffering and violence as it aims to preclude all escape, negating hope for salvation or relief in either a heaven beyond or in an absolute nothingness. However, the reverent, loving, romantic, halo of holiness that Nietzsche superimposes upon this amoral, vicious world—virtually a Medusa—as much as it may help to accommodate us to material reality also interferes with our apprehending that reality in its ordinariness and unadorned truth, free from romantic illusions.

In his having proposed the doctrine of eternal recurrence, one can wonder whether Nietzsche believed that for the most part, people are presently not strong enough simply to "be here now" without some kind of mythological conception of the world to keep them materially focused. Not all existentialist doctrines contain such an elaborate mythological apparatus.

To secure the existential meaning Nietzsche seeks, it could be enough to realize that every moment is unique, that it will *never* return, and that whatever one does at the present moment can never be reversed. At every moment, one inscribes content indelibly into the tablet of eternity and there is no turning back as the clock runs out. Indeed, Nietzsche realized this himself:

> In his heart every man knows quite well that, being unique, he will be in the world only once and that no imaginable chance will for a second time gather together into a unity so strangely variegated an assortment as he is: he knows it but he hides it like a bad conscience—why? (Nietzsche 1983: 127)

We mentioned in the Introduction that one of the existentially relevant themes in the nineteenth century is the highlighting of freedom and its disengagement from rationality. Nietzsche speaks frequently about the importance of creating new values to replace the presently unhealthy ones, and to do so requires freedom. In tension with this proposition, Nietzsche criticizes the notion of free will, speaking as if our given power levels merely play themselves out mechanically (Nietzsche 1966: 28–29; Nietzsche 1986: 34–35). If the latter is so, then his overriding project of formulating therapeutic prescriptions to heal a nihilistic culture becomes pointless in the face of such determinism.

Nietzsche's critical attitude toward free will can be explained as an artifact of his resistance to otherworldly hypotheses, among which is the idea of an absolutely free will, independent of the body, which we find in Kant. He appears to have accepted Kant's view that metaphysical knowledge is unattainable, and to have consequently restricted his philosophizing to the material world that we can know—a world that Kant, as well as Schopenhauer, described in thoroughly mechanistic terms. Following suit, but rejecting both Kant's and Schopenhauer's admission of dimensions beyond the spatiotemporal world, Nietzsche inherited a mechanistic view of nature as inherent to the perspective of life within which he was trying to express his culturally therapeutic aims. The counterproductive upshot is that if it is taken too literally and penetratingly, as opposed to being regarded superficially as merely a health-producing myth, this mechanism undermines the strong sense of freedom and creativity that his outlook crucially requires as a means to new values.

On the redeeming side, Nietzsche's thought displays a structure that embodies the notion of authenticity that prevails across existentialist thought. Reluctant to draw any essential differences between humans and other animals, he emphasizes in particular how we are living beings, and accordingly, how we ought to align ourselves as best as possible with the nature of "life itself." The most authentic humans are the ones who are what they ought to be as healthy forms of life. We can speak in this context of someone becoming a "genuine human," "real human," or "true human."

A true example of a thing arises when that the thing is what it ought to be. This is a kind of truth as self-correspondence, or better, self-realization or self-actualization. The moral intonation of this conception issues from Kant's moral theory, where to be a moral person, one exemplifies in one's behavior the idea of acting consistently, which is Kant's way of expressing the imperative to behave rationally. The situation is similar in Aristotle's moral theory: a human being is a being whose purpose is to act rationally, and a good human being is one who acts rationally well.

In these cases, the human being is defined with a given potential, and the task is then set to become an authentic, genuine, or true person by realizing that potential. Throughout existentialist thought, we can see this structure of self-realization reiterated. In Heidegger and Sartre, human beings are defined as self-questioning beings, and the task of becoming authentic is to be as self-questioning as possible. In Sartre and in Kierkegaard, humans are defined furthermore as free beings, and the task of becoming authentic is to express one's freedom as purely as possible.

In Nietzsche, human beings are defined as essentially living beings, and the task of becoming authentic is to be as *true to life* as possible, which translates fundamentally into being as healthy as possible. For Nietzsche, this ideal is too high for any presently existing human beings, so he expresses the ideal of supreme health in the image of the superhuman-yet-to-come. Attaining the ideal of being perfectly free is yet another ideal that proves to be too high for the human being, as we have seen in Kierkegaard, and as we shall see in Sartre.

With respect to Nietzsche, we should note the existential price that his outlook pays for saying "yes" to life so enthusiastically. It amounts to saying "no," not to suffering, which Nietzsche acknowledges, but to death. In the doctrine of eternal recurrence, we never absolutely die, but are reincarnated everlastingly as a set of exact reiterations of our present selves. In feeling supremely healthy, we also do not feel as if we will ever die. In becoming one with life itself, our sense of individuality submerges and our death is absorbed comfortably into a great flow of energy without any attendant anxiety. In feeling proud to sacrifice oneself to create some upcoming superhuman, the reality of one's own upcoming annihilation is obscured.

It is easy to confuse overcoming the fear of one's death with denying the reality of one's death, and in Nietzsche, the existentialist anxiety that issues from reflecting upon one's own death is noticeably diminished. Nietzsche embodies an important aspect of the existentialist outlook, namely, the idea of being down to earth as much as possible. In his projects of life affirmation and the rejection of otherworldliness, the reality of our personal death nonetheless becomes surrounded and absorbed by the ocean of forces that Nietzsche refers to as life itself. As we will see in the next chapter, Martin Heidegger advances existentially over Nietzsche, as he develops a down-to-earth outlook that more explicitly highlights our presence in the world as finite and anxious individuals who are continually facing death.

# 4

# Martin Heidegger (1889–1976)

When one apprehends the world as an overwhelming and amazing mystery, philosophy begins. This occurs in everyone's experience at one time or another, but not everyone dwells upon the perplexity in a persistent, soul-moving, or life-affecting way. As a matter of routine, the universe as a whole remains mostly out of sight, as more immediate and manageable concerns dominate, consume, and define our surroundings. Wider issues and a broader perspective may come to light during times of crisis or loss, potentially destabilizing one's world and opening the doors to change, but faith often appears consolingly to reestablish the status quo, confirming that everything will work out independently of any need to philosophize, worry, reflect, or modify one's perspective.

It remains peculiar nonetheless that the physical world is always "just there" before us, and that upon reawaking each morning, one's clothes are in the same place they were left the night before, one's bed is in the same position, and the rest of the world continues as it did previously, with the same contours, people, and challenges. A treasure chest that some pirates buried on a desert island centuries ago remains exactly where it was set, waiting right now for its discovery under the sand. That the world goes on without us lends a strange quality to our presence and existence.

Space and time extend further than we can imagine, as our efforts to comprehend them eventually draw a blank. Moreover, any piece of the world—a mountain, a stone, a grain of sand—can be divided into smaller and smaller units, endlessly, until nothing remains but the dimensionless points of empty space. We are always in the middle, immersed, centered, and suspended in infinity both large and small—an infinity that for others who observe our departure, does not disappear for them as it does for us, when we leave the worldly scene through death.

Such reflections can suggest that if the nature of "all that is" could somehow be fathomed, a fundamental philosophical understanding would follow. As a starting point for inquiry, and for an entrance into Martin Heidegger's thought, one can ask the simple and straightforward question, "What *is* Being?" Going a step further to take into account the world's *significance*, and thematizing thereby the uncertainty that surrounds life's ultimate meaning, the question can be more determinately formulated as expressing a concern with the "meaning" of Being. This is how Heidegger conceives of it in his most influential book, *Being and Time* (1927):

> Do we in our time have an answer to the question of what we really mean by the word "being"? Not at all. So it is fitting that we should raise anew *the question of the meaning of Being*. But are we nowadays even perplexed at our inability to understand the expression "Being"? Not at all. So first we must reawaken an understanding for the meaning of this question. Our aim in the following treatise is to work out the question of the meaning of Being and to do so concretely. Our provisional aim is the Interpretation of *time* as the possible horizon for any understanding whatsoever of Being. (Heidegger 1962: 19)

By "Being," Heidegger is not referring to an empty, virtually meaningless conception that includes indiscriminately everything one can think of, excludes nothing, and says nothing specific. In contrast to this abstract conception of Being, he is referring instead to the full, seamless, actual, and complete reality of everything that is, in its inexhaustible detail, existentiality, and multidimensional richness.

With this more weighty and realistic conception of Being in mind, it follows that for Heidegger, the word, "Being," signifies an unfathomable manifold of existence, and not an undeveloped seed or abstract philosophical point that will take millennia to mature into perfection, as Hegel's philosophy envisions. Being is already fully here and now in its richness, waiting to disclose its depths to us.

Observing the world and people around him, Heidegger finds that the existential reality of Being has been obscured by our cultural surroundings. We have been conditioned to live within a perspective that makes it difficult to appreciate the most crucial philosophical questions, such as the question of the meaning of Being. Before offering any answers, he sets out to clear the ground by explaining in detail why, in contemporary life, these philosophical concerns are not entering people's consciousnesses with sufficient urgency.

Heidegger's view—implicit in his earlier writings and explicit in his later ones—is that far-too-influential within the culture at large has been an essentially mercenary, mercantile, and selfish outlook, which reinforced through its enlistment of natural science, technology, and business, regards everything it encounters disrespectfully as an object to be measured, used, or otherwise exploited. This objectifying outlook, he maintains, has been preventing people from developing their inherent appreciation of themselves as existent beings, and he believes that our human task is to dissipate that fog as much as possible.

Heidegger compares to Nietzsche in this respect, who, only a few decades earlier, felt similarly that he was speaking and writing philosophically within and to a culture whose overall perspective was too weak and distracted by otherworldly attractions to face the world honestly, healthily, and courageously. Their differences notwithstanding, both philosophers perceive that the advance and cultural domination of science and technology both inhibits philosophical awareness and renders people insensitive to existential realities.

## 4.1 The obfuscating effects of objectification

To appreciate how difficult it is to apprehend clearly our existential situation, we can begin with the elementary way in which we express ourselves in language. A sentence has a *subject*, which usually refers to some things such as a table, a chair, a door, and so on—Aristotle referred to these common physical items as "primary substances"—and a *predicate*, which assigns to the item a property, quality, or "universal," such as red, loud, large, sweet, and so on. We say that the table is brown, the chair is hard, the forest is thick, the water is rushing, and so on.

This simple grammatical structure of "subject and predicate" implicitly conveys the message that the world is constituted by a set of things with properties. To complete the picture we can include relationships, either between the things, or between the properties, or between the properties and the things—greater than, smaller than, louder than, and so on—and consequently assume that the world is built from the ground up metaphysically, out of individuals, universals, and relations, regarded as the elementary units.

Here, the word "substance" is revealing. Considering the meaning of the prefix, "sub" (under), it reveals itself to be akin to the word "understanding." When we understand something, we typically aim to discern the core or essential support of the thing in question. Even as applied to people, which are not properly "things," we believe that we can understand a person well by formulating an idea of what is invisibly motivating below the surface of the person's changing clothes, appearances, physical body, gestures, and such, namely, the person's constant and true character. To discern that substantial character, we ask ourselves after observing and reflecting upon the person's diverse behavior, for example, what the person wants fundamentally.

In this case, the grammatically suggested structure of a "substance with qualities" is transferred over and applied to our understanding of persons to yield the idea of a "conscious subject" with qualities, where the conscious subject is conceptualized implicitly as a kind of integrated and persisting "thing," "object," "substance," or "soul." Considered in general and more expansively, this style of thinking in terms of things, objects, and substances soon becomes abstractive and scientific: to understand the world around us, we search for fixed definitions, constant characters, or formulaic constancies that underlie changing appearances, as in mathematics, chemical descriptions, and the laws governing gravitation or thermodynamics.

In the history of Western philosophy, a well-known example of this style of substance-centered or object-centered thinking is in the seventeenth-century philosophy of René Descartes (1596–1650). He described the physical world as an "extended" substance and reflective human beings as "thinking" substances, referring to himself accordingly as a "thinking thing."

We can also recall the philosophy of Baruch Spinoza (1632–77), who—writing in the decades immediately following Descartes—described what he believed to be ultimate reality, namely, God, as a substance as well. According to Spinoza, this infinite substance, which includes everything without remainder, is a single individual (i.e., all of reality) which has an infinite number of attributes, two of which, as per Descartes, are extension and thought, and the rest of which are inscrutable. A noteworthy aspect of Spinoza's conception of God relevant to our appreciation of Heidegger's conception of Being is that despite how Spinoza refers to God as a "substance," Spinoza regards

God's depth of being as so richly multidimensional, that it goes far beyond anything we can imagine or completely specify. Heidegger maintains the same about "Being."

The above-described, objectifying style of thinking that we find in Descartes and Spinoza persists, somewhat softened, in the later eighteenth-century philosophy of Immanuel Kant. Arguing controversially that human beings do not have the capacity to know the nature of ultimate reality, Kant nonetheless refers to that reality as an unknowable "thing-in-itself," suggesting implicitly that this reality is a mind-independent "thing." He also uses the word "object" in reference to ultimate reality. Taking a small step away from the objectifying style of thinking, however, Kant avoids using the concept of "substance" to characterize the thing-in-itself, arguing that this concept gives us only a limited and exclusively human way to think about our experience.

These examples, ranging from Aristotle to Kant, represent a long and persistent tradition in which a cluster of closely related terms—substance, thing, object—is used, sometimes as a whole, sometimes in part, sometimes straightforwardly, sometimes tempered, to characterize the ultimate reality of either the world or the human being. In reference to the physical world, the broader upshot of this style of thinking is that our surroundings eventually present themselves as an inanimate, alien, and confronting being—a being whose uncaring, thing-like appearance tends to generate the defensive, if not fearful, reaction that we humans would do best for ourselves to harness, dominate, and control the physical world, lest the mindless turbulence of natural forces destroy us by accident. With respect to humans, the upshot is that human subjectivity tends to be reduced to an insensate objectivity, either implicitly or explicitly, with a consequent erosion in our attitudes of mutual respect.

Herein lies the problem for Heidegger. Neither is the physical world a completely hostile being, nor are people objects through and through. People, especially, are not primarily objects to be used, dominated over, or defined essentially in terms of their efficiency or performativity. Human relationships, moreover, are not essentially business relationships.

It remains that our basic grammar, our immediately external orientation toward the world, our interest in understanding nature analytically and dissectively for practical use, self-defense, and survival, all reinforce each other to sustain a worldview that involves interpreting our surroundings as merely a set of objects to be used and controlled. As an expression and continuation of this attitude, philosophical questions and answers find themselves formulated in terms of objects, substances, and things. The staggering practical success of contemporary natural science goes far to legitimate this object-oriented mentality in philosophical thinking, leading many to believe that the human mind or consciousness can be entirely reduced and understood in the vocabulary of brain chemistry, physiology, or some other physicalistic discipline.

The nineteenth-century philosophical spirit brought some challenges to this object-centered style of metaphysical thinking, for it was realized more clearly that self-conscious human beings are just as much a part of reality as is everything else. It is not as if the rocks, stars, sunlight, and storms, all of which apparently have no subjectivity, are more real or privileged beings in contrast to humans. Reality flows through every being equally, constituting us as much as it does the flowers and the ocean. All beings are equal in this respect, and nothing is essentially alien. It is one and the same fundamental energy that beats our heart, moves our diaphragm, grows the flowers, shines the sun, and renders us self-aware. Since humans are questioningly aware of themselves and of the infinite space and time that surrounds them, their being is especially valuable and pronounced in this grand scheme of things.

If so, then we can turn directly to ourselves for metaphysical understanding. If, as a matter of self-knowledge, we can grasp our ultimate being—the being that is *closest* to us—then we will simultaneously grasp the ultimate being of the rest of existence. This insight epitomizes the critical reaction to Kant by philosophers such as Hegel and Schopenhauer, who believed that Kant was too skeptical about the possibility that humans can have absolute knowledge of themselves. Heidegger follows same insight in *Being and Time*.

Hegel's and Schopenhauer's criticisms of Kant accordingly involve rejecting the view that ultimate reality is best characterized as exclusively some kind of "thing" or "object." Hegel himself regarded it as a developmental process that embodies the structure of self-consciousness; Schopenhauer regarded it as the inner being of everything as "Will."

Kierkegaard, we have seen, took a similar line in his advocacy of truth as subjectivity and his associated denial that objective, scientific means can grasp the nature of God or the absolute.

These more metaphysically confident, assertive, and subject-focused positions arise from shifting the primary locus of philosophical inquiry toward oneself, and away from external objects. The logic is this: assuming that we can understand ultimate reality by understanding the human being's own reality, since humans are just as much an expression of reality as anything else, and if human beings are not primarily objects, then neither should one expect Being primarily, and certainly not exclusively, to be an object. "Being" contains individual objects, or beings, such as tables, chairs, the earth, stars, and moon, but Being as a whole is not an object like a table, chair, or celestial body. It is rich, inscrutable, and bottomless beyond the limits of any individual being or entity. It includes our existence, our subjectivity, and our very wonder about Being. One could say that in its manifestation in the human form, Being wonders about itself.

In his effort to understand ourselves and the world, Heidegger follows the path of philosophers such as Hegel, Schopenhauer, and Kierkegaard insofar as he recognizes that if we are going to focus on the human being, or more precisely, focus on what it is concretely, or *existentially*, to be a human—living, breathing, reflecting, acting, caring—then scientific characterizations need to be replaced and transcended by an outlook that is more true to our directly experienced, everyday condition.

In *Being and Time*, Heidegger consequently opposes the alleged primacy of the scientific, object-oriented, efficiency-governed outlook by developing an answer to the general philosophical question of the meaning of Being through a non-scientific conception of what it means to be human, namely, a phenomenological and presumably more metaphysically disclosing conception. We can also refer to this as an existentialist conception, since Heidegger attends carefully to the qualities of our daily, down-to-earth, first-hand experience of the world in this effort toward self-understanding.

## 4.2 Human being as "being present"

Just as the physical world is for us "just there," we ourselves are "right here and now," present on the scene, thinking constantly about this, that, or other things. Since we are right here and now, present on the scene, we do not stand *apart* from the world, observing it from a distance as if we were located invisibly outside of space and time, detached, coolly and objectively uninvolved as a theoretically ideal scientist might be. From the very start, each of us is immersed in the world and is immediately present within it. We are part of the world, or more exactly, we "dwell" within it, just as fish are always already both within and constituted by the water in which they swim.

We humans realize that we are here—indeed, astonishingly and puzzlingly so—and are consequently beings that are "present" to ourselves in the world. Heidegger refers generally to human being as "being present," or as "being there" on the scene. His technical word is *Dasein*. *Da* means "there"; *sein* means "to be." In ordinary German usage, *Dasein* means "concrete existence."

The philosophical project in *Being and Time* is thus to make *Dasein* transparent to itself, where *Dasein* is understood to be human being in its down-to-earth, existentially immersed, living, perceiving, questioning, self-aware, acting reality. Heidegger aims to arrive at concrete self-knowledge and to disclose the deeper truths of the universe thereby:

> Thus to work out the question of Being adequately, we must make an entity—the inquirer—transparent in his own Being. . . .This entity which each of us is himself and which includes inquiring as one if the possibilities of its Being, we shall denote by the term "*Dasein*." If we are to formulate our question explicitly and transparently, we must first give a proper explication of an entity (Dasein), with regard to its Being (Heidegger 1962: 27).

Centuries ago, aiming to hit philosophical bedrock, Aristotle formulated an inventory of the most basic kinds of things and qualities of which we humans can be aware, which he set out in a list of ten "categories." In linguistic terms, his ten categories specify the different states of being that can be either a subject or a predicate of a proposition. Aristotle appears to have formulated his list of ten categories non-systematically, simply by reflecting carefully and deeply about the world and the basic ways in which we think. The categories are (1) substance, (2) quantity, (3) quality, (4) relation, (5) place, (6) time, (7) being in a particular position or posture, (8) having a particular condition, (9) acting upon some other thing, and (10) being acted upon by some other thing.

Two thousand years later, inspired by the fundamentality and philosophical longevity of Aristotle's set of categories as they identify possible objects of awareness, Immanuel Kant also formulated a set of categories that characterize the most general ways in which we must think about ourselves and our world. Specifically, Kant set out a list of twelve different logical shapes in terms of which our understanding organizes given sensory information and contributes to the rational construction of our experience. Kant's twelve categories are (1) unity, (2) plurality, (3) totality, (4) reality, (5) negation, (6) limitation, (7) substance and accident, (8) cause and effect, (9) reciprocity, (10) possibility, (11) existence (*Dasein*), and (12) necessity.

More systematic than Aristotle in the construction of his list of categories, Kant derived his set of categories from a standard set of twelve elementary logical judgments that prevailed in the logic texts of his time, regarding each logical judgment as the basis for a respective category. For instance, he describes the application to our experience of the logical form of judgment, "If . . . then . . . " as the activity of the category (i.e., the pure concept) of "causality." The events in the world appear to be thoroughly connected in network of causal relationships because we connect them that way ourselves by projecting the "if . . . then . . . " format.

Kant's categories are essentially logical functions, reconceived as the elementary ways that our understanding gives a rational structure to the manifold of raw sensory information. More technically and broadly stated, his categories of the understanding are basic logical functions that, in their application to the raw sensory manifold, transform into basic epistemological functions.

The purpose of both Aristotle's and Kant's sets of categories is to identify philosophically in the form of a firm listing, what is fundamental either to the objects that we apprehend, or to our ways of apprehending those objects. In *Being and Time*, Heidegger likewise expresses an interest in setting forth such elementary dimensions of human thought and experience. The difference is that he starts with a more concrete, phenomenological conception of the human being. This issues in the construction of a set of categories, but categories of a different kind. Heidegger calls them *existentiales*, preferring this term to "categories" insofar as *existentiale* refers to the core structure of a being best described as a "who" (namely, us), rather than as a "what."

When Kant formulated his list of twelve categories, he conceived of the human being in more of a detached, non-historical, less realistic, almost scientific way. Isolating human understanding as a concept-containing-and-processing sector of our mind, he sought to outline the structure of the understanding as a specific mental faculty, independently of its being filled with any sensory contents, as one might describe a piece of a computer's hardware. Kant consequently identified twelve abstract conceptual forms, or categories, of the understanding that operate in conjunction with the structures of other mental faculties.

Heidegger, in contrast, philosophizes from within a context that regards people as situated initially and fundamentally within ordinary, or average, daily scenes. We dwell in the world from the very start, situated in a community, handling objects, eating, sleeping, laughing, reflecting, and so on. Within *this* kind of realistic social context, Heidegger's philosophizing about and identification of fundamental human structures—ones that we can reiterate are now being conceived of as "existential" structures—originates, emanates, and is grounded. Heidegger, like Aristotle, nonetheless derives his set of fundamental existential structures of human being simply by observing and reflecting carefully about what it is like to be a human being.

With this phenomenological approach, Heidegger rejects the essentially Cartesian and British Empiricist account of human knowledge which maintains that we are initially and immediately aware of mental images, and then, as a matter of inference from those images, become indirectly aware of the existence of physical objects, that is, the external world, which the mental images, like photographs, represent. The account is problematic because it begins our philosophizing unrealistically in a self-enclosed, solitary mental theatre where our perceptions are restricted to and are identified with private mental images. By accepting this as the philosophical starting point, it becomes difficult to break out of one's solitary confinement into a sphere of publicity, since it remains forever impossible to tell whether one's mental images refer to anything that is mind independent.

Heidegger argues that the above epistemological impasse is an illusion, for one cannot coherently formulate the skepticism-generating hypothesis that we always think immediately and exclusively about our mental images, as if living in a waking dream, without first having assumed to the contrary that we are initially situated in the physical world, directly perceiving external objects in a transparent way. The self-enclosed, Cartesian position makes sense only by assuming a prior starting point and grounding in the real world, sitting, for instance, before the fire in one's nightclothes, wondering philosophically whether or not one is perceiving the physical world accurately and reliably, as did Descartes himself. In this respect it is a secondary and derivative position. In opposition to this, Heidegger maintains that our "being-in" the world is the initially given condition, and that "being-in" is an *existentiale*. Any reasonable philosophy must subsequently admit at the very outset, that we find ourselves always already in a world filled with other people and things ready-to-hand in space and time. Philosophizing can only reasonably and realistically start with our being-in-the-world.

The same kind of argument challenges the alleged fundamentality of the scientific outlook, when this outlook is understood to presuppose an initial standpoint wholly detached from the objects it intends to observe. To the contrary, insofar as we are immersed in the world and dwell within it, there is no way to observe any object as it is in itself. Either we inevitably influence the object while observing it, or our immersion in the world requires us to observe the object from a particular angle or perspective.

## 4.3 Other people and the obscuring of personal authenticity

If we are situated fundamentally "in" a world with other people to begin with, then our consciousness is infused with sociality from the very start. Our sense of individuality consequently emerges and develops within a social context and the influence of other people. From our own individual standpoint, all other people are nonetheless "the Others" for us, and from the standpoint of each of those other people, each of us to them is among "the Others." As individuals, we each stand against "the Others," and from the standpoint of others who perceive us, we each constitute "the Others."

The other person with whom we speak might be a close friend, someone passing by on the street, or a person selling vegetables in a marketplace, but beyond and in addition to this, there is a general conception of "the Other" that derives more impersonally from the social collectivity in which we are situated. This generic conception becomes apparent when in daily life, for example, we hear that "they" say that we should tell the truth or respect others, or that certain groups of people are the enemy or are our friends. As these directives and opinions come to us, no one in particular stands as their source. It is what "they" say, rather facelessly. Heidegger refers to this general conception of the Other as "the They" (*das Man*).

In the course of ordinary living, it is impossible to avoid absorbing public opinion, or "the They," as part of our personal identity. We inevitably identify with the average group or society at large to some extent and dilute our sense of individuality in the process. Indeed, it is easy to become submerged in a sea of comforting and security-bestowing social labels and values. Upon identifying strongly with the role of mayor, waiter, cook, student, parent, member of the board, youth group, political party, and so on, to the point where one virtually defines oneself *as* the social role, and little more, however, it can become difficult to appreciate that as unique individuals, we are actually and humanly far more than what these roles, labels, armbands, flags, uniforms, and insignias circumscribe for us.

At the extreme, publicity and "the They"—by thinning-out, obscuring, and rendering superficial one's self-conception—can lead a person to forget what it is like to be a unique individual. Under such clouded conditions, people can *hide from themselves*, identifying excessively with social roles or labels, and failing to face their personal realities by bringing their social roles to the forefront, like shields or blankets. The social roles or labels become literally "cover stories" for people.

Adopting such cover stories is to some extent inescapable, for they are constituents of our social situation. The awareness of personal uniqueness always blends with the awareness of being one among many other people and having a place within the community. In view of this, the concrete human situation is accordingly tension-ridden: as we stand *with* others in a social context, we also stand *against* others as individuals, knowing that we are each placed specially in the world. Heidegger consequently describes our social situation with a precautionary tone that draws attention to the existential danger of becoming too absorbed in the average, everyday, generic world of "the They":

> We take pleasure and enjoy ourselves as *they* [man] take pleasure; we read, see, and judge about literature and art as *they* see and judge; likewise we shrink back from the "great mass" as *they* shrink back; we find "shocking" what *they* find shocking. The "they," which is nothing definite and which all are, though not as the sum, prescribes the kind of Being of everydayness. (Heidegger 1962: 164)

The Other is proximally "there" in terms of what "they" have heard about him, what "they" say in their talk about him, and what "they" know about him. Into primordial Being-with-one-another, idle talk first slips itself in between. Everyone keeps his eye on the Other first and next, watching how he will comport himself and what he will say in reply. Being-with-one-another in the "they" is by no means an indifferent side-by-side-ness in which everything has been settled, but rather an intent, ambiguous watching of one another, a secret and reciprocal listening-in. Under the mask of "for-one-another," an "against-one-another" is in play. (Heidegger 1962: 219)

Heidegger is concerned that if this kind of "group-think" or social "everydayness" infuses itself too deeply into our personalities, the likelihood of obscuring who we are as unique individuals will increase dramatically, leading us to fall into a condition of regrettable inauthenticity. The unique presence that each of us has is an essential, real, and existentially salient aspect of what it means to be a human being here and now on the scene, and as a matter of being true to oneself, it should not be obscured. We all wear uniforms, but these uniforms should not be allowed to take over our personality to the point where we begin to lose sight of our uniqueness as individuals.

The threat of losing contact with an essential aspect of oneself becomes obvious upon asking who "the They" *is*. The answer is that "the They" is no one, or nobody, in particular. Allowing social everydayness to define one's personality too extensively is an invitation to transform oneself into a "nobody": when others face us, they find themselves addressing a predominantly generic and personally inscrutable sociality. They may shake our hand eagerly as "the mayor," or as "the parent," "the cousin," "the tailor," "the soldier," "the movie star," or "the doctor," but in the process they do not come close to touching who we are as individuals. They touch a generic conception instead. They touch only the uniform.

Insofar as an exaggerated identification with social roles or prevailing social values is a manifestly inauthentic way to be a human—it is cartoonlike, actor-like, disingenuous, and pretending—we all consequently confront the problem of how to acknowledge our primordial and inescapable sociality in a way that does not entail losing ourselves in an ocean of social labels, roles, idle talk and daily chatter. To resolve this difficulty, Heidegger envisions a more authentic balance between sociality and individuality that places a greater existential weight upon our sense of individuality, given how the extensive absorption of public opinion into a person's character can disable the appreciation of the uniqueness and freedom of each individual.

The influence of "the They" upon our sense of self cannot be underestimated. The moment we begin to speak, the objectified presence of other people substantially enters our consciousness in the vocabulary and grammar of our community's natural language. Language is a communal medium by nature that brings together individuals through its general concepts and shared meanings, and which significantly overlooks individual differences. This is precisely why it is easy to lose oneself and hide from oneself by identifying strongly and superficially with social labels such as "musician," "chauffeur," "teacher," "parent," and such.

Appreciating this problem and working toward an existential solution, Heidegger identifies dimensions of human experience that have the contrary and counterbalancing effect of highlighting and intensifying our awareness of ourselves as unique individuals. Specifically, he finds that the experience of anxiety and the anticipation of death serve this purpose well.

## 4.4 Authenticity and individuality

Although everything happens in the present, human beings have a special ability to imagine time extending endlessly into both the future and past. We can consequently reflect upon our history and make plans that anticipate years of activity. This ability to comprehend time adds an incomparable richness to our experience as well as an unprecedented control over nature and other living things. Unlike humans, the awareness of most animals extends itself imaginatively into the future for only a second or two beyond the present moment at best. The human imagination, however, can project beyond the present moment endlessly, not to mention mysteriously, into the future and the past. This expanded awareness of time and our capacity to imagine the future especially are essential to our being human. We care deeply about the future and our actions follow accordingly.

The ability to make long-term plans also reveals our freedom: with a gaze toward an uncertain and open future, we can choose what we want to do and the kind of people we want to be. Our sense of individuality is accentuated thereby, as is our sense of responsibility. As we envision the actualization of our unique potentialities, we distinguish ourselves from others and become aware uncomfortably that with respect to ourselves as individuals, we can never be fully at home in the average, everyday social world, filled as it is with traditional and generic social labels which prescribe ways that everyone indiscriminately and equally should behave.

Insofar as we feel separate and alienated in view of our individual freedom, anxiety arises. Although disturbing, anxiety is an existentially productive feeling, contrary to what one might expect: Heidegger observes that anxiety "individualizes" Dasein, recognizing how this feeling illuminates our condition as free, self-questioning, self-directing human beings. Resonating well with this is his definitive statement that "Dasein is an entity for which, in its Being, that Being is an issue" (Heidegger 1962: 236). The self-doubt which issues from our ability to reflect upon our worldly place confirms that we are each fundamentally free and essentially on our own. Anxiety, in sum, helps reveal the human condition more authentically.

Freedom is not the only dimension of our basic human situation which provokes an individuality-intensifying anxiety. Equally telling is the awareness that we will die. In ordinary life, perhaps when watching a crowd of people in a marketplace, it seems obvious that each person is a separate individual going his or her own way, and with this separateness comes a persistent and haunting worry: we are each born to know that death awaits, and that when that day or night finally arrives, no one can die in our place. Existentially speaking, we each die alone, no matter how many friends and family members might surround and console us during those final moments.

Here, once again, "the They" steps in to tranquilize our anxiety and to stun the authentic appreciation of our human condition. The only death we can ever experience is not our own, but that of some other person as an external observer. Newspaper obituaries read similarly, cemetery headstones look very much alike, funeral rituals repeat the same words, and behaviors during times of bereavement assume a programmed quality: one acts properly in view of how they say one should behave. Moreover, exposure to the products of the entertainment industry intensifies the illusion. Death is presented as a common occurrence, where children who grow up watching television and movies see thousands of deaths portrayed before they finish elementary school. Yet in this, they are being prevented from developing an understanding of what death is. "The They" sedates and obscures the awareness of our upcoming death and of death in general.

In addition to the anesthetizing social context of "the They," the natural reluctance to bring suffering upon oneself stands in the way of an authentic appreciation of death. In his novella *The Death of Ivan Ilyich* (1886), Leo Tolstoy honestly and realistically presents the typical thought-processes involved:

> "Three days of frightful suffering and then death! Why, that might suddenly, at any time, happen to me," he thought, and for a moment felt terrified. But— he did not himself know how—the customary reflection at once occurred to him that this had happened to Ivan Ilych and not to him, and that it should not and could not happen to him, and that to think that it could would be yielding to depression which he ought not to do, as Schwartz's expression plainly showed. After which reflection Peter Ivanovich felt reassured, and began to ask with interest about the details of Ivan Ilych's death, as though death was an accident natural to Ivan Ilych but certainly not to himself. (Tolstoy 1960: 102)

Heidegger's observations about how "the They" cloaks an authentic awareness of death are embodied in Peter Ivanovich's reaction to Ivan Ilyich's death. To appreciate death in a more true-to-life, existentially human way, Heidegger maintains that one should acknowledge continually and reflectively that death could come at *any* moment. Death is always close by and beside us, and it casts a quiet and threatening shadow over each moment. Kierkegaard said the same:

> If the answer to our question is affirmative, the question then arises as to what death is, and especially what it is for the living individual. We wish to know how the conception of death will transform a man's entire life, when in order to think its uncertainty he has to think it in every moment, so as to prepare himself for it. We wish to know what it means to prepare for death, since here again one must distinguish its actual presence and the thought of it. (Kierkegaard 1941: 150–51)

Complicating our attempts to come to authentic terms with death is the impossibility of imagining death itself as an experience. From our first-person standpoint, we can have nothing more than a simulated confrontation with the absolute nothingness that awaits, akin to imagining where we "were" two thousand years ago, or where we will "be" two thousand years from now. As we try to imagine such a condition—and since there is literally nothing to imagine here—the only conclusion is that we were nowhere and will be nowhere. Of death itself, there is no experience. At best, we can imagine death as falling asleep one night, never again waking up, and never realizing that one did not wake up. Such thoughts defy the imagination and it is natural to shudder from them, wondering eventually why one exists at all.

The difficulty in confronting squarely and courageously one's death as absolute nothingness is understandable, but the confrontation is an unavoidable and persistent feature of being human. Even when submerged in "the They," denying as did Peter Ivanovich that one's death will arrive one day, perhaps soon, there remains a part of us—Heidegger calls it our conscience—that keeps the fact of our upcoming death present to us, dimly and subconsciously. In the back of our minds, our conscience realizes with a measure of guilt, how we continually defer facing death, pretending that our death is never going to happen, and that the bell will always toll for someone else. For Heidegger, listening to the call of conscience, self-consciously rendering that call more explicitly manifest, being honest with ourselves, and resolving with a strong will to maintain a steadfast gaze upon death are the paths for achieving a more authentic appreciation of our human condition.

It is worth reflecting that Heidegger's prescription to acknowledge that death could arrive at any moment is presented in the same spirit as Nietzsche's doctrine of eternal recurrence. Heidegger urges us to render each moment meaningful as if it were our last, and highlights the priceless value of the present thereby. To the same effect, Nietzsche proposes that we imagine the infinite reiteration of each and every present moment, and similarly renders each moment supremely meaningful. The two thinkers share a deep interest in fashioning and shaping attitudes that will help us to live in the most meaningful way: Heidegger achieves this through "death-affirmation"; Nietzsche, through "life-affirmation."

They believe—as does Camus, as we will see—that living optimally involves maximizing the meaning of each moment. Both aim to extinguish the feelings of nihilism and meaninglessness that erode a genuine appreciation of the human condition. Both believe that an existential approach to life is enlivening, enlightening, and contrary to the psychological emptiness that arises in connection with hopelessness, suicidal attitudes, and nihilism.

## 4.5 Sociality, poetry, and the fourfold

In *Being and Time*, which was published in 1927, Heidegger establishes that human beings are an amalgam of sociality and individuality: we are individuals who grow up within a social world from the very start. He observes furthermore that the social world of modern times has assumed in an overwhelming way, an individuality-obscuring and freedom-robbing form, namely, an impersonal form dominated by "the They." As an antidote, he stresses the importance of experiencing anxiety in the light of our freedom, and in the anticipation of death that could come at any moment, appreciating how anxiety positively individuates and reveals to each of us, our respectively unique presence in the world.

Sociality inevitably integrates us into a community through the shared values it imparts to everyone, but in the form of "the They," it also significantly obscures who we are as finite, individual beings. The more that this kind of sociality dominates our awareness, the less authentic our sense of self and world can be. Conversely, the more that a strong feeling of individuality integrates our awareness, the more authentic we can become. Neither sociality nor individuality is ever to be completely dissolved—they exist together like the poles of a magnet—but on the spectrum between an extremely inauthentic and an extremely authentic sense of self, Heidegger advocates the intensification of individuality in *Being and Time* as the path to genuine human being.

By the time we reach 1947, twenty years later, in the "Letter on Humanism"—a text whose target is Jean-Paul Sartre's existentialism—Heidegger's early prescription to intensify one's sense of individuality had become tempered by a more pronounced and positive recognition that the social medium of language permeates our awareness. He says revealingly in the letter that "language is the house of Being. In its home man dwells" (Heidegger 1977: 193). Language articulates our consciousness, and it is the vehicle through which we become intelligently aware of Being.

Heidegger's approving portrayal of language in his later work is evidence of a significant turn (*Kehre*) from the Kierkegaardian, traditionally "existentialist," individuality-emphasizing position expressed in *Being and Time*. A prime expression of sociality is language, which provides a sense of community and an awareness of historical tradition. Language also establishes the expressive foundation, value-set, and network of background expectations that any person must presuppose to launch a detailed interpretation of his or her surroundings. By characterizing language as the house of Being—and here we speak of a "house" as a dwelling where we are comfortably at home, rather than as a prison-house which confines and constrains us—Heidegger affirmatively values language, and presents sociality as having a powerful, constructive, and supportive role in human existence. Within this context, the quest for authenticity translates into the question of how to use the communal medium of language in an authentic way.

Heidegger's recognition that language is deeply constitutive of human being has the effect of relaxing the tension and opposition between sociality and individuality, since sociality-as-language is now seen as thoroughly permeating a person's sense of individuality. Not any kind of language, however, will serve well to accentuate and express individuality. It would signal a significant loss of ourselves, for instance, to become immersed and absorbed in daily chatter, common conversation, and the unimaginative recitation of ossified public opinion characteristic of "the They."

For Heidegger, an alternative kind of language, namely, the semantically resonant language of poetry, offers a more authentic way to speak and to be. In line with this, Heidegger himself speaks poetically in the very expression of his view, using a blend of poetic, philosophic, and religious language. Poetry's creative and innovative quality, as well as its ability to break and transform ordinary, frozen, stock meanings, lends the speaker a stronger sense of individuality, as well as a way to express and embody freedom. In its multidimensionality of meaning, poetic language also presents the multidimensional character of Being itself, and is consequently a carrier of truth: "The nature of art is poetry; the nature of poetry, in turn, is the founding of truth" (Heidegger 1971: 72).

Insofar as poetic language manifests the multidimensionality of Being, Heidegger's thinking after *Being and Time* can be appreciated as having turned more directly toward exploring ways to develop an open awareness of Being itself. This contrasts with the *Dasein*-oriented project revealing the nature of Being in general by articulating the specifically existential foundations of human being per se.

Heidegger's direct approach to Being accordingly presents us with two opposing conceptions of sociality, one negative and one positive. The negative conception is interpretable as a rethinking, transformation, and extension of the negative conception of sociality as "the They," which is salient in *Being and Time*. Retaining its objectifying generality, impersonality, and opposition to human beings as unique individuals, "the They" is carried forth and absorbed into a conception of social relationships characteristic of a world regarded as a one-dimensional, computational, calculatingly and technologically governed, mercenary, mercantile, objectifying, scientific, exploitative arena of human activity. Within this outlook, a river or mountain is framed merely as a natural resource or standing reserve to be plundered and used up. People, similarly, are reduced to and represented by, for instance, impersonal lines of numbers on accounting sheets.

This all contrasts with the more authentic, existentially truer conception of sociality and world attitude as poetic, nature-respecting, friendly, creative, and multidimensional. Here, authenticity is conceived of as coming into a positive, poetic appreciation of one's place in the world—a world toward which one feels reverence.

Despite the modifications in Heidegger's emphasis and approach, he continues to philosophize in an existential manner, for his vision remains down to earth and resistant to otherworldly realities. In arriving at this point, however, we have set aside what has become the more familiar existentialist characterization of the human being as fundamentally alienated, anxious, and alone—a position that Jean-Paul Sartre embodies more distinctively. In the Heideggerian appreciation of our essential and natural oneness with the surrounding cosmos, fear of death and feelings of isolation dissolve in being at home in the world.

Heidegger characterizes this truer human condition in a fourfold way, as being (1) related to the earth as our home, (2) expansively appreciative of our physical situation within the infinity of sky and stars that surround us in all directions, (3) aware of ourselves realistically as finite, mortal beings, and

(4) reflective of our place in the universe through an array of hopeful religious overtones. Each of these four aspects relates to and illuminates the others in an organic unity that defines the elementary human condition.

Depending upon the cultural situation, people's religious attitudes will assume a variety of forms, but to be human is nonetheless to carry an attitude of reverence toward one's surroundings, realizing as we stand together on earth, unable to understand ourselves or the cosmos fully, how everyone naturally fills themselves with hopes and dreams of better lives and some type of salvation. These four dimensions—earth, sky, mortals, and divinities, which Heidegger refers to as "the fourfold" (*das Geviert*)—constitute a nexus that circumscribes and characterizes the elementary human condition as we find ourselves here on earth, and which in its integrated aspects is the existential context through which we grasp our being and genuine dwelling in the world. Fully to realize one's place poetically within the fourfold is the lifelong task of an authentic human being.

To conclude, Heidegger's thought is instructive in how its earlier and later forms, if extrapolated and intensified beyond what Heidegger was philosophically intending, allow us to distinguish two different styles of existentialist thought, namely, individualistic and holistic. It is important, though, to appreciate this in contradistinction with how Heidegger himself conceived of his philosophizing, where such an opposition is not thematized. He rather understood his later philosophy as not involving a fundamental change of standpoint from *Being and Time* insofar as his main concern was always to understand the meaning of Being. The later work simply gives less emphasis to the analysis of *Dasein* and greater attention to how human beings dwell in the world. Throughout his work, it is important to add, Heidegger recognizes how we are essentially social beings and are not fundamentally isolated individuals, as we encounter in Sartre's outlook. With this in mind, we can nonetheless identify two different styles of existentialist thought that Heidegger's work intimates.

The individualistic style celebrates the presence of the individual person insofar as the individual stands against the world at large, comes to realize his or her freedom of choice, appreciates that he or she will die someday, and suffers feelings of anxiety, uncertainty, and intense responsibility. The contrasting holistic style is equally down to earth, but regards the individual without a feeling of radical isolation as an aspect of, and as being essentially integrated with from the very start, the wider cosmos.

The main problems that human beings face accordingly differ in each existentialist style. Within the individualistic style, the leading concern is how to find oneself and express oneself as a unique individual. Within the holistic style, the main problem is how to find oneself and express oneself as a manifestation and voice of what ultimately is, whether this reality is described as nature, considered as a dynamic whole, as Being, understood in a multidimensional way, or as some other, non-otherworldly kind of all-encompassing existence.

# 5

# Jean-Paul Sartre (1905–80)

Although it is always helpful to consider a philosopher's historical and personal context, Jean-Paul Sartre's milieu is particularly illuminating for his philosophy. In 1905, he was born into a middle-class Parisian family of moderate social prestige: his mother's Alsatian father Charles [Karl] Schweitzer was a successful language teacher and author of a German language textbook used widely in French secondary schools; his paternal grandfather, Eymard Sartre, was a doctor and an author of medical texts. Sartre's father, Jean-Baptiste, was an officer and engineer in the French Navy. Albert Schweitzer—a musicologist, medical missionary in West Africa, theologian, historian of Christianity, and Nobel Peace Prize recipient (1952)—was Sartre's mother's cousin, who in the year of Sartre's birth, published a well-received study of the composer, J. S. Bach.

Surrounded by the books in his grandfather's library and reading enthusiastically at an early age, some unfavorable events tempered Sartre's relatively good fortune. When Sartre was only fourteen months old, his father died from an intestinal disease contracted while serving in Indochina. His young mother pampered Sartre thereafter, allowing his hair to grow into long, girlish curls, but when they were eventually cut, the shocking contrast made Sartre feel terrible about his physical appearance—an appearance soon worsened by an affliction in his right eye that set it off to the side and eventually left it sightless. In the western coastal city of La Rochelle, where Sartre moved at the age of twelve after his mother's remarriage, he was bullied at school by his less sophisticated classmates who resented his superior intelligence and Parisian roots. Adding to his sense of isolation, Sartre's relationship with his stepfather, Joseph Mancy, a civil engineer and business executive, remained distant. Short in stature and with a history of being bullied, Sartre later took up boxing.

Returning to Paris from La Rochelle at the age of fifteen, Sartre's improved circumstances led to his enrolment at the Lycée Louis-le-Grande at the ages of seventeen to eighteen and the École Normale Supérieure at the ages of nineteen to twenty-four, two of France's finest educational institutions. After serving two years in the army after graduation, he became a high school teacher in the northern coastal city of Le Havre at the ages of twenty-six to thirty-one, the city that inspired the setting of his first novel, *Nausea* (1938).

These were intellectually exciting times for Sartre, a highlight of which was his residence in Berlin during 1933–34 at the ages of twenty-eight to twenty-nine where he developed his interest in Husserl's and Heidegger's phenomenological approach to philosophizing. Sartre had learned of their growing influence five years earlier in 1928 from a visiting Japanese scholar, Kuki Shūzō—Kuki was then forty; Sartre was twenty-three—who had been studying with Husserl in Germany. Emmanuel Levinas, who also had been studying with Husserl and Heidegger, published a book in 1930 that reinforced Sartre's attraction to phenomenology. In 1933, Raymond Aron, one of Sartre's friends, who had recently returned from teaching in Cologne and Berlin, further encouraged Sartre to visit Germany.

After having absorbed the phenomenological philosophical outlook and returning to France, Sartre continued to teach at various high schools until he was drafted into the French army in 1939 at the outset of the Second World War. He was thirty-four at that time. Soon captured by the Germans and confined to a prison camp for nine months (June 1940–March 1941), he thereafter resumed high school teaching until 1944, devoting himself exclusively to literary activities and political activism in favor of Marxism in the decades to follow. Simone de Beauvoir (1908–86), who he met during his college days, remained Sartre's soulmate and companion throughout his life.

Sartre's most significant work during his early period is the well-known existentialist study, *Being and Nothingness* (1943), upon which we will focus, written in the midst of the Second World War. The ideas for this book grew during the rise of fascism in Spain and Germany (Italy had set the scene and example, having had fascist leadership since the 1920s) and they matured in occupied France at the height of Germany's domination over Europe—a time when people's loyalties were being tested, and when the choice either to collaborate with or resist the German invaders was often fatal.

From one point of view, Sartre's existentialist conception of the world is bleak: the world is an absurd accident, and we are fundamentally frustrated, alienated beings, immersed inextricably and uncomfortably in an endless expanse of inanimate, senseless material. Throughout our lives we struggle to make ourselves at home in the world, but our fate, with nothing thereafter, is to die unfulfilled. In this effort, we spend most of our time living in bad faith, avoiding and denying our freedom, as artificial titles, social roles, and concepts that have no substance in reality infiltrate and ossify our self-conceptions with a false sense of stability.

Despite the frustrations in the human condition he describes, Sartre's philosophy is also liberating. He regards our creative capacities as virtually unlimited, where no one, whether it be family, friends, enemies, strangers, or the institutions within which we live, can dictate contrary to our will how we should act or how we should conceive of ourselves. Our choice either to affirm or deny external pressures and circumstances is absolute. Whether we realize it clearly or not, each of us stands against the world as an autonomous and responsible individual, with no ultimate authority, either on earth or elsewhere, to whom we need answer. Every moment is filled with new potentialities, and with respect to the seemingly heavy weight of our past, we can always set it aside and start afresh.

## 5.1 "Being-in-itself" versus "being-for-itself"

### Being-in-itself

The contrasting sides of Sartre's outlook reflect the distinction between "being-in-itself" and "being-for-itself"—a key opposition in *Being and Nothingness* that expresses an irreconcilable combat between the inanimate physical world and our conscious awareness. To appreciate this confrontation between dead objects and active perceivers, it helps to recall Sartre's phenomenological philosophical style. He is not speculative, imaginary, otherworldly, or starry-eyed in his orientation, but is observational and down to earth as he aims to describe with a minimum of interpretive projections and overlay, the qualities of experience as they directly present themselves.

With respect to Sartre's approach, consider exactly and objectively what is directly perceived when looking at, say, a cup on the table or an apricot cocktail in a glass, as was popular in Sartre's world of French cafés. First of all, the cup is set off against a background. It must be so set off, lest it blur perceptually into its surroundings. A necessary condition for perceiving any given object is that the object is situated within and against some background. The background context is necessary, and it establishes how we interpret the perceived object. A plastic cup presents a different meaning when set upon table in either a picnic ground, an elegant restaurant, or a jungle hut. Within the linguistic context, a closely related principle applies, sometimes even more radically. Notice how the word "bark" changes its meaning when set among different sets of surrounding words, as in, "The tree has no bark" and "The dog has no bark."

In its sheer appearance as a patchwork of colors, the cup is also open to a variety of interpretations. It is perceptually indistinguishable from, say, a hologram with the identical coloration. It is indistinguishable as well from an appropriately painted piece of cardboard. By reducing our perceptions to their basic elements—in the present case, the set of color patches from which our perception of the cup is built—the extensive and permeating influence of interpretations, projections, and assumptions typical of our ordinary engagement with the world becomes apparent. We see a person sitting across from us at the table, but we do not see the back of that person's head. We see only the perceptual presentation facing us, assuming as a matter of interpretation, that the person's head has a back to it.

When attending either to what we have observationally before us as the physical world, or to any particular physical object, the primary existential fact is that the world is "just there." We each find ourselves within this world, and as far as can be discerned, there is no reason for its existence. It is something given, showing itself as an accident and appearing to be absurd.

Moreover, as noted earlier, the world of physical objects extends spatially and temporally forever, with for us no alternative but to be situated within this infinite expanse. Physical objects are also endlessly divisible, with only more of the same materiality presenting itself to perceive and divide. From a phenomenological standpoint, the physical objects in our experience have no discernable inner being or underlying substance of a different metaphysical kind: to be a physical object is to be that which when divided presents only more materiality. An "object," as we commonly use the term, amounts to nothing more than its present perceptual presentation in conjunction with all of the other possible ways it might present itself. There is nothing metaphysically hidden inside the world in which we find ourselves and live.

Sartre accordingly describes the world of "objects," or "being-in-itself," as a being that is "glued to itself." Thick throughout, physical reality is massive, solid, uncreated, dead, and incomprehensible. A way to appreciate this condition is to imagine the physical universe as it was eons ago, long before there were any sentient beings, as a mass of energy and material unaware of its very existence. It would be an exaggeration to describe being-in-itself as corpselike, but the reality experienced when apprehending a corpse is of the nature of being-in-itself. It is disconcerting, somewhat repulsive and potentially frightening, a bit threatening, and definitely "other."

Not everyone apprehends the physical world in this blunt, graphic, and desolate way, so steeped in everyday habit and idealizing as we are, but there are occasional moments when the traditional and hypnotizing web of values and interpretations briefly falls away and "the stage sets collapse," as Camus says. When the illusions generated by ordinary routine and average everydayness dissolve, we apprehend more realistically the raw material that was always there before us. When looking into the mirror and squeezing one's cheek, there is only a blob of flesh. When shaking someone's hand, there are only the bony protrusions of another skeleton meeting one's grasp. A person smiles only to display at the opening of a digestive tube, a set of calcium outgrowths called "teeth."

Sartre experiences this existential reality—one can call it the "this-ness" of things—as nauseating and unsettling, as well as truth-disclosing. Such moments of enlightenment and disillusionment compare to how a superficial, idealized, and romanticized image of another person—as in a flattering painting or polished photograph—is quickly brought down to earth once pimples, tiny hairs, and earwax objectively inform the picture. For Sartre, this disillusioning quality inheres in all objects as they present a truth repulsive, gritty, and with respect to our existence, steeped in mortality.

## Being-for-itself

Having an experience of existential nausea, however, is not a prerequisite for appreciating the difference between the world of inanimate objects, or "being-in-itself," and consciousness, or "being-for-itself." Consider a brain, either one's own or that of another, as an example of being-in-itself. Were we surgically to explore the brain for conscious awareness, there would be nothing tangible to discover. We would perceive water, electricity, a variety of tissues, correlations between physical brain states and reported experiences, but not the experiences themselves, and eventually become puzzled about how brains can embody consciousness at all.

At the same time, we each directly, undeniably, and obviously experience the world through an outwardly extending openness that we call consciousness. We are aware of the objects in the world and through them upon reflection of our own presence. As consciousnesses, we are each an opening toward the world, although every effort to grasp that opening yields only a conception of consciousness as weightless, intangible, and inaccessible as a possible object of experience. This must be so, for consciousness is not an object. As opposed to the physical being of the world, consciousness is, phenomenologically considered, an insubstantial and elusive emptiness or nothingness, which is nonetheless not nothing at all.

Consciousness, for Sartre, is always consciousness of something. It is always about some object that lends it content. As an active awareness, consciousness is directed outwards, away from itself, toward something that is other than itself, for this is how it knows and acts. Even when consciousness aims reflectively for self-knowledge, it must comprehend itself as an object. Hence in every effort to know itself, a falsification of consciousness occurs. Since there is no "thing" or "object" that is consciousness, a scientific, formula-amenable, object-centered knowledge of consciousness is impossible.

Alternatively expressed, it is impossible to get "behind" our consciousness to grasp definitively the being of consciousness. There is no "being-in-itself" of consciousness that we can positively comprehend. Our situation compares to describing the holes in a metal screen with references only to the metal wires that constitute the screen. Phenomenologically, we have before us only the objects of which we are aware, combined with the awareness that we ourselves are aware and open to the world. The opening itself, however, is inscrutable and in this sense is a "nothingness."

Sartre describes consciousness paradoxically by saying on the one hand that consciousness is what it is not. Since our awareness is filled with the objects we apprehend, we naturally identify with those objects and become absorbed in the world that contains them. I look at a tree, aesthetically appreciating its form, and the tree fills my consciousness. I greet a friend on the street and smile, and my friend's face fills my awareness. I read a page of a book, and the words and thoughts consume my attention.

From this identification with objects arises our sense of being-in-the-world. The being of these objects and the world as a whole remains nonetheless of a different kind than that of consciousness. To the extent that we identify with objects and feel at home in the world, consciousness is involved in identifying with what it "is not." Few, however, realize that as consciousnesses, we are metaphysically not that with which we identify so naturally, necessarily, and ordinarily.

Sartre adds that consciousness is not "what it is." Since consciousness is always consciousness of some object, it has the character of springing away from, or out of, itself in its directedness toward some object. Like a constantly pointing arrow or directive, consciousness is always projecting ahead. It is always jumping forward. As it turns away from the emptiness and openness that it is, consciousness is not what it is.

These considerations coalesce into a characterization of consciousness as a constant directedness toward objects, as an inability to know itself, and as an openness toward the world that immediately gravitates into self-deception. Consciousness is necessarily conjoined to the world of objects—without that world it would have no content and be nothing at all—but the world to which it is conjoined is alien. It is an object, not a subject. As a condition for knowledge and to become anything specific, consciousness must fasten itself to what is antagonistic and opposed to it.

This characterization of the human condition initially sounds pessimistic, even tragic. Sartre realizes further, though, that the sharp distinction between consciousness and the world implies that consciousness is free from the physical world. Unlike that world, consciousness is not an object of any kind. The difference between consciousness and the world is indeed so pronounced that we can speak of ourselves as being absolutely free.

In a primal and sovereign ability to say "no" to anything whatsoever, we find our absolute freedom directly manifested. If asked to take a bribe or collaborate, we can always say no. If asked to participate in a corrupt institution or in a war, we can always say no. Resistance is always an option, and at the extreme, suicide is an ever-present possibility. On a less dramatic scale, lifestyle and career choices can always be changed. A decision to fight an addiction can always be made, as can a decision to be more sharing and benevolent. Since consciousness is not of the physical world, the determinations of that world always stand to be challenged through new and alternative interpretations. Everything that presents itself to us is subject to doubt, and every supposed authority is subject to question.

Sartre's distinction between "being-in-itself" and "being-for-itself," in sum, expresses the contrast between the physical world whose determinations inevitably infuse themselves within us through our environment and physical constitution, and our consciousness—which, phenomenologically considered, is nothing physical and hardly anything at all—from which extends our freedom to defy and deny those physical determinations.

Three basic aspects to our human situation thereby emerge: (1) the physical world as it is in itself, inanimate, senseless, thick, and absurd; (2) our consciousness in its purity, entirely free from the physical world, as the locus of our possibilities, our creativity, and our ability to question; (3) our ordinary condition as beings immersed in the world of daily activity, always thinking of objects and absorbing consequently into our self-conceptions, the world's deadening weight.

## 5.2 Bad faith

Bad faith is to be what one is not, namely, an object. Bad faith is not to be what one is, namely, free. Consciousness itself, as we can now discern, is a being whose immediate immersion in the world, both as knower and as actor, puts it in bad faith. Although each consciousness has an absoluteness and purity that can defy any determination impressed upon it from the outside, it finds itself inextricably situated within a world whose being is not conscious. Resisting to a significant extent, the objectifications that the world naturally infuses within and imposes upon us, is nonetheless possible.

Being-at-home-in-the-world—the predominant and concluding hope of many social and visionary philosophies—is consequently an illusion, for it involves identifying with objects in a manner that misleadingly minimizes and obscures our differences with them. We blend with objects when feeling at home in the world, as when comfortably riding a bicycle or effortlessly playing the piano. The existential truth, though, is that metaphysically speaking, the bicycle or piano are entirely different kinds of being than my consciousness. Feeling alienated in our self-awareness, rather, is the fundamental truth of the human situation.

For the sake of being healthy, cultivating an imaginative blend with the world is an attractive and desirable project, often accompanied by the belief that all is one and that individuality is itself an illusion. Such a cosmically communal enterprise remains self-deceptive and in bad faith nevertheless, for the nature of consciousness precludes its success from the very start.

By contrast, Sartre's understanding of bad faith is grounded squarely upon our freedom. As absolutely free to choose, we have full responsibility for our situation and what we have made ourselves, at least insofar as we can say "no" to it, and insofar as we have chosen it. By not negating our condition, we accept it, and by accepting it, we assume responsibility for it. I have no control over a disaster that occurs in a distant part of the world, but insofar as I choose to continue living in a world that contains disasters, I remain a party to that world, and as a party to that world and member of the world community, I, along with everyone else, have a responsibility toward the activity that goes on in that community.

Suppose one's job and surrounding community have become unsatisfying, due to events that were not in one's control. Perhaps an incompetent executive has been installed or maybe the economic situation has downturned. Still, there is no one at which to point a finger legitimately to relieve oneself of responsibility for the situation. One made the decision to accept the job and to live in that community. On the broader, global scale, the same applies. Each of us is a part of humanity, sentient beings, and the world as a whole. We may be "thrown into" the world, but the choice is ours either to remain living, or to return to the nothingness from which we emerged.

Appreciating the raw truth of being-in-itself may be difficult and nauseating, and it may be disturbing to recognize that being-in-itself is absurd. When facing outwards, existential nausea awaits. Turning inwards toward consciousness, though, offers neither escape nor consolation. Since consciousness is absolutely free, the accompanying awareness of our responsibility produces a different kind of pain, namely, anxiety. When facing ourselves, a substantial responsibility awaits, comparable in spiritual weight to the material thickness of being-in-itself.

Assuming responsibility for everything—taking upon oneself the sins of the world, in a sense—is difficult and foreboding, if not crushing. Most shun the burden and few want to be blamed. The typical reaction is to escape from freedom by objectifying oneself in countless ways. To alleviate anxiety, people cling to objects, suppress their inherent freedom, forsake their authenticity, become part of the crowd, and hide behind an assemblage of titles, labels, roles, awards, factions, and faiths—ossifications that furthermore neutralize in their idealizations the impact of existential nausea.

Sartre witnessed prime examples of bad faith during the Second World War, but the problem is perennial. For instance, the orders issued by military leaders or their political superiors, presently and in the future, will sometimes be criminal, and the soldiers who execute those orders will be relieved of, and will relieve themselves of, responsibility for the aftermath, precisely because soldiers take an oath to follow orders. Disobeying entails imprisonment and in wartime, sometimes death.

Similar kinds of rationalizations attend most social labels and roles, all to the effect of obscuring a person's responsibility and supreme power of choice as an individual. Michel, the mayor, excuses himself by explaining that "the mayor"—an abstraction—was responsible for the destructive decisions that issued from the mayor's office, and denies that "Michel," the concrete individual, was involved in any of the decisions.

This way of thinking is unacceptable to Sartre. In its close attention to existing reality and concrete individuals in all of their respective details, the existentialist philosophy of *Being and Nothingness* protests against this escapist, excuse-generating mentality. Sartre's theory of freedom and human authenticity may be unable to criticize the small handful of individuals who do not take cover behind their social titles and institutional power, and assume full responsibility for their morally questionable actions, but such individuals are rare. Sartre sees how people are usually false to themselves as human beings, lacking either the courage or insight to assume full and respectable responsibility for their actions as individuals. To these individuals, he speaks of bad faith.

## 5.3 Other people

Consciousness is free, but it is also vulnerable. Since consciousness is not an object, it contains nothing substantial that can outweigh the heavy presence of being-in-itself. The infinite physical world thus presents itself as a threat to consciousness. Moreover, insofar as we, as consciousnesses, are nothing more than openings onto the world with the ability to question, our sense of personality, or ego, filled with its history and attendant complexities, is also saturated with artificiality. The personal content that we conceive of ourselves as having is only provisionally stable and is always questionable. When two of these inherently vulnerable consciousnesses encounter each other, like a pair of masks without any determinate faces behind them, tensions arise.

The interpersonal tensions stem from consciousness' very nature. Since consciousness is always consciousness of an object, when looking at another person, or when being looked at by someone else, each person automatically objectifies the another. When someone looks at us, we become self-conscious in both senses of the word. The other person feels the same when looked upon. Moreover, just as it is impossible to know oneself as the pure opening onto the world which one is, it is impossible to comprehend any other people in their true being as consciousnesses. When perceiving oneself and others, we have before us a set of objectified consciousnesses which can never commune perfectly as such solidified images.

The upshot is that on the person-to-person level we consequently experience the same kinds of deceptions that arise in our relationship with the inanimate world. With respect to being-in-itself, as mentioned, we can imagine ourselves as being organically unified with the rest of the world, imaginatively feeling the spirit of nature flowing through us and within us, like a small patch of ocean that flows along with the great current. Since consciousness is not of the same metaphysical kind as being-in-itself, however, these imaginative projections that would have us blend seamlessly into the world are self-deceptive and unreal.

The same holds for our relationships with others. We can hold hands and sing; we can cheer together in a stadium; we can have the most intimate conversations and look deeply into each other eyes; we can enthusiastically refer to each other as "comrade," "brother," "sister," and "family." Such experiences stimulate the feeling of being at one with another person or group. Again, the communal feelings are illusory: one's imagination has obscured how the other person's consciousness is inaccessible and masked by his or her artificial "ego" or "personality."

To appreciate the illusions involved in interpersonal perception, it is remarkable how a painting, motion picture, or even a drawing of a face can produce virtually the same feelings we have when an actual person looks at us. The paintings and other images are inanimate objects whose form generates the appearance and illusion that one is being looked at, despite how the perception is literally of only paint, moving light images, or a set of lines on a piece of paper. Operating here is the same mental process through which meanings are apprehended in written inscriptions. When actually being looked at, an existing consciousness stands behind the person's physical appearance, but that consciousness is a nothingness that presents a mask for our perception. Everyone is in fact invisible to one another.

Consistent with his theory of consciousness, Sartre maintains that our primary efforts to commune with other people—either through love, sex, control, or submission—are frustrated by consciousness' objectifying quality. We fall in love with someone, but upon elevating that person to the most precious being in the world for us, we do not blend or commune, but rather impose a distance between ourselves and the beloved person. We have sex with someone, but insofar as our own ecstasy eventually consumes our attention, we do not blend or commune, but instead become distanced between ourselves and our partner. We try to control another person to see a reflection of ourselves, but the other person's consciousness is not an object, and is not the kind of being that can be comprehended and controlled. We try to submit to another person, as to a priest, politician, movie star, or respected elder, aiming to fill ourselves with the other's will, but in doing so we use the person to satisfy our self-interest, and introduce a distance between ourselves and our supposed superior. In sum, each of us stands alone, unable truly to suspend our individuality in the expanded awareness of social communion.

We can face this existentially frustrating situation with an effort to be as authentic as we can—a difficult project that inevitably involves compromise. As immersed in the world, the social order supplies the roles, labels, and values in terms of which we live. This imposition notwithstanding, it is possible to work creatively with these materials, choosing and transforming them through our freedom to construct a personal style, rendering oneself into a self-created work of art, or self-made character. The materials with which we construct ourselves are contingent, artificial, and historically conditioned, but our hand is free to work upon them artistically.

Moreover, one's fundamental choices can always be modified to alter one's character in an act of self-questioning. It may be impossible constantly to question oneself as a matter of practice—if self-doubt were a constant endeavor, then action would freeze—but this does not entail sinking into ossifying, unreflective habit. Assuming responsibility is difficult, but it neutralizes the temptation to rest content behind the artificial construction called "me," no matter how original one's presentation may be.

## 5.4 Critical reflections

### Sartre's Crypto-Christianity

*Being and Nothingness* is a paradigm of existentialist philosophy. In a down-to-earth manner, Sartre emphasizes how the spatiotemporal world is the only world that there is, as he simultaneously magnifies our freedom, individuality, and capacities for creativity and authenticity. To this he adds a substantial measure of anxiety, solitude, alienation, both from other people and the world at large, combined with stern reminders to accept our responsibility for ourselves and the world.

Sartre's oppositional attitude toward being-in-itself nonetheless reveals some traditional and historically conventional features of his existentialist views. Specifically, they harbor a crypto-Christianity that, in Roman Catholic France, goes some distance in accounting for his existentialism's dramatic popularity.

Descartes's dualism—a philosophy that acknowledges two independently existing but also interacting substances, extension, and thought—renders life after death possible. Our bodies die, but our souls independently endure. Sartre does not recognize consciousness as a substance, let alone an enduring one, but he maintains in a dualistic fashion that consciousness and the world are of different metaphysical kinds. He portrays being-in-itself as gritty, repulsive, nauseating, and as a kind of glue that undesirably infects a consciousness that is inherently pure and free. As such, the world of being-in-itself is one from which to recoil. Some versions of Christianity, as in monasticism, ascribe a negative value to the physical world as well, as a field of fleshly depravity.

In traditional Christianity, salvation is believed to be actualized in a world beyond, whereas for Sartre, we have only this world and the sheer effort to become more authentically human. Sartre offers no world beyond, but he acknowledges a quality of oneself, namely, one's being as a pure consciousness, that is, entirely free from the physical world. The freedom of this pure consciousness is absolute and virtually godlike in its power of choice, as Descartes acknowledges in his Fourth Meditation. Sartre urges that we realize this freedom to live more authentically, and this amounts to a prescription to embody the absolute aspect of ourselves in the physical world as much as possible. Framed in this way, Sartre's existentialist project can be viewed as an atheistic analogue to the Christian prescription to embody the absolute aspect of ourselves—typically conceived of as God's spirit within the human being—as best as we can. Sartre's position that we ought to assume responsibility for the world, moreover, recalls the image of Jesus as an individual who takes on the sins of the world.

Interfering with the effort to achieve authenticity, though, is the nature of consciousness as always being aware of some object, and hence, as always having its purity infected with something alien. The infection is inescapable and is a condition for any knowledge we might have. In its engagement with the world, this condition of consciousness compares to original sin, for consciousness' practical existence is involved from the outset by a kind of adulteration that issues from our existence on earth and defines the finite human condition.

Sartre recognizes no life after death, and he denies the existence of any extraterrestrial God or higher authority anywhere outside of ourselves. This has an anti-Christian and rebellious ring to it, but at the core of Sartre's existentialism are analogues to central Christian concepts, subliminally appealing to the Christian consciousness. We can refer to this as the crypto-Christianity in Sartre's existentialism. Given how Kierkegaard developed existential themes explicitly within a Christian context a century earlier, and is one of the inspirations for existentialist thought in general, the presence of Christianity in Sartre's outlook is to be expected.

## Heidegger's "Letter on Humanism"

In Paris, five months after the Second World War ended in Europe and a month after its conclusion in Asia, Sartre gave a public address in October 1945 entitled "Existentialism Is a Humanism." Existentialism was popular at the time, and Sartre aimed to reinforce some of his leading existentialist ideas for the general public by defending existentialism against criticisms from communist and Christian fronts. The essay was published in 1946 and is now quoted frequently to initiate discussions of Sartre's existentialism.

In the months following Sartre's address, Jean Beaufret (1907–82), a French philosopher sympathetic to Heidegger, sent some questions to Heidegger, asking him for his own thoughts on existentialism and humanism. The response was Heidegger's "Letter on Humanism," published in 1947, twenty years after *Being and Time*. Since Heidegger's philosophy is also existentialist, the similarities and differences between the two outlooks reveal the paths existentialist thought can alternatively take.

Sartre distinguishes in his essay between two kinds of existentialists, atheistic and Christian, adding that despite the differences, their common ground as existentialists resides in their agreement that existence precedes essence, and that philosophizing should ground itself in subjectivity, that is, in the first-person perspective. For Heidegger, Sartre's characterization of existentialism is questionable.

In Sartre's existentialism, the subjectivist grounding is the experience of consciousness, phenomenologically considered, as it faces the world. In Heidegger's, according to Sartre, the subjectivist grounding is the experience of *Dasein*, or human being. In *Being and Time*, Heidegger states that "to work out the question of Being adequately, we must make an entity—the inquirer [i.e., Dasein; the human being]—transparent in his own being" (Heidegger 1962: 27) and that "an analytic of Dasein must remain our first requirement in the question of Being" (Heidegger 1962: 37).

In his quest to understand the meaning of Being, Heidegger attends to the human being in its existential involvement in the world. His approach is not subjectivist in an individualistic, self-centered, Cartesian sense, but is human-centered, operating on the assumption that if we can understand the specific reality of the human being, then we will be in the position to generalize this knowledge to illuminate reality in general. Sartre has this human-centeredness in mind when he refers to Heidegger's view as grounded in subjectivism.

In a turn from the position expressed earlier in *Being and Time*, however, Heidegger presents in his Letter on Humanism an approach to understanding the meaning of Being that is noticeably less subjectivist. He describes human beings as capable of allowing Being to reveal itself through and within them, if they adopt an open, caring, non-objectifying, poetic attitude toward the universe. Humans, he maintains, can put themselves into an appropriate frame of mind and "stand in the lighting" of Being. His inquiry no longer proceeds by specifically examining human being as the take-off point for generalizing toward the more comprehensive meaning of Being, but engages and communes directly with the richness of Being itself.

This approach to Being has a more "open air" feeling reminiscent of the ancient Greeks, contrary to the modern, Cartesian, self-enclosed philosophical atmosphere of a single, isolated subject of experience, certain only of itself, which in an effort to break free from its first-person—or in a more expanded Kantian version, human—enclosure engages in the project of discovering whether it can know anything beyond its own condition. Heidegger unsympathetically describes this modern way of thinking as subjectivism, which he associates with Sartre's existentialism, and which he rejects in 1947 as a characterization of his own outlook. In his Letter, Heidegger denies that he is an existentialist.

Sartre's position remains nonetheless that an absolute starting point is required to eliminate uncertainty and arbitrariness in one's theorizing, and that the first-person awareness of oneself—the Cartesian *cogito*—is precisely this proper starting point. Sartre is also convinced that it is impossible to transcend human subjectivity insofar as our absolute freedom, which allows us to make something of ourselves, resides exclusively and unsurpassably in our subjectivity.

As a form of existentialism, Heidegger's later starting point can be praised for its down-to-earth, refreshing return to the daylight realism of the ancient Greeks. In Sartrean terms, though, its enthusiastic immersion in the world either forgets or ignores how consciousness objectifies everything it knows. Heidegger believes that since Being is not an object—he distinguishes importantly between Being and beings (i.e., objects), revering the former and demoting the latter in its contrasting superficiality—it is on a plane beyond the objectifying state of mind. Immersing oneself in Being is consequently unproblematic. By contrast, Sartre regards Being—as being-in-itself—as nothing but an object, uninspiring and inanimate, emphasizing moreover that consciousness is such that it cannot know anything at all without conceiving of it as an object.

It is to their credit that the differences between Sartre and Heidegger do not undermine their mutual assault on objectifying styles of thinking, forcefully regarded in their views as incapable of providing philosophical truth and insight. Natural science with its cause-and-effect mechanistic outlook, the technological interpretation of nature and people, "the They," bad faith, calculative reason, inauthenticity, as well as knowledge conceived of as mere utility or pragmatism together stand as expressions of their concern with how blind almost everyone is to the truth of what it means to be human. Sartre regards this blindness as an unchangeable feature of the human condition; Heidegger more optimistically believes that people are capable of saving and enlightening themselves, if they open themselves up to Being.

Heidegger's outlook is more visionary, difficult to prove, and exemplary of the kind of philosophizing that Sartre self-consciously tries to avoid in his advocacy of a subjectivist starting point. Despite this vulnerability, the visionary aspect of the Heideggerian perspective is more consoling and philosophically comprehensive in its primal and caring orientation toward Being. Conceived of multidimensionally, and as defying objectification in its overwhelming mystery and hidden dimensions, Being as such allows Heidegger to introduce the phenomenon of language in a significant role as "the house of Being" in which we dwell, as we saw in the previous chapter. In addition, he ascribes a more substantial role to history and defines genuine freedom in social, rather than individualistic terms.

Less attractively for those who highly value their absolute autonomy, Heidegger subordinates the human being to Being, urging ideally that humans should play the role of "shepherds" of Being, as opposed to "lords" over individual beings or objects, with which he associates Sartre's position. Just as Heidegger rejects Sartrean existentialism and subjectivity as primary departure points for philosophy, he rejects humanism insofar as it portrays humans as all-important, primary beings.

Unlike Sartre, Heidegger displays a reverence for Being that compares well to devout theists' reverence for God. He holds furthermore that Being flows through all of us in a positive way, strongly opposing the Sartrean position that being-in-itself is a threatening and degrading alien that threatens our freedom and infects consciousness with what consciousness is not.

The differences between Sartre and Heidegger are marked, and they reflect their opposing attitudes toward the world: Heidegger's world is a friendly, supportive, multidimensional dwelling place that we simply fail to appreciate as such, blinded as we are by the narrow-mindedness of technologically oriented and mercantilist society; Sartre's world of inanimate and endless being-in-itself is unfriendly, massive, hiding nothing, and standing in perpetual opposition to the human effort, expressed uniquely by each individual, to be free.

## 5.5 Conclusion

Sartre's attitude toward the world follows philosophically from his phenomenological method: if we reflect carefully, we find nothing tangible that is "consciousness," and if we attend carefully to what we think about, we encounter nothing but inanimate objects. This yields a sharp and unbridgeable "either/or" division between consciousness and the world. Sartre accordingly rejects the ideal of an "in-itself-for-itself"—a perfectly amalgamated and reconciled object/subject, which, when conceived at the most comprehensive and completed level, he equates with God—as a contradiction. We strive to become one with the world, and do so moreover in bad faith, failing to realize that ultimate satisfaction is impossible.

Along with the phenomenological method comes Sartre's allegiance to the first-person standpoint and subjectivism as the necessary starting point, all flowing originally from the influence of Descartes's philosophy. The split between consciousness and the world, and the accompanying emphasis that our freedom allows us to start completely afresh, is a position that exudes the modernistic spirit. The hallmarks of modernism include the idea of completely starting over, setting aside past history, being creative and making something entirely new, and we can locate Sartre's existentialism as among the many phenomena that characterize early-twentieth-century modernism.

Sartre eventually subordinates his existentialist views to his later Marxist ones, and we can observe how the idea of absolute freedom is itself qualified in Sartre's own exposition. We do not have the freedom to turn into butterflies, nor do we have the freedom to control our immediate emotional reactions to circumstances. We have the freedom to say no, and the freedom to work slowly at a change in personality, but material conditions—our facticity—significantly circumscribe our potentialities for freedom. In some societies, as is well known, if we are born with a skin color, religion, sex, or socioeconomic status that is frowned upon by those in power, then certain possibilities are tightly closed off for us.

Once it is admitted that our individual freedom is limited realistically to negations, reinterpretations, and reformations of given circumstances and materials, and that at the physiological level, our consciousness is affected unavoidably by the simplest glass of wine, doubts arise regarding the philosophical desirability and effectiveness of the phenomenological method for composing a complete philosophy. More attractive would be a method that is able to comprehend wider dimensions of human experience, such as language, history, and freedom socially conceived—dimensions that Heidegger indicates in his Letter on Humanism.

Sartre does not become a Heideggerian in his later years, but Heidegger's Letter on Humanism helped spur Sartre's interest in social philosophy. Influenced more by Hegel and his analysis of the master-slave relationship, Sartre's quest for a method led him to Marxist social philosophy—the unsurpassable philosophy of our time, as he later wrote—which, with its advocacy of a dialectical logic, has the power to reconcile "either/or" oppositions. With the admission of dialectical syntheses, the phenomenological foundations of Sartre's existentialism weaken and his existentialism wanes, for such syntheses reinforce the possibility of diminishing significantly our alienation from the material world, from other people, and from ourselves.

6

# Albert Camus (1913–60)

## 6.1 Life and works

Unlike Jean-Paul Sartre, whose background was thoroughly Parisian, Albert Camus grew up in Algeria, a predominantly Arabic nation, when it was a territory under French control. Camus's father's family was of French descent, his mother's, Spanish. Like Sartre, Camus never knew his father, Lucien Camus, who at the age of twenty-eight, was killed in the First World War when Albert was less than a year old. Prior to entering the French army, Lucien had been a laborer on a wine-producing estate earning a meager, but sustainable salary. After his death, Camus spent his childhood in poverty, living in a three-room apartment in Algiers with his mother and older brother, grandmother, and two uncles. Camus's mother, Catherine, worked as a cleaning woman. She was partially deaf and could neither read nor write.

Camus's talents and exceptional intelligence were apparent from an early age, and he received a scholarship at the age of eleven to attend one of the most prestigious preparatory schools in the country, the Lycée Bugeaud (presently the Lycée Émir Abdelkader). After he graduated, he enrolled in the University of Algiers. Although Camus enjoyed sports, especially soccer—he played goalkeeper for a respected Algerian sports club—an attack of tuberculosis ended his participation when he was seventeen. The disease followed Camus throughout his life, recurring several times in the decades to come.

Camus's lung disease caused him to leave his mother's apartment and move in with his uncle and aunt to recuperate, since their home was more spacious and less crowded. It was also more financially secure and intellectually inclined than his immediate family. Camus remained at his uncle's residence during his final years at the Lycée and first year of university studies, developing his interests in philosophy and publishing some articles under the guidance of his teacher, Jean Grenier. In 1935, he joined the Communist Party, although his official affiliation with the communists would be short-lived.

Aspiring to be a teacher, Camus completed his degree in 1936 at the age of twenty-three with a thesis on Plotinus and Augustine. His medical history, however, prevented his entrance into the profession, and this led to a shift in his career interests toward politics, journalism, and theatrical writing. Camus subsequently organized a theatre group and composed several plays that presented communist ideals, some of whose performances were prohibited by the local authorities. Critical of the Communist Party's weakness on the issue of colonialism, though, his party membership came to an end in 1937.

With a strong interest in justice, Camus continued to develop his literary talents, publishing essays and joining the staff of a new and open-minded newspaper, the *Algiers Républicain*, where he did some court reporting. His work for the newspaper also included writing book reviews, one of which was a review of Sartre's first novel, *Nausea*, published in October 1938, where Camus praised the work's philosophical depth and literary imagination, while also noting how Sartre's philosophical ideas sometimes conflicted with the novel's aesthetic composition.

The *Algiers Républicain* closed in January 1940, soon after the start of the Second World War in September 1939. Again, for reasons of health, Camus could not enlist in the French army to fight the Germans, and he left Algeria for Paris in March, where he worked for *Paris-Soir*, a well-known newspaper. By June, only three months later, most of France, including Paris, had been taken over by the Nazis. By December, Camus no longer had his position at the newspaper, now German controlled, and he returned to Algeria to continue work on *The Myth of Sisyphus* and *The Stranger*, both of which he would publish with great success in 1942. He also worked on *Caligula*, which became one of his most well-known plays, published in 1944.

While in Algeria, Camus suffered another attack of tuberculosis, which necessitated a convalescent lifestyle during 1941 and 1942 while the war was raging in Europe. At the end of 1942, he returned to occupied Paris, where his two works were making a splash.

In Paris, Camus's literary success allowed him to socialize easily with other intellectuals and writers, most notably Jean-Paul Sartre, with whom he remained good friends until the end of the war. As an indication of their close association, although the plans did not fully materialize, Camus worked with Sartre in 1943 on a production of Sartre's play, *No Exit*, where he was scheduled to play Garcin, the leading male role.

During this time, Camus publicly worked for the Gallimard publishing house reading manuscripts; privately and secretly, he was active in the French Resistance as the editor in chief of *Combat*, an underground newspaper, continuing in this position until 1947, through its change from a clandestine to a mainstream publication. Among his editorials for *Combat* was a response to the nuclear devastation of Hiroshima, published on August 8, 1945, two days after the explosion, where he stated that the existence of nuclear weapons now indicates that the most important fight is the one for peace, since it appears that mechanical civilization is moving into its ultimate phase of barbarism, and that science is consecrating itself to organized murder.

As the war ended, *Combat* addressed how French collaborators should be treated. Camus initially advocated the death penalty for extreme violations of human rights, but when he saw how justice was unfairly meted out after the war's end, he rejected capital punishment. His opposition went so far as to sign a petition to block the execution of Robert Brasillach, a playwright, poet, novelist, scholar, anti-Semite, advocate of fascism and the German occupation, editor of the influential collaborationist newspaper, *Je suis partout* (*I am everywhere*), and public voice who had called for the execution of left-wing politicians and all members of the French Resistance. Had the war a different outcome, Brasillach would have been in favor of Camus's own execution.

The petition did not prevail, and Brasillach was executed by a firing squad on February 6, 1945. Simone de Beauvoir attended his trial and refused to sign the petition. Neither did Sartre sign. Persisting thereafter in his opposition to the death penalty, Camus urged the United Nations to advocate the worldwide probation of capital punishment in an address he gave at Columbia University on March 28, 1946, titled "The Human Crisis." The crisis he had in mind was how people have grown too accustomed and indifferent to the torture and death of others.

Camus's postwar years were marked by the publication in 1947 of *The Plague*, his most successful novel at the time, and in 1951, *The Rebel*, a lengthy philosophical and historical work wherein, among many other topics and discussions, he criticized the Soviet Union as a terrorist regime. The criticism aroused the animosity of communist sympathizers, including Sartre, who condemned Camus.

Despite his subsequent alienation from French academic circles, Camus maintained his steadfast resistance to injustice, publishing short stories, novels, and plays, among which were *The Fall* (1956) and *The Exile and the Kingdom* (1957). He continued to work in the theatre, and in 1957 was awarded the Nobel Prize for Literature, which commended his sensitivity and insight into the problems of the human conscience that had become pronounced during the preceding decades. Seven years later, in 1964, Sartre was also awarded the Nobel Prize for Literature, but he declined the prize.

Camus's achievements and abilities notwithstanding, he sometimes experienced anxiety and depression, often in compassionate view of the plight of impoverished people in the world. He was particularly troubled by the Algerian war for independence, since he could identify closely with both sides of the conflict. On the afternoon of January 4, 1960, at the relatively young age of forty-six, Camus was involved in a terrible car wreck: the car in which he was a passenger sped out of control and crashed into a tree on a country road outside of Paris, ending his life.

## 6.2 The feeling of the absurd

In the 1955 preface to *The Myth of Sisyphus*, published fifteen years after the book was written, Camus explains that his fundamental concern in the book is whether life has any ultimate meaning in the absence of eternal values and God. Within a context where, from a metaphysical or objectively true standpoint, whatever values we recognize are not written into the fabric of the cosmos, but are temporary artifacts of our own creation, it remains unclear whether life is worth living. There is a question of why suicide is not the appropriate response. The book's first line accordingly reads, "There is but one truly serious philosophical problem, and that is suicide" (Camus 1955: 3).

Camus is not the first philosopher to address the question of life's meaning in view of the nothingness that time and death appear to deliver. It characterizes the interests of Arthur Schopenhauer (1770–1860), among others, who, reflecting upon the perishability of all individuals, finds no meaning in earthly existence per se, but discovers satisfaction in transcendent, otherworldly states of consciousness. It is also Friedrich Nietzsche's concern, who contrastingly rejects all transcendent meanings, advocating instead the creation of values that promote health and power on earth.

Camus's own approach to the question of life's meaning is motivated by situations where our existence seems empty, and where depression and suicidal thoughts arise in response to life's apparent meaninglessness. He understands this emptiness as arising from a feeling of divorce, or disengagement, between oneself and the rest of the world, where one's entrenchment in daily activity is suspended, and where life presents itself as ridiculous. This is the feeling of the absurd and regarding it as valid, he considers how, upon such a foundation of meaninglessness, life can still be rendered meaningful. Whereas Heidegger regards the disengagement from average everydayness, or *das Man*, to reveal our individuality and to open a path to authenticity through anxiety in the face of death, Camus discusses how such a disengagement reveals the absurdity of our ordinary lives and how it opens a path to authenticity through a confrontation with meaninglessness.

Camus refers to the absurd as a "feeling," but it is not a mere pathology where a person loses the motivation to engage with the world in a socially healthy and normally participatory manner. The feeling emerges when a certain fact is realized, namely, that everything will dissolve and be forgotten. In the distant future, the sun will explode, the earth will be incinerated, and it will be as if humans never existed. Upon realizing how time constantly erodes whatever meanings we presently live by and respect, like ocean waves that dissolve a sandcastle, a feeling of emptiness and puzzlement arises as one asks what ultimate meaning our lives could have.

One conclusion is that since we live amid a vast and insensate universe, it makes no difference what we do and that to become engaged enthusiastically in worldly affairs—even the distinguished affairs of statesmanship, which from an astrophysical perspective also fade to nothing—is willfully to steep oneself in illusion. To respect the truth, it is important to resist this illusion—an illusion issuing from our immersion into *das Man* or "the They"—by setting out a lifestyle that is consistent with universal transience, and that puts into a clear perspective the daily world of ordinary work, newspapers, dinner parties, politics, movies, sports, and all activities that tend to obscure the awareness that everything is fated to dissolve and that all life is condemned to death.

Objectively supporting the feeling of the absurd is the long-term recognition of time's passing. Buddhism—an outlook that focuses upon the alleviation of suffering through a heightened awareness of the world's transiency—also acknowledges that change is fundamental to existence. Buddhism's insight is that much suffering, especially psychological suffering, stems from the error of holding on to perishable things—possessions, loved ones, social status, hopes, and dreams—as if they were imperishable. To appreciate that it is metaphysically misguided to hold on to perishable items as if they were imperishable, as if a tomato, grape, or beautiful flower could last forever, is to be more enlightened. Camus's discussion of the absurd rests equally upon the assumption that the world is constantly changing, but his response to how we should address such a world, as we shall see, is more combative than Buddhism's tranquil and compassionate approach.

Camus discerns that if we take a distanced view upon our daily life, it will display a structured routine, a schedule, and repetitiveness that can appear absurd. Imagine a fast-forward movie of oneself that presents how one rises each day, dresses, eats, goes out, returns home, and so on, and that accentuates the repetitiveness and mechanical quality of the overall routine. The meaning of one's activities fades from such a standpoint. Camus adds the example of a person talking in a telephone booth, gesturing in excitement, and how, without being able to hear what is being said, we wonder from a distance why the person even exists, removed as we are from the person's self-enclosed world of meanings. Looking at oneself in the mirror, and seeing one's face as a mass of flesh, disengaged from how one's personality animates it, also easily generates the feeling of the absurd.

Such experiences erode the meanings within which one ordinarily dwells, and reveal the world to be a stage, or theatre, upon which we are the tiny players. The thought is Shakespearean, but Camus renders it more existentially pressing, for in the experience of the absurd, the stage sets collapse to reveal the oblivion beneath the stage. That we persist as actors in this theatre, knowing that we are in a mere play—a play of sights and sounds, a play that is not serious, a play that is theatrical—enters significantly into Camus's various reactions to the feeling of the absurd. He is convinced that this feeling is central to the human experience, and that it requires a thoughtful response in relation to the question of whether life is worth living.

## 6.3 Escapist reactions to the absurd: Hope and suicide

Camus more specifically defines the feeling of the absurd as an outcome of a contradiction between our inherent drive to understand the world as a meaningful unity and the world itself that resists our efforts to comprehend it. It is absurd that we are driven to make sense of something that will not make sense. The phenomenon, he observes, is exclusively human and it has no objective, mind-independent existence. It appears and dies with us.

There are three contributing constituents: (1) the nonrational world, (2) our inherent quest for a rational understanding of things, aiming for full comprehension, and (3) the incompatibility of the two. To make light of either the world's incomprehensible quality or our desire for comprehension is to undermine the tension and confrontation with the truth of our existential situation. Camus consequently criticizes all views that fail to acknowledge the tension, noticing how they either soften one of the elements of the relationship or dissolve the relationship altogether. Just as Sartre regards bad faith as a weak-minded response to our inherent freedom and responsibility, Camus similarly regards as inauthentic, views that escape, diminish, or deny the feeling of the absurd.

It can come as a surprise that Camus officially resists the label, "existentialist," but part of the reason is that he interprets traditionally labeled existentialist philosophers such as Lev Shestov (1866–1938), Karl Jaspers (1883–1969), and Søren Kierkegaard (1813–55) as escapist thinkers. He maintains that although they acknowledge the absurd human condition, which is a point in their favor, when they confront the absurd, they transform it into an inspirational idea that indicates with hope and faith, an inscrutable, transcendent, salvation-promising reality beyond the spatiotemporal world.

For Camus, their approach to the absurd obscures how preposterous our human condition is, for as it places a halo of religiosity upon the absurd, it obscures how there will be no answers, payoff, or transcendent value when death arrives. Insofar as Camus associates "existentialism" with religious interpretations of the absurd, he rejects the label, convinced that the absurd entails a life without hope, without appeal, and without any consoling religiosity.

Since our human condition absurdly involves conflict between our desire to comprehend and a world which frustrates that desire, as well as a conflict between our perishable bodies and our desire to persist, Camus concludes that to live genuinely is actively to confront these conflicts, persevering and embodying the contradiction between our desires and the world. Suicide is not an option, for self-destruction annihilates the absurd. One should be like the person condemned to death who, fully aware that death is approaching, fights it defiantly with every available opportunity and energy, aiming to live as long as possible. We are all condemned to death, so this defiant attitude is a model for everyone who intends to live authentically. True human beings never surrender.

Such is the context of Camus's statement that what counts is the "most" living in terms of sheer longevity, and not the "best" living in terms of quality or intensity. Many people would think otherwise. By asserting that quantity of life is preferable to quality of life, he is saying firstly that in the cosmic scheme of things, or objectively speaking, everything is meaningless and the value of each experience is zero. At the same time, he adds that our awareness of this emptiness reveals that our situation is absurd, as we realize how we thirst for meaning and life in the face of a meaningless and deadly universe. It remains for us to be true to ourselves, and sustain our absurd situation for as long and lucidly as possible. Our lives may be objectively meaningless, but being authentic demands that as a matter of defiance—as a matter of preserving the tension between our desires and the world—we aim for longevity.

The philosophical quest for absolute understanding, as well as the natural desire for the longest life possible, is as absurd as a person who, when battling a group of machine gunners, attacks them with a sword. To display this kind of unrestrained defiance, however, is to have an authentic attitude toward life. Expressed more succinctly in a single act, being true to oneself is to throw a final confronting word at a firing squad, just when they are about to pull their triggers.

One can consequently applaud thinkers such as Hegel, Leibniz, and Whitehead for having constructed some of the most remarkable and inspiring philosophical systems which, despite their imperfection, are among the most penetrating and comprehensive visions of the world as a rational, coherent unity. Insofar as they fought a losing battle in a grand way, these philosophers are among the prime examples of absurd living, although they might not have realized it. Similarly, with respect to longevity, people who struggle for exceptionally long lives—eating well, exercising regularly, and so on—without deeply considering the human condition and the ultimate futility of their labors also embody the absurd.

A lucid absurd lifestyle, however, requires that one defies the world's incomprehensibility and fatality, knowing well that the effort is hopeless. Within this state of mind, each moment is of the same value, not as a set of equally worthless moments, but as a set of equally precious ones. This is to be cognizant of the flame of life that one is determined to keep burning as long as possible, regardless of the oncoming and extinguishing wind.

## 6.4  Absurd lifestyles: Expenditure, creativity, and revolt

Camus outlines a variety of lifestyles that embody the spirit of the absurd and accentuate its aspects to different degrees. We can refer to them respectively as lifestyles of expenditure, creativity, and defiance, each of which has its limitations. The lifestyle of expenditure is most familiar to readers of Camus. After considering each in turn, we will introduce a fourth kind of lifestyle implicit in Camus's writings that can be understood as more fundamental than the three he explicitly sets forth, as it comprehends and integrates them into a single attitude.

### Lifestyles of expenditure

Assuming that there is no life after death and that in time all will be forgotten, Camus begins by describing a kind of absurd lifestyle that displays "expenditure." His examples are not exactly models to copy, but share a basic attitude that can inspire and guide comparable ways to live in view of the absurd. This attitude is to live with no further interest than to extract the greatest appreciation from each passing moment, or to "expend" life to the fullest. He states, for example, that one can aim to have as many sexual experiences as possible, or to play as many roles as possible, or to visit as many different places as possible, or to conquer as many territories as possible. The representative figures are Don Juan, the actor, the traveler, and the conqueror.

A variety of different lifestyles can embody the spirit of these examples, for what matters is not the activities performed per se, but one's attitude toward them. An author's aim can be to write as many books as possible, a social worker's can be to help as many people as possible, or a milk delivery person's can be to deliver as much milk as possible, owing merely to an intrinsic enjoyment of writing, helping, or delivering.

The activities can have a moral quality or social benefit, but as Camus describes these lifestyles—consider how the seducer, Don Juan, uses people for his own pleasure, or how the conqueror deals death to many people—morality is tangential and of no immediate concern. The point is not to work for an eternal good or reward, either in this world or the next, but merely to experience the present moment in its rich immediacy and to expend life without reserve. One can be dedicated to a single grand goal, except that from the standpoint of the absurd, attaining the goal is unimportant. The actual "goal" is to live fruitfully from moment to moment within the scope of that wider plan. If one were to die in the middle of the process, it would make no difference.

Following Camus's conception of the absurd, the lifestyle of expenditure is governed by a self-conscious refusal to live for eternal values, the future, or otherworldly realities, turning away from all conceptions of the future or "the beyond" that harbor hope, an expectation of salvation, an appeal to a higher being, or the achievement of a moral balance. On the face of things, it is self-centered, self-gratifying, down-to-earth, immediacy-centered, and independent of other people's welfare. Helping others within this lifestyle is fine, but the lifestyle is not itself motivated by acting from duty or compassion toward other people. Helping others can issue as a side effect of extracting a self-centered enjoyment of the moment, but this would be merely consistent with what morality requires, with no merit involved.

Camus's examples of the seducer, actor, traveler, and conqueror give the impression that since the lifestyle of expenditure is aesthetically motivated and involves no moral value in relation to duties toward others, rights, obligations, and such, the lifestyle is morally bankrupt and consequently undesirable. Camus values this kind of lifestyle nonetheless, because he sees it as being true to our human condition. It is motived by a respect, perhaps not for other people, but for the truth. He considers it a dignified manner of living, for by continually acknowledging the pointless position in which we find ourselves, it is an honest life that does not harbor any illusions about our likely fate.

As a matter of consistency, though, if there is a general respect for the absurd, along with a general respect for the idea of expending life to the fullest, then one should respect this idea of expending life to its fullest in others as well as oneself. This would introduce some moral constraints upon absurd lifestyles of expenditure, since there would be some care not to transgress the efforts of others to live life to the fullest. The logic here echoes a conception of liberty that goes back to the French Revolution, as expressed in the fourth article of the 1789 Declaration of the Rights of Man and Citizen: liberty is the freedom to do whatever one wants, as long as it does not injure someone else. Such a morally tempered approach to lifestyles of expenditure is more consistent with Camus's general interest in social justice and respect for others, despite how he highlights disreputable figures such as the seducer and the conqueror.

## Lifestyles of creativity

Since lifestyles of expenditure depend upon one's attitude, even the most ordinary lifestyles can respect the absurd. Living exclusively for the moment is the aim. If, more ambitiously, fame happens to be sought, then that fame must be experienced and enjoyed. Posthumous fame subsequent to having been thoroughly unappreciated during one's life, as was true for Friedrich Nietzsche and Vincent van Gogh, is pointless. If solitude is the preference, then the solitude must be enjoyed. If creativity is one's love, then constant and consistent creativity is called for.

When considering the life of an artist, an absurdist approach would be to create as many works of art as possible, finding value in the act of creativity for its own sake. An absurd artist can consistently engage in a single, grand project, not especially for the sake of completing the project, but to experience the joy of creation from moment to moment. In this respect the absurd artist differs little from the other absurd figures mentioned above.

Camus is particularly attracted to the absurdist artist, however, for both the subjective attitude that the artist embodies—which, as we shall see, goes beyond living merely to enjoy life in the passing moment—and the kinds of artistic product that can result. Concerning the latter, he advocates the creation of artworks that convey the spirit of absurdism. His novel *The Stranger* is an example as it serves beneficially to communicate the absurdist message to others, just as his earlier plays conveyed the spirit of communism. Underlying this prescription is a conception of "good" art, where a work of art is deemed good, if it effectively conveys the preferred philosophy at hand. This is a common, as well as controversial, way to characterize good art, since it is so partisan. Marxism follows this path in its preference for social realism as the allegedly most revolutionary and desirable art.

Camus has something more interesting to say about the value of artistic creativity, though, and this concerns how the act of creativity involves a joy that surpasses sensory pleasure. To be creative is to act freely—and we can recall how the existentialists put a premium on freedom—and when one is creative, there is a tendency not to be conformist and mechanistic, at least in principle. Being creative within the boundaries of the ordinary values is common enough, as when acting in the service of advertising, propaganda, or an established bureaucracy, but a more effective and pure expression of freedom resides in creativity that challenges the status quo.

The joy in being creative is an upshot of what is absolute in us, namely, freedom. When discussing Sartre's crypto-Christianity in Chapter 5, it was noted that Descartes's Fourth Meditation describes our capacity to affirm or deny any given proposition as a virtually godlike capacity. Camus appreciates this capacity, and regards it as a source of joy that confers intrinsic value upon each moment in which we are creative. This is unlike Sartre's position in *Being and Nothingness*—a work published a year after Camus's *The Myth of Sisyphus*—where freedom stands as an absolute capacity within us, but as a source of profound anxiety. It is also unlike Kierkegaard's position, where freedom is the occasion for anxiety and dread.

In *The Myth of Sisyphus*, Camus traces the idea of freedom's quasi-divinity to Dostoevsky, who presents it through a character named Kirilov. A year in advance of Sartre's assertion of freedom's fundamentality in *Being and Nothingness*, Camus wrote the following:

> "For three years," says Kirilov, "I sought the attribute of my divinity and I have found it. The attribute of my divinity is independence." Now can be seen the meaning of Kirilov's premise: "If God does not exist, I am god." To become god is merely to be free on this earth, not to serve an immortal being. Above all, of course, it is drawing all the inferences from that painful independence. If God exists, all depends on him and we can do nothing against his will. If he does not exist, everything depends on us. (Camus 1955: 79–80)

Camus concludes his discussion of the absurd artist by acknowledging that a creative person with a lucid, absurdist awareness creates not in view of God but of nothingness, knowing that the resulting artifacts will dissolve. When being creative, which often involves struggle, he appreciates nonetheless and more immediately, that in addition to the intrinsic value creativity confers, the involved struggle can be a vehicle for overcoming illusion, and can assist in sustaining an awareness of the absurd.

## Lifestyles of defiance

The figure of Sisyphus in *The Myth of Sisyphus* has a curious position in the book. Camus does not mention Sisyphus in the main text, but introduces him as an absurd hero in an independent, four-page concluding segment. Given the book's title, it is still evident that Sisyphus's situation, attitude, and behavior reveal an essential quality of the absurd and the absurd attitude toward life.

Sisyphus's importance is in how he represents the absurdist ideal of persistently adopting a defiant attitude in a thoroughly hopeless situation. To appreciate this kind of defiance, we can recall once again Descartes's characterization of the godlike part of us, namely, the capacity to affirm or deny any given proposition. This is our ability to say "no" in any given circumstance, even to the point of committing suicide. Sartre highlights this capacity in an extreme example, when he explains how there is no escape from the total responsibility that our absolute freedom entails:

> If I am mobilized in a war, this war is my war; it is in my image and I deserve it. I deserve it first because I could always get out of it by suicide or by desertion; these ultimate possibles are those which must always be present for us when there is a question of envisaging a situation. For lack of getting out of it, I have chosen it. (Sartre 1956: 708)

Like Sartre, Camus appreciates that saying "no" is an act of freedom, and he grounds his concept of the absurd upon our saying "no" to the meaninglessness of the universe and our eventual annihilation. Death is to be avoided, and our acts of creativity "give colors" to the void, knowing that these colors and meanings will fade. Being able to say "no" is central to Camus's outlook, more so than the prescription to expend life pleasurably to the fullest, which is only one among a set of absurd lifestyles. Its centrality is evident upon noting how this idea carries through substantially into Camus's later works, where it is at the basis of his 1951 book, *The Rebel*. The first lines are thus:

> What is a rebel? A man who says no, but whose refusal does not imply a renunciation. He is also a man who says yes, from the moment he makes his first gesture of rebellion. A slave who has taken orders all of his life suddenly decides that he cannot obey some new command. What does he mean by saying "no"? (Camus 1956: 13)

Sisyphus is himself a rebel, and he exemplifies the attitude of complete defiance within the absurdist, existentialist context. He is a slave, condemned to hard labor for having loved life and sensuosity beyond his allotted time, where his punishment, pointlessly and forever, is to roll a rock to the top of a hill, only to have it roll down once again upon reaching the summit. Working hard, struggling, day in and day out, he faces the constant challenge to raise the rock, but the challenge has no bearing on anything. Sisyphus's plight compares to the human situation for Camus, except that death gives us a reprieve. Most importantly, he conceives of Sisyphus engaged meaningfully and happily in his empty and painful struggle, describing him as appreciating his physical strength as he works, as well as his willpower to defy constantly the gods who imprisoned him.

As a matter of critical reflection, we can consider the philosophical limits of a conception of freedom that is defined exclusively as the ability to say "no." This is the spirit of pure disagreement or, alternatively described, universal doubt. If allowed to take over one's disposition toward the world completely, a danger arises in saying "no" today to some given viewpoint or proposition that happens to be presented, and then saying "no" tomorrow to its opposite, merely because one is basically defiant and disposed to say "no" whenever something appears to be in opposition to oneself. This kind of universal rebellion, however, is self-destructive as one becomes contradictory in the long run, leaving oneself with no position to stand upon consistently. Hegel, in his account of the skeptical consciousness in *The Phenomenology of Spirit* (§§202–05), makes these observations.

It is to Camus's credit that he does not overplay the skeptical, nay-saying attitude and recognizes that although creativity involves the negation of what is given, it involves more than that. We do not simply say "no" to what is given, but introduce and impose new forms upon what is being negated, and this transforms the hollow skeptical attitude into a positive, formative, and visionary one. Camus discusses his own artistic creativity in this positive light when he shows his concern to help those who have been downtrodden:

> But from my first articles to my latest book I have written so much, and perhaps too much, only because I cannot keep from being drawn toward everyday life, toward those, whoever they may be, who are humiliated and debased. (Camus 1955: 150)

Just as the idea of rebellion, or of saying "no," surpasses the lifestyle of expenditure in a more penetrating expression of absurdity, the idea of a constructive, focused style of creativity surpasses the idea of pure rebellion. This opens the way for considering in Camus's thought, a comprehensive way to understand the absurd human condition that combines into a single approach, the lifestyles of expenditure, creativity, and rebellion.

## 6.5 Conclusion: Life as deadly serious sport

Sisyphus embodies how life can be subjectively meaningful in the most objectively meaningless circumstances. We create meaning for ourselves. In Sisyphus's case, that which provides meaning is not the sensuous pleasure that he enjoyed on earth, for Sisyphus lost this when he was condemned to hard labor in the underworld. Providing meaning for him is a defiant struggle against his imprisoned situation and the gods who imprisoned him. Sisyphus stands as an image for everyone in his persistence against a hopeless situation, but for those who perceive their daily work as hopeless in a more local way, he is additionally inspirational. Camus characterizes Sisyphus as a proletarian hero, stating that "the workman of today works every day in his life at the same tasks, and this fate is no less absurd" (Camus 1955: 90).

Sisyphus's importance in Camus's presentation of the absurd allows us to reiterate a significant point, which was mentioned above: Camus subordinates the idea of living each moment merely for sensuous pleasure, expending life on that register, to that of living in constant revolt, defiance, or rebellion. This rebelliousness does not involve sensuous pleasure as much as it involves the expression of freedom. Don Juan steps aside as Sisyphus presents the absurd life more effectively, as he works for nothing, and yet works defiantly.

When considering Camus's advocacy of the absurd life, with its emphasis upon how everything will dissolve in conjunction with its prescription to live exclusively for today, one cannot help wondering why Camus remained throughout his life so passionately committed to social justice, political issues, and the abolition of suffering. If everything will eventually dissolve, it is unclear why he, or anyone, should care.

Camus's respect for human dignity helps explain his passionate attitude, which is implicit in his prescription to be true to oneself—to be authentic—by facing and preserving our absurd situation. Associating dignity with authenticity, as well as with nobility, Camus recognizes that everyone can see the truth and can conduct themselves accordingly in a dignified and noble way. This capacity is worthy of respect. We may be objectively worthless as individuals, destined to disappear in time, but as we stand upon the human stage right now, our capacity for reflection and freedom confers dignity and nobility upon our acts of defiance.

Being able to say "no," as in the purely skeptical mentality, does not entail being particularly creative. Nor does it entail a life of sensuous pleasure. Since children can simply say "no," it is a rudimentary expression of our freedom—a capacity that by itself does not imply the absurdist lifestyles of expenditure and creativity. Moreover, each absurdist lifestyle has its limitations. The life of expenditure does not capture the more deep-seated meaning of rebellion that is independent of the search for pleasure; pure rebelliousness can gravitate into skepticism and can ignore the importance of being positively creative; while immersed in its joy, creativity can lose sight of the importance of remaining defiant.

Inherent in Camus's views is a way to integrate all three kinds of lifestyle. To appreciate this, we can recall his enthusiasm for the game of soccer, from whose play which he was traumatically and repeatedly excluded as a result of tuberculosis. We can also recall his fondness for the figure of actor, or theatrical player, which is one of his examples for the lifestyle of expenditure. There is the play of the game, along with the play of the theatre.

Playing soccer or any sport well requires an engaged and serious concentration on the game. Playing well also involves pleasure, opportunities to be creative, and questions of morality: one can play to win at all costs, cheating if need be, or one can play with dignity and self-respect. One can play despicably, or one can play with pride and integrity. One can play hard and doggedly, or one can give up after a disappointment. Throughout this, despite the game's seriousness, we know that it is ultimately only a game, transient, and eventually to be forgotten.

These thoughts apply to living well with an absurdist attitude toward life: all the world is a stage, or a play, but the play is fatal to every player. We can choose how to play, and we can play out our lives such that each moment is enjoyable, creative, competitive, struggling, unsurrendering, and dignified.

The thought of "life as a deadly serious sport" thus provides a fourth model of how Camus conceives of rendering life meaningful in the face of emptiness. Since the game of life is one we must lose, there are no winners and everything consequently depends upon how we play. The optimum choice for Camus is to play as tragic heroes in view of the truth, as actors in a deadly play, where in constant view of our eventual failure, our nobility and integrity persists in the refusal to give up the game and its theatrics.

Camus's thought is frequently discussed in comparison and contrast to Sartre's, but among the existentialist writers we have surveyed, his closer kinship is to Nietzsche, who was inspired by the sportsmanlike one-upmanship of the early Greeks, as well as their springtime performances of tragic plays. The Greek notion of *agon* inspired Nietzsche's conception of the will to power, whose antagonistic substance involves the spirit of competition, expansion, and combat, all within the context of an objectively meaningless world. Both thinkers maintain that we are solely responsible for creating meaning, and for recognizing intrinsic value in the act of creation. Nietzsche refers to these creative energies as the will to power; Camus refers to them as the positive expressions of the spirit of rebellion.

# 7

# Simone de Beauvoir (1908–86)

Although Jean-Paul Sartre's *Being and Nothingness* is over 800 pages in length, only a brief section at the book's end addresses ethical matters. In Sartre's 1946 lecture "Existentialism Is a Humanism," the ethical focus is more salient, but it is also brief. For the first extended study devoted to existentialist ethics, we need to look at Simone de Beauvoir's 1947 work *The Ethics of Ambiguity* (*Pour une morale de l'ambiguïté*). The book was influenced by *Being and Nothingness* owing to her close working relationship with Sartre, but Beauvoir's conception of existentialist ethics is more concrete: whereas Sartre sets out a theory of absolute freedom and urges our immediate realization of how free we actually are, Beauvoir closely examines the conditions for realizing our freedom, cognizant of the constraints imposed by our given social contexts and our interconnections to other people.

Simone de Beauvoir was born in Paris on January 9, 1908, into a family that was economically well-off when she was very young, but that lost most of its money after the First World War. This left Simone without the prospects of a dowry and the associated opportunities for a socially well-thought-of marriage. Excelling superlatively in her academic studies, she passed her baccalaureate exams in mathematics and philosophy at the age of seventeen, and at the age of twenty-one, she completed her master's degree with a thesis on Leibniz as well as the *agrégation*, the civil service teaching qualification exam. Beauvoir was the youngest person to pass the exam to date, but not only did she pass the exam, she came in second, with Sartre coming in first.

Beauvoir worked thereafter in secondary schools until 1943, teaching in Marseille, Rouen, and Paris, at which point—now at the age of thirty-five—she had her teaching license revoked as the result of an accusation that she had been involved in a sexual affair with one of her seventeen-year-old female students some years earlier. From then on, Beauvoir lived as an independent author. This period from 1943 until her death in 1986 was that of her most influential works which include *She Came to Stay* (1943), *The Ethics of Ambiguity* (1947), *The Second Sex* (1949), *The Mandarins* (1954), and *The Coming of Age* (1970). Beauvoir is most widely known and respected for *The Second Sex* (*Le Deuxième Sexe*), a landmark study in feminist thought.

## 7.1 The ambiguous human condition: Mind versus body

Beauvoir understands the human condition as characterized by a duality, or "ambiguity," as she calls it, that has over the centuries been described in a variety of ways. In its basic formulation, it is characterized by the distinction between body and mind: each of us has a body that is a physical object among all other physical objects in the world, but each of us also has a consciousness that is intangible and mysterious in nature, for when we open up a body surgically to examine the physical brain, we find only the brain, and no consciousness. And yet, we each experience an "opening" toward the world that we call "consciousness" through which the world is disclosed to us.

This split between mind and body entails a separation between people as well: aside from how our bodies are in respectively separate physical locations, I have an individual experience and you have an individual experience, but I cannot experience or "be" your experience and you cannot experience or "be" my experience. We are each isolated from one another objectively and subjectively.

This mind-body split underlies the philosophical distinction between idealism and materialism: although physically my body is nothing more than a vanishing point in an infinitely expansive universe, my mind, when reflecting upon this situation, is that which in its thought contains the entire universe within which I am defining myself as a mere speck. My mind "is in my head" from the materialistic perspective and my head "is in my mind" from the idealistic perspective. As the history of philosophy has shown, there is no easy reduction of one perspective to the other.

Sensitive to these kinds of impasses, Beauvoir resists trying to reduce mind to body, or idealism to materialism, or vice versa, and believes it to be more honest to start one's philosophizing by accepting the paradox, dualism, or ambiguity within which we are situated, and work forward from there. She describes our inherent double-aspectedness as that of our each being one person among billions on the one hand, tending toward insignificance in the face of an overwhelming physical universe, while at the same time being absolutely free individuals from the standpoint of our first-person awareness:

> He asserts himself as a pure internality against which no external power can take hold, and he also experiences himself as a thing crushed by the dark weight of other things. (de Beauvoir 1947: 11)

Each of us is to ourselves a completely free consciousness, while in view of our bodies, each of us is an object in the world as a whole and in the eyes of others. This ambiguity can also be described as the opposition between subject and object, or between subjectivity and objectivity. In the terminology of *Being and Nothingness*, the ambiguity is expressed by the tension between consciousness, the "for-itself," and the physical world, the "in-itself."

With respect to human interactions and ethical relationships, the ambiguity is reflected further in how, recognizing that we are mutually free beings, we treat each other with respect, while we also treat each other instrumentally as means to our self-centered ends. Neither perspective can be dissolved or explained away; every person interacts with every other in terms of both.

Beauvoir, like Sartre, maintains that God does not exist, that each individual is absolutely free, that the physical world is intrinsically meaningless, and that values issue from the choices people make. Such assumptions, citing Dostoevsky, are understood usually to imply that "everything is permitted," thus rendering meaningless the idea of an existential "ethics."

This, however, is not the end of the matter. Beauvoir observes the following about an ethics that issues from and expresses our ambiguous condition:

> An ethics of ambiguity will be one which will refuse to deny a priori that separate existants can, at the same time, be bound to each other, that their individual freedoms can forge laws valid for all. (de Beauvoir 1947: 26)

Beauvoir does not assert or assume out of hand that it is impossible for people to agree to respect laws and create a morality for themselves. Universally applicable moral laws are possible, but they do not come from above or beyond. They originate from people. We can construct them and choose to respect the laws as such. Within most other systems of thought, no choice is involved in the fundamental moral regulations, since they issue from an external or objective source through which they derive their authority. The regulations might come from God, as in some traditional religious views. They might come from a fixed rational human nature, as in Kant's moral theory. Insofar as the cosmos has no intrinsic moral fiber, everything is indeed permitted in an ultimate sense, but people can still formulate moral laws for themselves, despite how they will disappear and be forgotten with the extinction of the human race.

Beauvoir appreciates that the majority of people in the world assume to the contrary that there are preexisting moral laws given by God or by some other authoritative source, but she regards these people as failing to see the truth, and compares their perspective to that of children. When children are growing up, they are presented with a world already formed, filled with rules, values, and authoritative adults who impose and institute those rules and values. To the child, the rules and values appear to be objective, solid, and unconditional. Beauvoir maintains that when adults assert the existence of unconditional values that derive from a source external to human beings, they are merely carrying forth the outlook that was presented to them when they were youngsters.

Despite how everyone is responsible for themselves in principle, social pressures are difficult to resist, for it is common knowledge that departures from the status quo are often severely punished. It is said that a soldier is always free to disobey any given order, but people naturally cling to life, a good soldier's sense of duty can be strong, and under conditions of war, the price of disobeying an order could be immediate execution.

Achieving an increased exercise of one's freedom can require an extraordinary amount of self-awareness and willpower, and with respect to the ability to exercise their inherent freedom, people consequently fall into different categories. Recognizing this, Beauvoir presents a ranking of people that ranges from benighted individuals who do not appreciate their freedom at all to those who display a clear awareness of their actual, groundless, value-free condition.

This philosophical style of formulating rankings appears in a variety of philosophers—the most complicated, thorough, systematic, and articulate of these is perhaps Hegel—where the philosophy's ideal is set out and where alternative perspectives are positioned in a hierarchy that approaches the philosophy's ideal. Since ideals differ among philosophers, rankings accordingly differ. Kierkegaard sets the aesthetic, ethical, and religious outlooks in a series that advances toward the latter. Nietzsche speaks of the weaker common people, the relatively higher people, and beyond the higher people, the extremely strong, superhuman type. For Camus, the arrangement is simpler, with only two levels. The "everyday man" is at lower level and the "absurd man" is at the higher, where the latter includes figures such as Don Juan, the actor, the traveler, and the adventurer. For Sartre and Heidegger, inauthentic individuals contrast with the authentic ones. For Beauvoir, where "ethics is the triumph of freedom over facticity," her highest types realize their freedom in concrete contexts most effectively. These are the genuine, true, authentic human beings.

At the lowest end of Beauvoir's hierarchy are people who, as she describes them, perceive the world as a dull, dead place, and who are unimaginative, uncreative, apathetic, unloving, empty, and in a sense, fearful of the world. She refers to them as "subhumans" (*sous-hommes*). In German, one would call them *Untermenschen*—a type that, using Nietzsche's phrasing, stands as the polar opposite of the *Übermenschen*, the superhumans. For Beauvoir, the subhumans are not feeble pain-avoiders, as Nietzsche would have it, but are substandard individuals who live at a great psychological distance from realizing their inherent freedom and the possibilities of giving life meaning. They "take refuge in the ready-made values of the serious world," and define themselves and their lives by hiding behind "labels."

Such people are immersed in Sartrean bad faith, are noticeably unreflective, and blindly follow prevailing social movements and customs. They are at the lowest level in that they tend to regard themselves as objects, like soldiers or slaves, rather than as free beings, "dead" to themselves in their lack of vitality, generosity, and sensitivity. In Sartrean terms, they identify more with the inanimate physical world, or the "in-itself," as opposed to their own free consciousnesses, or the "for-itself." Of the subhuman type, Beauvoir has a dim view, saying that "in lynchings, in pogroms, in all the great bloody movements organized by the fanaticism of seriousness and passion, movements where there is no risk, those who do the actual dirty work are recruited from among the sub-men" (de Beauvoir 1947: 64).

At a slightly higher level are the "serious" people who have a more explicit sense of their freedom, but who adopt the ready-made values of the status quo, put themselves under arbitrary constraints thereby, and poorly exercise their inherent freedom. Like the subhumans, these people are disposed to escape their freedom by adhering to what they consider to be fixed, unconditional values. Those who fit Kierkegaard's "ethical" stage, such as Judge William, are in this category.

Moving closer to the genuine, free individuals are the nihilists, who see the illusion of believing in unconditional values, but who react to it with futility, feeling that nothing matters. This condition can take a variety of destructive turns, ranging from suicide, to skepticism and bitter irony, to frivolous and shameless hedonism, to vicious and self-destructive quests for power. Beauvoir partially sympathizes with the nihilist, but adds that something important is missing:

> The nihilist is right in thinking that the world *possesses* no justification and that he himself is nothing. But he forgets that it is up to him to justify the world and to man himself exist validly. (de Beauvoir 1947: 81)

> The fundamental fault of the nihilist is that, challenging all given values, he does not find, beyond their ruin, the importance of that universal, absolute end which freedom itself is. (de Beauvoir 1947: 82)

At the top of Beauvoir's hierarchy are creative, essentially artistic, self-determining people. These individuals are best at exemplifying how freedom is the source of all values, and are best at giving life meaning. She writes:

> Freedom is the source from which all significations and all values spring. It is the original condition of all justification of existence. The man who seeks to justify his life must want freedom itself absolutely and above everything else. (de Beauvoir 1947: 34)

Underlying Beauvoir's view and expressed in the above excerpt is the Kierkegaardian theme of becoming a true person by coming into contact with the absolute, godlike, aspect of oneself. Just as God created the world freely and with self-determination, creative people produce new worlds. They give style to their personal character, or develop new styles in social movements, literature, music, or the visual arts, or serve as cultural leaders who set the programs for the future.

That Beauvoir's ideal of the creative individual follows as the next stage from the nihilistic outlook is worth reflecting upon, for the ideals espoused by Hegel, Schopenhauer, Nietzsche, and Camus also emerge from a penultimate nihilistic phase. In each case, nihilism represents a crisis point that contains the potential for awakening and salvation: a person hits rock bottom in utter frustration after projects, lifestyles, or outlooks that were aiming to secure meaning in life fall apart, but after a period of total emptiness, a new, more viable, and apparently more permanent source of meaning presents itself. It is instructive that the above theorists have different conceptions of the outlook that emerges from the nihilistic condition.

Hegel's discussion of the unhappy consciousness mentioned in the introduction moves from the nihilistic dark night of the soul to a priestlike figure who integrates and harmonizes the tension between mind and body, the unconditioned and conditioned. Schopenhauer, after being overwhelmed morally by the terrible presence of suffering in the world, judges the spatiotemporal world to be worthless, and surmounts this nihilistic condition by entering a state of otherworldly, ineffable, desire-free, peaceful awareness. Nietzsche, agreeing with Schopenhauer that the spatiotemporal world is filled with suffering, denies that a convincing, concrete form of salvation can be achieved by attending to otherworldly realities, or to past civilizations such as that of the ancient Greeks, or to some anticipated perfect society to come. He overcomes nihilism by transforming his attitude toward suffering: he rejects the entire moral evaluation of the world that led Schopenhauer to condemn life, and affirms life as a whole with a love of the fundamental, pain-filled struggle for achieving something higher than ourselves on earth, not is some realm beyond. Camus, like Nietzsche, appreciating that from the standpoint of infinite time, everything will dissolve into nothing, overcomes nihilism by finding meaning in the immediate experience of the present moment in conjunction with embracing struggle, competition, and life-as-sport. Unlike Nietzsche, though, he does so with a strong sense of social responsibility for all people, especially the disadvantaged.

Beauvoir criticizes Camus's absurdist ideals of Don Juan and adventurer in *The Ethics of Ambiguity* as being too nihilistic, but she shares with him a similar social conscience: they both acknowledge that each person is free and that life is essentially meaningless in an objective sense, and encourage us to create meaning with a sensitivity for the plight of people who suffer. Both Beauvoir and Camus advocate social activism to increase freedom in the world.

Beauvoir's rationale is more philosophically developed than Camus's in that her theorizing is more attentive to our ambiguous condition. While appreciating that each person is absolutely free as a concrete individual, where no external control can be fully exercised over what will be chosen, she appreciates from a more abstracted perspective that each individually free person is also the instantiation of freedom in general, speaking as if "freedom" were a single entity that is embodied in this or that individual, as "blueness" is embodied in the blue sky and in a blue blanket. From this abstracted perspective, the only consistent position is that freedom does not contradict itself.

If we align our behavior in accord with the ideal that freedom in general is not to contradict itself, substantial social and moral implications follow: every choice that each person makes ought not to inhibit or oppress the choices of others. The implied ideal is impossible fully to realize, but it serves morally and regulatively to guide people's decision making. The struggle for increased freedom in society will never end, given the ambiguity between the specific freedom of the individual person and freedom in general—"no action can be generated for man without its being immediately generated against men"—but this does not imply that the goal of realizing freedom throughout society is not meaningful.

## 7.2 The ambiguous human condition: Individuality versus sociality

As mentioned at the outset, Beauvoir formulates the ambiguity of the human condition in view of the distinction between mind and body, following Sartre's main distinction in *Being and Nothingness* between "consciousness" (the "for-itself") and the physical world (the "in-itself"). As *The Ethics of Ambiguity* unfolds, another distinction soon predominates, namely, that between "individuality" and "sociality." Recognizing via Heidegger's influence that people are social by nature—being-with-others, as Heidegger maintains, is a primary feature of human existence—Beauvoir does not advocate at her highest ranking, selfish, purely individualistic modes of creativity, but ones that recognize and respect the freedom of other people. Her highest types have a deep-seated moral consciousness. In this respect, her view is unsympathetic with Nietzsche's amoral love of life.

Beauvoir's existentialism is grounded in a more Heideggerian, socially infused conception of freedom than Sartre's more individualistically oriented conception. She arrives at this position by drawing out the implications of Sartre's conception of absolute freedom more explicitly and concretely, developing Sartre's own advance in a more socially conscious direction as expressed in his 1946 essay "Existentialism Is a Humanism." Beauvoir and Camus had their personal differences, but her view resonates well with Camus's own sense of social concern. Her understanding of existentialism is also closer to someone such as Martin Buber, whose existentialism, as we will see, emphasizes the importance of intimate and respectful social interaction.

With respect to realizing our freedom, the ambiguity between our individuality and our sociality presents itself as follows: although from the individual, personally subjective standpoint each of us is absolutely free, from the more collective, social standpoint, we are impressed from infancy with social content and values. The language we are taught to speak is permeated with values, many of which are morally questionable, as in the case of sexist meanings. Education, socialization, training, and so on work further to solidify each person's definition and self-understanding, the typical result of which is to congest a person's awareness of appreciating how free he or she actually is. In *The Second Sex*, for example, Beauvoir observes the following:

> Richard Wright showed in *Black Boy* how blocked from the start the ambitions of a young American black man are and what struggle he has to endure merely to raise himself to the level where whites begin to have problems; the blacks who came to France from Africa also have—within themselves as well as from outside—difficulties similar to those encountered by women. (de Beauvoir 2011: 830)

> As Virginia Woolf shows, Jane Austen, the Brontë sisters, and George Eliot had to spend so much negative energy freeing themselves from external constraints that they arrived out of breath at the point where the major masculine writers were starting out; they have little strength left to benefit from their victory and break all the ties that bind them: for example, they lack the irony, the nonchalance, of a Stendhal or his calm sincerity. Nor have they had the wealth of experience of a Dostoevsky, a Tolstoy: it is why the great book *Middlemarch* does not equal *War and Peace*; *Wuthering Heights*, in spite of its stature, does not have the scope of *Brothers Karamazov*. (de Beauvoir 2011: 841)

Upon this ambiguity between free individuality and ossifying sociality, Beauvoir develops a significant portion of her writings, speaking of the possibilities of revolution, the need for better education, and the importance of remaining open-minded and creative. Although not identical to the ambiguity between mind and body or between being-for-itself and being-in-itself, the ambiguity between individuality and sociality is akin to it insofar as language, labels, and established social values and roles work together to set people into fixed categories, often opposed to one another, as when one religious or nationalistic group goes to war with another, where each is convinced that their self-definition is absolute.

The "thickness"—like Sartre's "in-itself" that is "glued to itself"—and congestive resistance to change that our social conditioning involves, can be appreciated by considering how language permeates our consciousness and is necessary for thinking of anything determinate. Our consciousness may be absolutely free at its base, but as our awareness develops from infancy, the social consciousness that accompanies language acquisition renders the prescription to be as free and creative as possible, challenging, and daunting.

Sartre says to a person engaged in a war that suicide is always a possible way to express one's freedom and resistance to the war. Beauvoir, however, reveals the layers of social conditioning that inhibit such a radical exercise of freedom. She thereby sets the scene for later French poststructuralist theorists who, recognizing the weight of social conditioning, observe that liberation requires challenging the social labels and values that are embodied in the languages we speak. This can be done by adopting a more poetic awareness through which new vocabularies and ways of thinking about ourselves can emerge. In the field of French feminism, Luce Irigaray (b. 1930) makes important advances in this regard as she reveals how the languages we speak implicitly instill sexist attitudes.

These considerations should cause us to reflect upon the valuations implicit in Beauvoir's hierarchy of human types—a hierarchy that ranges from the subhuman, to the serious person, to the nihilist, to the genuinely free person. In *The Ethics of Ambiguity*, the only types that receive a positive presentation are the nihilist and the free person. The subhuman is condemned by the very word used to describe that unfortunate state of mind; the serious person is looked upon with the negative valuation that attaches to Sartre's characterization of those who live in bad faith.

The difficulty here is that Beauvoir importantly shows that the forces of socialization tend to lead people into conditions where they are virtually unable to discern that they are not realizing their capacities for freedom.

Some of the people who fit into Beauvoir's categories of the subhuman and serious are those who, as they stand among the oppressed, she hopes will someday become more enlightened and free. A word about her use of the term "subhuman" is consequently appropriate at this point.

At the lowest level of human being according to Beauvoir are the subhumans, among whom she includes morally repulsive individuals who engage in lynchings, murders, persecutions, and similar kinds of abhorrent activities. The word she uses is *sous-hommes*, the German equivalent of which is *Untermenschen*—a word that gained currency from the 1922 book by Lothrop Stoddard, *The Revolt Against Civilization—The Menace of the Under-Man*, published in German in 1925. The Nazis used the word *Untermenschen* to describe people who in their view were so inferior relative to Nazi ideals, that they ought to be treated as nothing more than servants, like tools, without respect. With a linguistic history of this kind, despite how Beauvoir mentions as examples of subhumans, those who committed atrocities during the war, it seems prudent for a theorist to hesitate to label any human being as a "subhuman," *Untermensch*, or "Under-Man."

This reveals a disappointing side to Beauvoir's sensibilities, for it appears that her extreme valorization of the ideal of freedom in the immediate postwar period led her to describe its opposite with the terminology that had been used ideologically by the oppressive forces that had occupied France only a few years earlier. At the same time, there is a humanly thoughtful aspect of her theorizing—an essential one—where she appreciates how socialization and a history of abuse can render a person virtually incapable of advancing beyond some of the lower levels of human moral development.

## 7.3 Beauvoir's ethics of ambiguity

At one point in *The Ethics of Ambiguity*, Beauvoir states that unlike other moral theories, existentialism gives a real role to evil insofar as it acknowledges that there are no ultimate or absolute prohibitions against behaving in a malicious manner. God does not exist and each of us is free. There is no afterlife and no tribunal therein where criminals will be judged and punished. People can choose to be violent, cheating, and disrespectful toward others, for our freedom is absolute and not constrained by rationality.

As we move from individual to individual in a concrete manner, as when counting people sitting in a room, each individual is free to choose differently from the others and each can make a choice not to respect rationality. Beauvoir argues that moral constraints follow upon choosing to be rational, however, for once one respects the absolute value of freedom in oneself, then consistently it must be respected in others. If freedom is to be instantiated as much as possible in one instance or situation, then it ought to be instantiated in other situations of the same kind. To express this idea, as noted earlier, she states that freedom must not contradict itself.

This style of moral theory is reminiscent of Kant's, which is based on the very idea of being consistent in one's behavior. Kant holds that one should act only according to maxims that can be generalized into universal laws, which is to say that one should not act inconsistently. Beauvoir's ethics of ambiguity is based similarly on a conception of freedom that calls for consistency from person to person insofar as that conception rationally requires that each person respect the freedom of others.

With this common link between people, one might think that Beauvoir would acknowledge with Kant, an ideal end-state toward which we morally and rationally tend, namely, a free society populated by mutually respecting people who live together peacefully. This, though, is not the case: on her more existentially grounded view that recognizes the ambiguity of the human condition—one more resonant with Nietzsche's conflict-filled conception of the world—there is no ultimate social condition of universally actualized freedom, liberation, mutual respect, and peace to expect:

> To the idea of present war there is opposed that of a future peace when man will again find, along with a stable situation, the possibility of a morality. But the truth is that if division and violence define war, the world has always been at war and always will be; if man is waiting for universal peace in order to establish his existence validly, he will wait indefinitely: there will never be any other future. (de Beauvoir 1947: 166)

This expresses the ambiguity in our human condition. From the rational standpoint, one might expect a good society to emerge someday, for each person has a rational aspect and rational capacity that if accentuated sufficiently could produce such a society. Since each person is free to choose as she or he wishes, without constraint, the chances are nonetheless high that there will always be a significant proportion of people who will choose evil, who will damage the social fabric, and who will stand apart from the world of peace, compassion, and mutual respect. Such is the tragic nature of our freedom.

Beauvoir's position has a realistic ring, for it is remote to expect that people will stop going to war, or on a lesser scale, stop being violent to each other. If it is only partially true that reason is the slave of the passions, as David Hume believed, irrationality can be expected to be incorporated perpetually into human life, with immoral consequences to follow.

Questionable in Beauvoir's view, though, is the particular argument she offers to ground her existentialist ethics, namely, that we are each obligated to respect the freedom of others, since freedom should not contradict itself. The argument itself may be acceptable in principle, but the philosophical disposition that underlies it is not especially existentialist, for it relies upon a conception of freedom as an abstract idea.

Beauvoir argues that "freedom" will unacceptably contradict itself if one person chooses to be rational while another chooses to be irrational, or if one person chooses to respect the freedom of others while another chooses not to. "Freedom itself" is violated in such a situation. This is exactly how the actual world is, though, so the notion of freedom upon which her argument is based, exists only in an abstract, philosophical sense as an unrealized ideal. Rather than being a down-to-earth, existentially centered idea, it derives from a different style of thinking that is more abstractive. Beauvoir's existential ethics consequently rests upon a philosophical style of thinking that runs counter to the spirit of existentialism, since the latter regards as foundational each person's concrete and absolute ability to choose in any way that is desired, without rational constraint. This is what it means to acknowledge the genuine reality of evil.

As we know from her feminist writings, Beauvoir has a powerful interest in eliminating oppression and in developing a complementary moral theory. This interest seems to be more important—and justifiably so from a social standpoint—than that of remaining entirely consistent philosophically with the existentialist premise that everyone is absolutely free. When taking the latter seriously, metaphysically, and primarily, it becomes difficult to require anyone to act morally. Moreover, Beauvoir speaks sometimes as if individuals are not to be held entirely responsible for their values, situation, and actions, due to the overwhelming weight of oppressive forces to which they were exposed since childhood.

We can note how Kant observes to the contrary, and more extremely, that even when it appears that a person is naturally irredeemable from a moral standpoint, we still hold the person responsible:

> There are cases in which men, even with an education which was profitable to others, have shown from childhood such depravity, which continues to increase during their adult years, that they are held to be born villains and incapable of any improvement of character; yet they are judged by their acts, they are reproached as guilty of their crimes; and indeed, they themselves find these reproaches as well grounded as if they, regardless of the hopeless quality ascribed to their minds, were just as responsible as any other men. (Kant 1956: 103)

If one agrees with Kant about our ordinary attitudes toward holding people responsible, then no one has an excuse, as Sartre maintained. Regarding Beauvoir's philosophical argumentation, the following is a suitable point of arrival—a point that reveals an ambiguity in Beauvoir's own outlook. There is a side to Beauvoir that agrees with Sartre that we are absolutely free. There is another side that resists holding people entirely responsible for their actions, beliefs, lifestyles, and such. The assertion of absolute freedom in each individual contradicts the idea that due to childhood conditioning, some people are not entirely responsible for how they behave and for what they believe. It also contradicts the idea that freedom is an abstract entity whose consistency needs to be maintained, for people can choose as they individually wish.

We can reasonably call this an ambiguity in Beauvoir's outlook, since neither is it easy to erase the proposition that people are absolutely free, nor the fact that we have some kind of foundational moral awareness, nor the evidence that some people have been so brainwashed since they were children that convincing them that they are free to be otherwise—that they need not, for instance, be essentially a soldier, waiter, representative of some religion, or nationality—is a virtually hopeless endeavor. Through her concept of ambiguity, Beauvoir tries to respect and philosophically balance these conflicting ideas.

Part Two

# Existentialism in Religion, Culture, Psychology, and Film

# 8

# Christian Existentialism

Christianity is an outlook that regards the personage of Jesus as centrally inspirational, where Jesus is understood to be more than an especially enlightened human being, as some versions of Buddhism understand Buddha, but an earthly embodiment of God. Given existentialism's extremely down-to-earth quality, a Christian existentialist can be characterized in principle as someone who affirms the human capacity to emulate closely, or even to become, an embodiment of God or of one of God's essential qualities, conceived consistently with how God is portrayed in Christian scriptures.

If Christianity's essential message is to live one's life in a way that exemplifies Jesus, then approximating such an embodiment would render a person into a living example of that toward which Christian existentialism—and some would argue true Christianity—aims. This down-to-earth emphasis upon becoming a Jesus-figure involves a primary attention not to God per se as an otherworldly, supernatural being, but to the realistic, morally acting, often tortured, embodiment of God on earth, along with the ways we can embody that figure.

We have seen that Kierkegaard is a Christian existentialist in this respect, for he emphasizes the importance of experiencing the divine quality of absolute freedom when making an ungrounded leap of faith—an anxiety-ridden experience that he describes as infused with fear and trembling. He attends specifically to the anguish that issues from the tension in being a finite human being that is nonetheless absolutely free.

In general, the Jesus-figure need not be presented as a tortured being, for it is possible that a thoroughly gratifying ecstatic experience can result when a person embodies divine qualities. Assuming that pure love and care are among God's essential characteristics, a deeply loving and caring person could be regarded as a Jesus-figure and true Christian. Since anxiety in the face of death is among the keynotes of existentialist philosophy, however, a Christian existentialist image of Jesus would tend to include a dimension of suffering in the face of death, if only by recalling how it is said that during his crucifixion, Jesus asked why God had forsaken him (Mk 15:34), or how, on the night before, he is said to have experienced severe anguish in the garden of Gethsemane (Mk 14:32). The basic Christian existentialist image of Jesus is sublime rather than beautiful, one can say.

There are related ways to be considered a Christian existentialist. One can develop a theory whose fundamental conception of the human condition is inspired and defined by existentialist concerns such as the meaning of life, freedom, individuality, and anxiety in the face of death, but where the prescriptive response to this condition is extracted from Christian scriptures and is not particularly existentialist in content. Paul Tillich's view is an example. He understands the human condition in existentialist terms, but he draws meaning from Christian scriptures and disagrees with how atheistic existentialist philosophy, as we find in Nietzsche, Sartre, and Camus, concludes that life is objectively meaningless and that we are alone and solely responsible for creating meaning.

There is some inherent friction between existentialism and Christianity insofar as Christianity grounds itself upon the being of God, understood as an otherworldly entity. To be thoroughly existentialist is to be completely down to earth, however, without looking beyond to extraordinary or otherworldly levels of being. In Christian existentialism, there is consequently a tension and need to arrive at a balance between the this-worldly and the otherworldly, where alongside the affirmation of what is this-worldly in the existentialist spirit, there is a reluctance to sacrifice the belief and ultimate dependence upon what is otherworldly.

When God is understood moreover and emphatically to be a rational being who created a fundamentally rational world, the tension between the this-worldly and the otherworldly is reduced, with a corresponding modification in the notion of Christian existentialism. "Existence" may remain the main focus, but by acknowledging that the ultimate rational ground of the universe resides in God as a rational being, worldly existence is no longer regarded as absurd, fundamentally alien, or the legitimate occasion for anguish in the face of it, but rather as essentially amenable to our spiritual hopes.

A theorist who employs this conception of God can be interpreted as either departing noticeably from the varieties of existentialist philosophy expressed by Kierkegaard, Nietzsche, Sartre, Heidegger, and Camus, and no longer aptly characterized as an "existentialist" per se, or claiming more competitively that the atheistic existentialist philosophers, at least, fail to grasp what true "existentialism" is. Jacques Maritain (1882–1973), inspired by the philosophy of St. Thomas Aquinas, adopts this stance as an advocate of what he calls "existentialist intellectualism." He writes the following:

> We have seen how the existentialism of Thomas Aquinas differs from modern existentialism, both because it is rational in type and because, being founded upon the intuitiveness of the senses and the intellect, it associates and identifies being and intelligibility at every point. (Maritain 1956: 147)

> Moreover, the very name of existentialism is, as regards atheistic existentialism, a name usurped. Neither being nor existence: such philosophies are in reality philosophies of action, either of *praxis* and the transforming action of the world, or of moral creation *a nihilo* and liberty for liberty's sake. This is why the very notion of contemplation has become unthinkable for them, and they have no other recourse than, in the fine scorn of ignorance, to stigmatise with the name of "quietism" the highest and purest activity of the intellect, the free activity of fruition of truth. (Maritain 1956: 141)

Among all of existentialism's philosophical representatives, Jean-Paul Sartre's atheistic existentialism is perceived by Christian existentialists such as Maritain, Paul Tillich (1886–1965), and Gabriel Marcel (1889–1973) as the arch-enemy of true existentialist thought. The degree of commonly recognized "existentialist" content varies among these Christian existentialists, but each maintains a down-to-earth focus while arguing against Sartre's atheism, employing contents either from existentialist theory itself, as do Tillich and Marcel, or from mainstream rationalistic philosophy, as does Maritain.

Since their theorizing is closer to "existentialism" as commonly understood, we will attend to Tillich's and Marcel's views in this chapter as representative of Christian existentialism, and will see that Marcel's version, insofar it centrally adopts some of Heidegger's insights about the nature of human being, has the most noticeably "existentialist" quality.

## 8.1 Paul Tillich (1886–1965)

Paul Tillich is influenced significantly by Kierkegaard's view that the human being is conflicted at the core: although we are finite beings and know we will die, we can imagine the infinite, apprehend the extensive universe beyond ourselves, reason that the universe has an ultimate ground, and even feel the infinite within ourselves. Our physical bodies are finite, but our minds have a capacity for transcendence.

Hegel expresses this tension in his discussion of the unhappy religious consciousness, as he describes how the unhappy consciousness yearns for God, sometimes feels God within itself, and yet is repeatedly drawn back into an awareness of its finite and seemingly insignificant character. Beauvoir refers similarly to the "ambiguous" human condition in that we are physical bodies subject to the laws of nature, while also free to create values. Tillich describes our condition and predicament as follows, emphasizing our finitude, and invoking Heidegger's notion of an *existentiale*, or fundamental structure of human being:

> Finitude as an existentiale is the double-sided experience of the existing subject as bound to transitoriness and as transcending it in the awareness of the trans-temporal. The existing subject is aware both of its belonging to the infinite and of its being excluded from it and surrendered to finitude. It is this duality that explains the profound melancholy that permeates classical Greek culture: the fact that, of all beings who have to die, men alone are called mortals in contrast to the immortals—the gods—in whom is embodied man's potentiality of transcending transitoriness. It is the same duality that explains the Old Testament idea that naturally man comes from dust and must return to dust and that he is transitory like the grass and the animals in the fields, but at the same time that this contradicts his essential destiny to participate in the divine eternity. (Tillich 1956: 743)

This excerpt displays Tillich's clear, philosophical style—one that is informed by an impressive command of the history of philosophy. He is a reliable expositor when discussing philosophical and theological issues, and proceeds typically by setting out the historical background of the problem at hand, the various solutions that have been developed to date, and then his own position in view of his predecessors.

Tillich understands atheistic existentialism, in his opinion represented best by Heidegger and Sartre, as the philosophy that most effectively conveys the cultural atmosphere of the early-to-mid-twentieth-century period—the period in which he lived—although he traces the general spirit of existentialist thought to aspects of Plato. Tillich's well-known book *The Courage to Be* (1952), accordingly addresses atheistic existentialist thought within a survey of conceptions of courage, all of which intend to respond effectively to the human condition. After completing his survey, Tillich presents his own conception of courage—one he regards as the most penetrating and profound conception—that provides a Christian solution to fundamental existentialist concerns.

As penultimate to his own conception, Tillich describes a particular kind of courage that is distinctive to atheistic existentialism, namely, a courage in the face of despair: upon realizing that the world is essentially and objectively meaningless, one summons the courage as a free individual to create meaning for oneself. This kind of courage is inherent in the prescriptive aspects of Nietzsche's, Sartre's, Camus's, and Heidegger's views. It is implicit in Nietzsche's appeal to the strongest individuals to provide significance to earth and life by preparing the way for the superhuman being. It is implicit as well in Sartre's advocacy of absolute freedom in a life of authenticity, in Camus's celebration of the rebellious and absurd person who appreciates the infinite value of every moment and lives exclusively for today, and in Heidegger's prescription that we act with resolve in the face of death.

Tillich remains dissatisfied with these efforts to create meaning, mainly because the groundlessness of human freedom that underlies atheistic existentialism provides no foundation for moral values. Beauvoir appreciates the same difficulty, but adds that nothing prohibits us from choosing a moral life, either. Tillich nonetheless regards this open-endedness as a problem, maintaining that the lack of moral foundations inherent in atheistic existentialism does nothing to prevent people from gravitating into fascist and communist affiliations—ones that were responsible for the deaths of millions of people during his lifetime. In response to atheistic existentialism, Tillich invokes a different kind of courage that respects and draws inspiration from a being that is beyond and immeasurably more powerful than finite human being and individually centered freedom.

Tillich adheres to the existentialist understanding of the human condition as one where each person is inherently apprehensive about and resistant to death's inevitable approach. Each person is consequently disposed to discover a "courage to be which is beyond the threat of non-being" (Tillich 1952: 152). He believes that atheistic existentialism is mistaken in its understanding of the person as a self-enclosed center of absolute freedom, for he observes that humans naturally look beyond themselves for salvation. Indeed, we can see this attitude motivating the early Nietzsche himself, when he interprets the experience of Greek tragic theatre as providing a "metaphysical comfort" in the awareness that we are each inextricably involved in and sustained by the energies of life itself that continue on despite the deaths of individuals.

Tillich advances the same kind of consoling solution to the problem of meaninglessness in the face of death as the early Nietzsche, except that in place of "life itself"—the trans-individual, earthly energy Nietzsche identifies—he refers us to a broader foundation, namely, "being itself":

> For everything that is participates in being itself, and everybody has some awareness of this participation, especially in the moments in which he experiences the threat of non-being. (Tillich 1952: 153)

Tillich personifies being itself as God, and accordingly recognizes inspirational and existentially sustaining experiences that involve relationships with God, either as a mystical union, a personal encounter, or deep conviction of God's approval of oneself. These experiences provide an unconditional assurance and ground for courage in the face of death—one that Tillich maintains is superior to the atheistic existentialist position that we are alone in a meaningless universe and have only our free, decision-making, value-creating individual selves upon which to rely. For Tillich, salvation from our existential condition of apparent meaninglessness can be attained only by opening ourselves up to God's infinite power:

> The acceptance by God, his forgiving or justifying act, is the only and ultimate source of a courage to be which is able to take the anxiety of guilt and condemnation into itself. For the ultimate power of self-affirmation can only be the power of being-itself. Everything less than this, one's own or anyone else's finite power of being cannot overcome the radical, infinite threat of non-being which is experienced in the despair of self-condemnation. This is why the courage of confidence, as it is expressed in a

man like Luther, emphasizes unceasingly exclusive trust in God and rejects any other foundation for this courage to be, not only as insufficient but as driving him into more guilt and deeper anxiety. (Tillich 1952: 162)

With a philosophical awareness, Tillich equates God with "the ground of being" or "being itself," and invokes the power of "being-itself" as a counterforce against nonbeing and death. One could refer to this power as that which is apprehended and appreciated upon tapping into the sheer and amazing presence of the world that appears in reaction to the puzzlement precipitated by the question, "Why is there something rather than nothing?" Upon identifying with "being itself" and considering the prospect of our death in view of it, Tillich believes that a consolation and strength will emerge in a courage sufficient to overcome any concerns about our finitude and apparent meaninglessness.

This is Nietzsche's "metaphysical comfort" transposed from the level of appreciating one's unity with "life itself" to the more expanded level of appreciating one's unity with "being itself." The means of salvation that Tillich suggests is thus a familiar one: we submit to and blend our individuality with a force higher than ourselves.

A thought-provoking aspect of Tillich's position emerges in contrast to Sartre. Like Tillich, Sartre similarly recognizes "being-in-itself" as metaphysically foundational, but he regards it as hardly a means to salvation. For Sartre, being-in-itself is "just there," present as an absurdity and as a being fundamentally alien and threatening to free, human consciousness. There can be no blend that is possible between the "for-itself" and the "in-itself," and the attempt to be God, as Sartre describes this effort, is contradictory. Sartre accordingly associates being-in-itself with death, since it is devoid of consciousness, like a stone. In radical contrast, Tillich speaks of a person's being grabbed by "being itself" in a transcendent and inspirational experience that provides strength and a sense of salvation.

Tillich intends his conception of God as the ground of being to be truer than conceptions of God that are mentioned superficially in political and propagandistic speech, truer than conceptions of God that separate God from the world too sharply, and truer than conceptions of God as a kind of tyrant—a conception of God that Tillich identifies as the actual, and misconstrued, enemy of atheistic existentialism. He aims to transcend these more familiar kinds of theism and introduces the locution, "God above God"—that is, the "God above the God of traditional theism"—to express a more refined conception of God. This is intended to be beyond precise, objective definitions, beyond arguments for God's existence, and beyond conceptions of God as an object or foreign being. God is conceived here as a being that one must experience through a profound and personal connection with the cosmos as a whole.

It is nonetheless instructive to recall the cosmological argument for God's existence at this juncture, the core of which is as follows: since the spatiotemporal world is a contingent existence, it is necessary to suppose a ground for that existence, namely, a being that is its uncaused cause—a necessary being that we call "God." If we admit the existence of such an uncaused cause, there remains a well-known gap in the argumentation when making the logical transition from "uncaused cause" or "necessary being" to "God." Postulating a necessary being at the ground of the universe does not by itself imply the intelligence, goodness, or other anthropomorphic characteristics such as caring, forgiveness, and compassion that are frequently ascribed to God. By defining God as the God beyond the God of theism, the appreciation of God's infinity is significantly enhanced, but it also increases the danger of losing God's spiritually attractive, humanly amenable qualities.

Tillich supplements his conception of God that is beyond the God of theism with contents from Christian scripture that render God into a being that accepts us in our finitude and can relate to us humanly. From a philosophical standpoint, such an external reliance on Christian scripture to render a sublime and ineffable God more human is questionable if only because not everyone subscribes in detail to Christian scripture. As we will see, Gabriel Marcel's version of Christian existentialism does not depend as heavily upon accepting scriptural details or any particular version of Christianity such as Protestantism or Roman Catholicism and is more philosophically attractive in this respect.

Despite how his outlook requires the acceptance of many biblical statements, Tillich is interested in developing a universalistic conception of salvation. With respect to the characterization of Christian existentialism offered at the outset, where the guiding interest is to emulate Jesus or become Jesus-like, rather than attend to God as an otherworldly being, Tillich observes that people at all times and places have reflected upon the human condition and have postulated a better world for themselves. Sometimes this better world is located beyond the spatiotemporal world; sometimes it is located on earth, usually in the future. Either way, it is natural for us to postulate a revised, improved, better world or "new being" as Tillich calls it. As one can anticipate, he maintains that Christianity and the image of Jesus provide the best conception of this new being:

> What, then, is the peculiar character of the healing through the New Being in Jesus as the Christ? If he is accepted as the Saviour, what does salvation through him mean? The answer cannot be that there is no saving power apart from him but that he is the ultimate criterion of every healing and saving process. We said before that even those who have encountered him are only fragmentarily healed. But now we must say that in him the healing quality is complete and unlimited. The Christian remains in the state of relativity with respect to salvation; the New Being in the Christ transcends every relativity in its quality and power of healing. It is just this that makes him the Christ. (Tillich 1957: 194)

This excerpt reveals the traditional nature of Tillich's outlook insofar as he does not recognize that any individual human being other than Jesus himself can be a complete or bona fide Jesus-figure. That is, he upholds a distinction between Jesus's assumed perfection and every other human being. Jesus as the Christ stands inspiringly as an ideal that we can try to approximate, but no one will ever fully embody or realize this ideal. In this regard, Tillich does not represent a version of Christian existentialism that allows for people to be filled with God's spirit in the same way as was Jesus.

To locate Tillich's position along a spectrum of alternative relationships between human and the divine, Hegel's characterization of the unhappy consciousness is useful in its outline of three general stages of relationships with God, or the absolute. The first is where God is conceived as a distant, otherworldly being to which we relate with yearning, devotion, and profound respect, but with a tragic sense of being disconnected and alone as individuals. Judaism's conception of God would be an example in Hegel's view. The second is where God materializes and appears in a physical form such as Jesus, but where this divine individual remains different and separate from everyone else, despite its earthliness and despite how we can derive inspiration and life-changing attitudes through faith and devotion to the ideal that the divine individual presents. This second stage is where Tillich's conception of Jesus as the embodiment of the New Being resides. The third conception is that through which Christian existentialism has here been characterized in its purest and most universalistic form, namely, where God is recognized as a being that is literally infusible in principle into any given individual, where a person can find God living within and throughout himself or herself, and where in light of this extraordinary, existentially fulfilling experience, otherworldly conceptions of God proportionally fade in significance.

## 8.2  Gabriel Marcel (1889–1973)

Gabriel Marcel has an illuminating philosophical project insofar as he allows us to see the religious dimension that remains only implicit and submerged in atheistic existentialists such as Nietzsche and Heidegger. Marcel shares Nietzsche's and Heidegger's perception that the modern world is spiritually ill and, like them, prescribes a remedy through an alternative outlook on life. His view is that the majority of people have lost an appreciation of our natural surroundings, other people, and the cultural world insofar as these are felt to invoke an atmosphere of respect and sacredness.

Speaking in general, Marcel observes that people have become content with petty materialistic relationships, mercantile concerns, and merely technical problems, and that this has narrowed their horizons and drawn them away from a more loving attitude toward others and the world that respects it as a sacred place. He consequently refers to our modern world as a "broken world," permeated with feelings of alienation and filled with people whose occupations have turned them into mechanical functionaries. Marcel's project is accordingly therapeutic: he tries to show the way out of this relatively inhuman condition into a more human, integrated one where a feeling of being at home in the world prevails. Explicit in his outlook is the religious quality of trying to save people from their depraved or "fallen" condition, as we see also, but for the most part implicitly, in Nietzsche and Heidegger.

In "Existentialism Is a Humanism"—a verbal address first given in October 1945 and later published in 1946—Sartre refers to Marcel as a representative of Christian existentialism. Aware of this, Marcel responds to Sartre's characterization in an essay of February 1946, "Testimony and Existentialism," where he presents a contrasting idea of what is existential—one understandable through the distinction between an "objective observation" and a "personal testimony." Marcel preceded with this an essay of January 1946 entitled "Existence and Human Freedom," where he criticized Sartre's view in detail.

In an objective observation—suppose I am perceiving a glass of water upon a table in a café—the glass of water is not itself affected by my observing it, for I could leave the table and the glass would remain as it is, perhaps observed by the other people who remain sitting. Similarly, it makes no difference to the observation per se, that "I" am observing the glass, since as a consciousness, anyone else sitting at the table could make exactly the same observation that the glass of water is on the table. Described as such, this situation conveys the impersonal quality of Sartre's central distinction between consciousness, or the "for-itself," and the physical world, or the "in-itself." Both are impersonal and are, moreover, empty of meaning. Consciousness is a "nothingness" and being-in-itself has no intrinsic value. Upon this distinction, Sartre develops his existentialism. Marcel regards it as a theory grounded upon the experience of objective observation, as one would have in standard phenomenology.

Marcel points out, however, that there is another aspect of human experience that Sartre's distinction between the "for-itself" and the "in-itself" does not capture, namely, the experience of appreciating something that is given to us in a personal way, or conversely, the experience of appreciating something that we personally give to someone else. One can give one's word, for instance, as in a promise. Or one can give a gift, as for a birthday. In such cases, it can be said that one "consecrates" the item in question, such that the item is given a positive, caring meaning: it is made "holy," or "special," or "sacred" in a broad sense. When giving one's word, one's word acquires a value in view of the truth. For Marcel, this is what is "existential," namely, the transmutation of an object from a merely meaningless, utilitarian item, to a personally meaningful one:

> By virtue of my giving it, the object, which had been until then merely a neutral thing, costing so much at this or that shop, acquires a new quality, a being-for-another, not for everybody in general but for this particular person. Clearly, this being-for-another is not an objective quality of the thing; the value of my present may lie in some memory, in some event which belongs to the life of my friend, who thus receives from me a genuine communication of myself, an expression of the manner in which he is

present to me. Such a communication is existential in the sense that it is quite different from the mere transmission of a thing which is meant to reach it destination unaltered. (Marcel 1948: 75)

As does the experience of objective observation, the experience of giving or receiving a gift resides in the phenomenological and existential sphere: a sense of specialness and personal meaning is accorded to that which is given or received, and this extends over and beyond the Sartrean, objective register of empty consciousnesses and meaningless physical objects. In reference to Christian existentialism, important for Marcel is that upon expanding this kind of awareness into that by which one regards one's life itself as a gift, one's orientation toward the world transforms: a sense of sacredness, holiness, or spiritual appreciation attaches to nature itself, along with one's presence within it.

Marcel hesitates to call this a "Christian" existentialism per se, since he appreciates that people who do not identify themselves as Christians, but who have a sense of the world as a sacred place also experience the reverent and thankful attitude he has in mind. Insofar, though, as God is assumed to be a caring, loving, and appreciative being, one can be regarded as a Jesus-figure when embodying these qualities in a penetrating way, where they govern one's overall character and outlook toward the world.

There is a question of why this attitude of appreciating individual objects, as well as the world as a whole, as "special," "holy," "consecrated," or "sacred," is particularly "existential" or "existentialist." It is easy to think that the Sartrean position is more down-to-earth, honest, and realistic, since it states objectively that the human condition is defined fundamentally by consciousness, which is initially empty and free, in conjunction with a world within which consciousness finds itself, or into which it is thrown—a material world that appears absurdly to be simply "there."

If existentialism is an outlook that concerns itself with defining the fundamentals of the human condition and with retaining a focus upon these fundamentals in a down-to-earth manner, though, then Heidegger's analysis of human being or what he calls *Dasein* would be perfectly existentialist in spirit. As we have seen in the chapter on Heidegger, his analysis of *Dasein* sets forth a list of *existentiales*, or essential features of what it is like to be a human, among which is the attitude of "care." To be human is fundamentally to be a caring being, and to be a deeply caring person is to be human in a most authentic way. In this respect, Marcel's emphasis upon the importance of being a loving and caring person expresses an outlook as existentialist as Sartre's. The difference is that they develop their respective existentialisms upon different aspects of what they conceive to be fundamental to human being.

With Marcel, an essential aspect of our being human impels us to regard our lives as a gift, for which the appropriate response and attitude is gratitude. The being toward which our gratitude is extended remains unknown—there are no plausible academic or mathematically styled proofs of God's existence—but our humanity directs us nonetheless toward having faith and hope in a being that would appreciate our gratitude. For many people, this would be God. Theism, or more generally, a positive directedness toward an intelligent, morally appreciative, transcendent being is part of our caring human nature.

The uncertainty and implicit anguish in such faith is that our feeling of gratitude could have no actual transcendent referent, for our belief in God could amount to mere anthropomorphism. We may be compelled by our caring nature to regard our lives as a gift and to feel grateful toward an unknown, transcendent being conceived in our intellectual and moral image, but in doing so, we might only be playing out an accident of nature, the intrinsic being of which is nonrational and absurd.

Aware of the inability to prove that God exists, Marcel appreciates that we live in an uncertain condition. The human condition is "ambiguous," if we were to import Beauvoir's terminology. Our human nature may impel us to feel at home in the universe, but we know also that we could be doing this within a senseless expanse of insensate matter. Still, this ambiguous awareness represents our existential condition more truthfully than asserting dogmatically that there is no God and that the universe is absurd, or asserting dogmatically that God exists and that the universe is thoroughly meaningful.

Kierkegaard intensely appreciated this uncertainty as well, and he based his outlook on the spiritual struggle it generates. Marcel is more optimistic, resting with the faith that our human nature is not alien to the rest of the cosmos. This is despite how when we address ourselves to the universe as a whole and ask toward the beyond why we are here, silence is the usual answer.

# 9

# Jewish Existentialism

## 9.1 Franz Rosenzweig (1886–1929)

Franz Rosenzweig is most well known for *The Star of Redemption* (*Der Stern der Erlösung*), a book written during his military service in the First World War. It dates from August 1918 to February 1919 and was published in 1921. Ludwig Wittgenstein's *Tractatus Logico-Philosophicus*, although written with a more mathematically and logically oriented philosophical temperament, is a comparable book in its profundity, published in the same year and written while Wittgenstein was also serving in the German army during the war.

Rosenzweig, as was coincidentally Wittgenstein, was from an assimilated Jewish family where religion was not a predominant factor, and it disposed him seriously to consider converting to Christianity in mid-1913, when he was twenty-six years old. A few months later he decided against it, apparently having been influenced by his reflections upon Judaism in conjunction with his participation in the annual religious ceremonies that highlight Rosh Hashanah, the Jewish New Year, and Yom Kippur, the day of atonement and holiest day in the Jewish calendar.

From that time until his death in 1929 at the age of forty-two, Rosenzweig's interests centered upon understanding the essence of Judaism and devoting his time to the Frankfurt Jewish community where he founded in 1920 the Freie Jüdische Lehrhaus (Free House of Jewish Learning), a center for adult Jewish education. Suffering gradual paralysis from 1922 onward, his early death was due to ALS—a disease of the neurons that control voluntary muscle movement.

Before the First World War, Rosenzweig was a scholar interested in Hegel's social and political philosophy, the result of which was his 1912 doctoral dissertation, *Hegel and the State* (*Hegel und der Staat*), published in 1920. To put Rosenzweig's views into perspective, it will help consequently to review some relevant aspects of Hegel's philosophy, some of which Rosenzweig adopts and many of which he contests.

In the background of their respective philosophies are religious affinities: Hegel regards Christianity as the most advanced religion; Rosenzweig adheres to Judaism. Both aim to formulate a theory of all reality; both are interested in social communities. According to Hegel's metaphysics in particular, everything ultimately has a logical beginning: all that presently is has its source in the abstract, contentless concept of pure being—a concept that develops of its own accord via an inherent logic of opposition and reconciliation to complete the realm of pure thought, where from there, it transforms into the spatiotemporal world with its characteristic hierarchy of living things. The sphere of human life and cultural development then follows, progressing historically with increasing systematicity, rationality, self-consciousness, and freedom. To this day, the process continues toward an ultimate point of social integration.

On the face of things, this Hegelian understanding of the world's origin appears to be implausible insofar as raw matter does not seem to be the kind of being that could arise from a condition of pure conceptuality, however detailed and complete that condition might be. Hegel's position can also be criticized along existentially motivated lines as remaining too content with tracing the broad patterns of world history while neglecting the concrete, lived quality of each individual human being's experience. Kierkegaard adopts this stance toward Hegel in his emphasis upon the experience of passionate inwardness. Rosenzweig shares Kierkegaard's reservations about Hegel's philosophical approach.

Nonetheless, Hegel was among the first philosophers of the early nineteenth century to include within his outlook an appreciation of the concrete details of historical phenomena. He disagreed with views inspired by the Enlightenment and its mathematically grounded scientific thinking that attend almost exclusively and merely to the abstract essence of whatever object or subject matter is under investigation, as if one could speak meaningfully about humanity in general without referring to individual people, or speak about religion in general without referring to the differences between specific religions.

Such considerations render it inappropriate to criticize Hegel flatly as a philosopher who has an unrealistic and insensitive attitude toward worldly realities, notwithstanding his relative lack of attention to aspects of personal experience such as passionate, subjective inwardness. His interest in understanding the world in a concrete way motivates his hallmark position that cultural phenomena need to be comprehended as organically situated within a developing historical context. As early as 1800, he expressed doubts about the abstractive philosophical attitude characteristic of the Enlightenment:

> "What is human nature in its purity?" This expression, "human nature in its purity," should imply no more than accordance with the general concept. But the living nature of man is always other than the concept of the same, and hence what for the concept is a bare modification, a pure accident, a superfluity, becomes a necessity, something living, perhaps the only thing which is natural and beautiful. (Hegel 1948: 169)

The necessity to which Hegel refers—we can call this an "existential necessity"—of a person's hair color, size, weight, and facial structure, for example, resides in how without such features there could be no existing physical body and living organism of which to speak. When considering furthermore the content and significance of various religions, Hegel is consequently not satisfied with the position that the apparently contingent, morally superfluous features of any religion (e.g., its regulations regarding dietary practice or the proper attire to be worn within religious buildings) should be ignored or dismissed in view of its essential and timeless (or what he calls "natural," as in the concept of God-given "natural" law) moral content. He rejects the essentialistic, "Enlightenment" style of analysis for a more historically grounded one. Referring to Judaism—albeit unsympathetically within the context of his developmental conception of history where as a matter of cultural progress, he understands Christianity as a spiritual advance upon early religions such Egyptian, Jewish, and Greek Religion—he states:

> To shudder before an unknown Being; to renounce one's will in one's conduct; to subject one's self throughout like a machine to given rules; to abandon intellect altogether in action or renunciation, in speech or silence; and to lull one's self into a brief or a lifelong insensibility—all this may be "natural," and a religion which breathes this spirit would not on that account be positive, because it would accord with the nature of its time. A nature demanded by such a religion would be a deplorable one; but the religion

would have fulfilled its purpose by giving this nature the only higher Being in which it found satisfaction and with which it was compatible. When another mood awakens, when this nature begins to have a sense of itself and thereby to demand freedom in and for itself instead of placing it in its supreme Being, then and only then can its former religion begin to appear a positive one. The universal concepts of human nature are too empty to afford a criterion for the special and necessarily multiplex needs of religious feeling. (Hegel 1948: 170)

Rosenzweig's understanding of Judaism—one that he is convinced transcends Hegel's allegiance to historical development—is at the other end of the spectrum:

In the whole Christian world, the Jew is practically the only human being who cannot take war seriously, and this makes him the only genuine pacifist. For that reason, and because he experiences perfect community in his spiritual year, he remains remote from the chronology of the rest of the world. . . . He does not have to wait for world history to unroll its long course [i.e., as Hegel would have it] to let him gain what he feels he already possesses in the circuit of each year: the experience of the immediacy of each single individual to God, realized in the perfect community of all with God. (Rosenzweig 1985: 331)

Here, both Hegel and Rosenzweig are insightful and implausible in different ways. Hegel sees that genuine spirituality should not be equated with merely acting in mechanical accord with a respected set of rules, but it is inaccurate to characterize Jewish spirituality in this way. Rosenzweig understands well that if one adopts a more timeless outlook, the nuances of history—ones often driven by petty and transient concerns, even in many cases of war—will present themselves as relatively insignificant in the greater course of things, but it is questionable to describe the Jews as being essentially the only group that embraces such an outlook.

Rosenzweig's above-cited characterization of the Jewish mentality nonetheless importantly reveals the central terms through which he comprehends reality, or "the All," namely, in reference to the fundamental philosophical triad of "God," "world," and "self," broadly conceived. Rosenzweig's terms are *Gott* (God), *Welt* (world), and *Mensch* (Man; Human), where, depending upon the context, the latter can refer to "soul," "self," "consciousness," or "person."

Although from a theistic standpoint where God is the ultimate being, one would say that everything issues from God, it remains existentially that from the standpoint of someone who aims to understand the universe in its totality, the situation is more complicated: an embodied consciousness faces a physical world that is simply "there," apparently independently of it, with a reflective awareness of being a finite entity that does not know all of the universe's mysteries. Underlying this "self versus world" relationship is the recognition of an absolute ground—the thought of God, as one might characterize such a ground—to yield a triadic relationship of "self," "world," and "God."

This triad is a familiar one in philosophical thought, most notably seen in Descartes's philosophy, who in his *Meditations on First Philosophy* (1641) begins methodologically with himself as a questioner and raises extensive doubts about the certainty of his knowledge of the external world. Discovering thereafter within himself the idea of God as an actual infinity—an idea he believes could not have originated from his own imagination—he becomes certain of God's existence and appeals to God's goodness as a guarantor of his clear and distinct perceptions of the external world. In this philosophical sequence, Descartes moves from the self, to God, to the world, starting from his uncertain, but existentially ineradicable condition as a person in the physical world trying to discover the truth. As a later historical antecedent to Rosenzweig's use of the Self-World-God triad, Kant's *Critique of Pure Reason* (1781/87) also features the ideas of soul (*die Seele*), world, and God as among the central metaphysical concepts that focus our rational efforts to understand the ultimate truth, or "things in themselves."

Now Rosenzweig interprets philosophies such as Descartes's that are based upon the Self-God-World triad and that as a matter of method either derive, reduce, or subordinate two of the terms to one of the others, as operating within an older, traditional, and questionable way of philosophizing. Ancient thought starts with the world and understands humans and the divine in terms of the world; medieval thought starts with the divine (God) and understands humans and the world in terms of God; modern thought starts with the self and understands the world and God in terms of the self, often advocating some version of philosophical idealism.

Rosenzweig offers a new way of thinking, conceiving of the triad from the general human standpoint as a balanced tripolarity, where each term is organically related to the others. Diagrammatically, he envisions the three terms as the points of an equilateral triangle, where the relationships between each pair of points indicate three additional intermediary points that when connected form a second equilateral triangle superimposed over the first. The point between God and world is "creation" (*Schöpfung*); the point between God and the self is "revelation" (*Offenbarung*); the point between the self and the world is "redemption" (*Erlösung*) in view of the existence of suffering and death. Rosenzweig's arrangement of the two triangles into a six-pointed star presents his philosophical understanding of the universe through the image of the Star of David. He calls this the star of redemption and the divine countenance, highlighting the importance of our relationship with God.

To appreciate Rosenzweig's insistence that each term of the basic triad, although organically related to the others, maintains its own identity and integrity, his presentation of the human situation is revealing, for he discerns how in the face of our finitude, we all experience an isolation from each other and from the world. In the very first sentences of *The Star of Redemption*, Rosenzweig speaks existentially about our anticipation of death, echoing Kierkegaard's notion of "fear and trembling," anticipating importantly one of the main themes to be developed only a few years later by Martin Heidegger in *Being and Time* (1927), not to mention effectively presenting the primary dualism in Sartre's existentialism between the "for-itself" (consciousness) and the "in-itself" (world), two decades before it appears centrally in Sartre's *Being and Nothingness* (1943):

> All cognition of the All originates in death, in the fear of death . . . each is bound to die, each awaiting the day of its journey into darkness with fear and trembling. . . . Let man creep like a worm into the folds of the naked earth before the fast-approaching volleys of a blind death from which there is no appeal; let him sense there, forcibly, inexorably, what he otherwise never senses: that his I would be but an It if it died. . . . With index finger outstretched, it directs the creature, whose limbs are quivering with terror for its this-worldly existence, to a Beyond of which it doesn't care to know anything at all. For man does not really want to escape any kind of fetters; he wants to remain, he wants to—live. (Rosenzweig 1985: 3)

Rosenzweig's reference to the "Beyond" reveals how when facing death squarely as a singular individual, a disposition naturally arises to direct one's attention toward what might reside beyond death, either to God specifically, or to the divine in general, or simply to a higher and more fundamental dimension beyond the transient earthly one, as Plato imagined. To understand clearly what awaits, the more philosophically, religiously, and existentially aware individuals aim to establish a spiritually satisfying relationship between themselves and this higher dimensional level of being. Rosenzweig conceives of this as "the experience of the immediacy of each single individual to God."

As is true for Kierkegaard, Rosenzweig wants to understand what a genuine God-relationship would be, given our condition as finite, perishable individuals. Kierkegaard, in his own effort to understand this, and hence, to understand what it means for him to become a true Christian, invokes the experience of absolutely soul-shaking faith that has been ascribed to Abraham, who was not a Christian, but a Jew living long before Jesus's time, and moreover, one of the most important leaders of the Jewish people. Through this Kierkegaardian example, as well as appreciating how Jesus himself was a Jew who experienced a close relationship to God, we can understand Rosenzweig's own decision not to convert to the established Christianity of his own time, for Abraham and Jesus, to cite only two examples, stand as examples of people who established an immediate connection to God in the absence of an institution or religion called "Christianity," and without using an external priestly figure as an intermediary to forge the connection between themselves and God. Contrasting with this, Rosenzweig maintains that the Christian relationship to God, as per standard Christian doctrine, typically involves an intermediary:

> The Christian dares to enter the presence of the Father [i.e., God] only through the Son [i.e., Jesus]. If the Son were not a man he would avail nothing to the Christian. He cannot imagine God himself, the holy God, could so condescend to him as he demands, except by becoming human himself. The inextinguishable segment of paganism which is innermost in every Christian bursts forth here. The pagan wants to be surrounded by human deities; he is not satisfied with being human himself: God too must be human. (Rosenzweig 1985: 350)

With respect to the idea of having an immediate relationship to God, Hegel's account of Christianity vis-à-vis Judaism in the *Phenomenology of Spirit* contrasts with Rosenzweig's, for Hegel—a theorist who rejects the epistemological adequacy of all "immediate" relationships—understands the history of religion in reference to the development of religious consciousness. At the initial, most primitive and abstract stage, God is conceived of as a distant, otherworldly, mysterious being toward which one can only pray and yearn unknowingly with deep feeling. Advancing upon this situation, God is then conceived of as coming down more tangibly to earth—Hegel has Christianity in mind—in the form of a divine human personage, different from everyone else, to whom people look for inspiration and guidance. The final stage is the realization that divinity resides as well within oneself, and that one is not, and never was, fundamentally alienated from God. Upon attaining this level of personal realization, the need for a priestly figure to serve as an intermediary between oneself and God dissolves, for one has become a priestly, Jesus-like figure oneself, understanding that God's spirit had been infusing one's inner being all along.

One can understand this third stage as being closely akin to Rosenzweig's "experience of the immediacy of each single individual to God," characteristic of Jewish spiritual experience. With this line of interpretation, the dynamics of the situation are thought-provoking, for in the experience of the immediate relationship with God, one implicitly refers to experiences such as those had by Abraham, Jesus, and many other religiously inspired individuals. Since the aim of many reflective Christians is to become genuine Christians by fostering a Jesus-consciousness within themselves—Kierkegaard exemplifies this understanding of Christianity, and it is revealing that his prime example of subjective inwardness is Abraham, whose faith in God transcended reason—an "experience of the immediacy of each single individual to God" describes what becoming a genuine Christian involves. Rosenzweig's own description of our relationship to God resonates with Kierkegaard's description of Abraham, whose trust in God was unconditional. Rosenzweig writes:

> To walk humbly with thy God—nothing more is demanded than a wholly present trust. But trust is a big word. It is the seed whence grow faith, hope, and love, and the fruit which ripens out of them. It is the very simplest and just for that the most difficult. (Rosenzweig 1985: 424)

Rosenzweig's understanding of the Jewish relationship with God coincides with this Kierkegaardian Christian aspiration, for such Christians do not regard the Jesus-figure as a necessary external mediator for a relationship with God, but regard him as a person to emulate by seeking for themselves a direct and comparable experience of the divine. In accord with this characterization of what becoming a genuine Christian involves, one can say that the Jewish and Christian religious experiences coincide. That Rosenzweig maintains that the awareness of God precipitates love supports the equation as well, given Jesus's embodiment of pure love.

Although Hegel's description of the historical development of religious consciousness appears to make sense at first sight, given its gradual progression from an initially abstract, indeterminate conception of the divinity to a more concrete conception that culminates with the realization of the divine within oneself, it can be questioned, since the historical development of religious consciousness appears to have been in the opposite direction. The first godlike personages were down-to-earth, anthropomorphic entities such as tree spirits, human-like gods, or deifications of the living ruler of the community, such as the Egyptian Pharaoh. Jesus as the "son of God" is not the first example of a human-divine religious personage. The more abstracted, unified, transcendent, otherworldly conceptions tend to come later, with the God of the Hebrew scriptures standing, in certain respects, as an early example of a more advanced mentality. Hegel's claim that the most abstract conception of the divine is the most primitive and spiritually immature, consequently does not seem to appreciate well that historically, the most primitive conceptions of the divine were the concrete, anthropomorphic ones—ones that Rosenzweig associates with paganism.

Despite Rosenzweig's acknowledgment that authentic, morally inspired God-relationships are possible, and that these relationships and associated experiences have an eternal aspect, he does not dissolve the individual person into a condition of pure universality or transcendent mystical oneness with God, but rather appreciates our finite condition throughout. In this respect, his outlook contains a strong existentialist aspect:

> The self is solitary man in the hardest sense of the word. (Rosenzweig 1985: 71)

> The self awakes to an ultimate individuation and solitude: there is no greater solitude than in the eyes of a dying man, and not more defiant, proud isolation than that which appears on the frozen countenance of the deceased. (Rosenzweig 1985: 71–72)

One might here recall the words of Jesus upon the cross, who stated in a loud voice as he approached death, *Eli, Eli, lema sabachthani?* which means, "My God, My God, why have you forsaken Me?" (Mt. 27:46).

## 9.2 Martin Buber (1878–1965)

Martin Buber—one of the most eminent Jewish religious thinkers of the twentieth century—writes with a religious consciousness, respectful of the cosmos and of the fundamental realities that govern it, but he does so with a sensitivity to the finite human condition, as do the Christian existentialists. His most well-known work, *I and Thou*, published in 1923, appearing four years before Martin Heidegger's *Being and Time* (1927) and twenty years before Jean-Paul Sartre's *Being and Nothingness* (1943), foreshadows themes that we find in Sartre's, Heidegger's, Tillich's, and Marcel's writings. Buber's existentialist aspect resides in his appreciation for the finite human condition as we inherently strive for a more distinct and meaningful awareness of the infinite, or what one can call God. His interests resemble Kierkegaard's, who strove to experience an authentic "God-relation" in his life.

Buber's outlook rests upon a distinction between two basic relationships that we have to the world and the things and people in it, reminiscent of the primary difference between Sartre's and Marcel's versions of existentialism. The first relationship is one where we regard other beings as inanimate objects, as things to use, as items that do not necessarily call for respect, and as merely factual matters. Buber refers to this as an "I-It" relationship, where the word "it" conveys the sense of the other being's relation to us as a mere "thing." We live in a physical world, our bodies are physical beings, we eat food, travel in vehicles, live in material dwellings and such, so the "I-It" attitude is appropriate in many contexts, simply as a matter of practicality.

The second relationship is one where we regard other beings in a close-knit personal manner, with a strong sense of human connection. The relationship between two caring friends, or the relationship between two people mutually in love with one another, expresses the level of sociality and intimacy that this relationship has ideally. It is not a cold relationship of sociality or of merely "being with" people, as typically found along a crowded street in a large city. It is even more intimate than ten thousand people at a sports event, cheering together in a stadium for their home team. The relationship is more "human" in the most caring sense. Words such as "brotherhood" and "sisterhood" come closer to the feeling involved. Buber refers to this relationship as an "I-You" (or "I-Thou") relationship, where the word "you" is the German *du*—a form of the word "you" that one uses with friends, family, and people with whom one feels a close personal bond. For Buber, everything in human life revolves around these two relationships, "I-It" and "I-You."

If we recall the basic distinction between "being-in-itself" and "being-for-itself" upon which Jean-Paul Sartre grounds his philosophy, it might be thought that Buber's "I-It" and "I-You" relations are essentially the same, with different wording. They are close, but Sartre's conception of "being-for-itself" refers at base to an empty, indeterminate, absolutely free consciousness, without personality. A specific sense of self, ego, or personhood comes later for Sartre as a social construction. From Buber's standpoint, this conception of the self is itself too impersonal and "I-It" oriented. There is consequently a deep difference between Buber and Sartre in this regard.

With further respect to Buber's place in the history of existentialism, he departs from the tradition established by Kierkegaard, Heidegger, and Sartre in that he does not assign a central place to the individual human being as such. Kierkegaard, for example, is concerned with the capacity for an individual to make a leap of faith and experience freedom thereby, and he wrote at length about the despair and anxiety that can accompany individual, personal decisions. Sartre similarly emphasizes the individual's absolute freedom and with respect to social relations, arguing that it is impossible to connect socially with other people in a complete, satisfying way, thereby leaving each person isolated. Heidegger, also impressed by the situation of the individual person, stresses how each of us must face death alone, typically with an accompanying experience of anxiety, although he appreciated more clearly that being with other people is also an essential aspect of our human nature.

Buber, however, emphasizes that as a matter of direct experience, every human being has an immediate and intimate social connection to others, and he accentuates this dimension of human experience in his philosophizing. It is apparent from the very beginning in infants, who as a rule connect personally with their mother for milk and sustenance, and who gaze at the mother or caretaker in an intimate social connection that is primal. The existentialist sense of isolation, anxiety, alienation, and feeling of being alone in the world comes later, after a period of socialization. Given this, Buber regards the "I-You" relationship as both philosophically central and fundamental to us as human beings.

Introducing a more reflective component into this picture, Buber sees that in the more mature person, this "I-You" relationship becomes present and active during times when people question their place in the universe, consider what resides at the foundation of things, and adopt an attitude of prayer. The natural human tendency is to address the cosmos in a personal manner—consider the history of mythology—and to construct images of ultimate being to which one can relate intimately. These are distinctively more intimate than conceptions of God as a thing, a "thing-in-itself," "it," "substance," "idea," or "form," and are akin to how Kierkegaard approaches God with a conception of truth as subjectivity, and conceives of the God-relationship as a personal one that extends beyond the constraints of objectively stated moral rules.

Buber has an existential orientation insofar as he appreciates how we are limited to our human condition and that if we are to regard the world and its ultimate foundations in a personal way, then this must be done in the here and now that we inhabit. This is the "presence" that Buber highlights when he discusses the "I-You" attitude toward the world. When extended to everything, this attitude brings the entire world of physical nature and people into a sphere of intimacy, caring, and respect that automatically generates a moral attitude toward whatever one encounters. One could say that as one intensifies and extends the application of the "I-You" attitude in one's life, the more reverent and truly human one becomes.

To render Buber's view with a stronger existentiality—more than he renders it himself—one can understand the "I-You" relationship to be as far as we can know, an artifact of our human being, or human condition. It would follow nonetheless that it is natural to regard the world in a moral way, as thoroughly humanized in a positive sense. Existentially, one might say simply that if we can grow to appreciate the kind of intimately social beings that we naturally are, then that would be sufficient to live a meaningful life. This is to resist being overcome by the "I-It" relationship throughout one's life, as would happen if a life project were defined by striving for money, using other people as mere things, and being selfish, that is, living in an essentially individualistic manner. For Buber, the unfortunate endpoint of this kind of life is to find oneself lost in the midst of nothingness and meaninglessness.

Buber, though, takes the extra step and although admitting that God's existence cannot be proven, he derives our human sense of personhood expressed in the "I-You" relationship from the eternal personhood of God, thus giving philosophical and metaphysical priority to God. In this conceptualization, we have more than the idea that our awareness of God is projected inevitably from our natural tendency toward intimate sociality, but that our sense of personal and caring intimacy is something we have as a projection of God, as we are created in God's image.

The circularity in the above reasoning notwithstanding, we find importantly in Buber a different kind of existentialist position expressed already in the early 1920s—one that does not locate the isolated, anxiety-filled human individual at the center of consideration. For Buber, this individual-centered outlook is benighted. He rather appreciates that we are intimately social beings from the start, that our natural connectedness with other people plays an essential role in how we conceive of our place within the cosmos, and that although we are woven into the fabric of material reality, our natural intimacy with other people remains a force stronger than that of selfishness and alienation from others.

We might ask what is particularly Jewish about Buber's existentialism. Despite his unwavering commitment to Judaism and the Jewish people, he writes *I and Thou* in a universalistic manner, speaking to everyone without any religious partisanship or bias. His book, though, communicates a sense of warm community at the basis of his view, combined with a theism that renders God as a being whose infinity and mystery cannot be captured in words, but who must be grasped in a personal manner, not unlike how Moses spoke with God. These features of close-knit community and theism are not unique to Judaism, but they are characteristic of it and when set in combination with Buber's emphasis upon achieving a higher awareness in the here and now, they go far in rendering Buber as a Jewish existentialist.

# 10

# American Existentialism

Martin Heidegger observes insightfully that the items we ordinarily and unreflectively use—cups, keys, eyeglasses, clothing, vehicles for transport, and so on—are usually taken for granted and tend to attract special attention only when they break down. A pair of eyeglasses functions transparently and virtually invisibly until the lens cracks and requires repair. One quickly jumps into a vehicle to reach some destination and it is only when the vehicle malfunctions that its mechanical workings become highlighted. When situations and objects break down, we take explicit notice.

A similar phenomenon occurs when we are speaking not of a pair of eyeglasses or other such use-item, but of networks of established and habitually accepted social relationships and values. A death in the family leads to reflections upon the roles of the individuals in the family; the breakup of a romantic relationship leads to a sense of loss, perhaps liberation, but inevitably thoughts about what one's desires and ideals in fact happen to be.

The same applies to entire generations of people who have experienced a collective loss, or large cohorts of individuals such as an army's soldiers who have suffered together in defeat. Such collective injuries have an impact upon cultural attitudes, often producing a sense of disillusionment. After a major war, for instance, it is common to see a rise in the popularity of philosophical outlooks that are concerned with the meaning of life. The "Lost Generation"—represented significantly by a group of American expatriate writers who lived in France during the 1920s—questioned the values of heroism, nationalism, and materialism that had inspired men to fight in the First World War. Immediately following the Second World War, the "Beat Generation"—where "beat" originally meant tired or beaten down—perceived themselves as misfits in the mainstream American society, personally unsuited for the postwar conservative, conformist, and materialist values of the "organization man." Similarly, many Vietnam War veterans who were disillusioned with the anti-communist justifications advanced in defense of the United States' role in the conflict, felt estranged from the 1960s' American culture upon their return and subsequently became peace activists in the Hippie movement. Common to these groups is a sense of alienation from prevailing cultural values.

The impact of these various meaning-seeking and soul-searching communities upon American society, especially during the 1940s–1960s, contributed to an atmosphere that rendered it receptive to the kind of existential thought that became popular in the United States immediately after the Second World War, namely, the atheistic existentialism advocated by Jean-Paul Sartre, Simone de Beauvoir, and Albert Camus, all of whom visited and lectured in the United States between the years 1946 and 1948.

The context in America into which French existential thought entered was different from that in postwar Europe where it originated. Aside from the initial attack on Pearl Harbor, the United States's territory was not significantly damaged through bombings, major battles, and house-to-house warfare during the Second World War. America was among the victors of that war, and as the most powerful country on earth at the time, it entered the postwar period with a sense of optimism, rather than disillusionment or need for reconstruction. This optimism tempered the reception of existentialist thought in the United States with more hopeful values and aspirations, where even among its enthusiasts, who despite their feelings of alienation, there were underlying hopes for either a successful assimilation into the mainstream through literary or artistic fame, or in later years, enhanced social status through peace protests intended to render society more loving and humane.

Among the various influences that existentialism had upon those who perceived themselves as outsiders in American society, perhaps the most authentically touched group was that of the African Americans, rather than the Beat Generation writers, avant-garde abstract expressionist artists, or hippies, many of whom were raised in relatively secure socioeconomic circumstances. Even into the 1960s, the African-American experience typically involved segregation, discrimination, systematic marginalization, and exclusion not simply from the most powerful and prestigious places in American society, but from ordinary conveniences such as public toilets and transportation, as well as education and housing.

It is not, however, as if the disillusioned and alienated Americans from the post-First World War and the post-Second World War all automatically gravitated to existentialist styles of thought. Adopting an intensely down-to-earth, individualistic, self-questioning, often anxiety-ridden, freedom-celebrating outlook was one among several options that included hedonism, sheer aimlessness, and the search for an alternative religious faith. The latter, for instance, is portrayed well in *The Razor's Edge* (1944), a novel by W. Somerset Maugham, where the main character, Larry Darrell, is modeled after the experience of the Lost Generation. Darrell begins well placed in Chicago society prior to the First World War, engaged to a beautiful woman, with the anticipation of lucrative work as a stockbroker. After enlisting to fight in Europe, he is exposed to violence and death in battle, where he is wounded and sees his best friend killed, and accentuating his anguish, killed while saving Darrell's own life.

Traumatized, disillusioned, and uncertain about his previously appointed path in life, Darrell postpones his wedding upon returning to the United States and decides to embark on a soul-searching journey to Paris. Although he embodies existentialist values of individualism, self-questioning, anxiety, and the quest for freedom, these eventually lead him to India, where he discovers the ancient philosophy of the Upanishads, through which he finds happiness and inner peace. In this case, Darrell resolves his spiritual crisis through classical Indian thought—a perspective that finds its way to America during the 1960s to define a lifestyle that attracts many in the peace-seeking counterculture.

## 10.1 The reception of existentialist philosophers in America

To appreciate the context through which existentialism became popular in America, we can trace in sequence the American reception of each of the authors we discussed in the first several chapters, namely, Kierkegaard, Nietzsche, Heidegger, Sartre, Camus, and Beauvoir, among whom the latter three were the most influential. Only after Sartre, Camus, and Beauvoir had their impact upon the American cultural scene did Kierkegaard, Nietzsche, and Heidegger come into a more general appreciation, despite the availability of all of Nietzsche's and some of Kierkegaard's works in English before the 1940s.

## Kierkegaard, Heidegger, and Nietzsche

The translation of Søren Kierkegaard's works into English was extensively achieved during the 1930s and 1940s by David Swenson (1876–1940) and Walter Lowrie (1868–1959). Their translations had the effect of introducing Kierkegaard's name and the concept of anxiety into some segments of American intellectual life, but Kierkegaard's thought did not catch on in a widespread way, notwithstanding Lowrie's efforts to popularize it. There were, though, some notable influences. The theologian Reinhold Niebuhr was influenced by Kierkegaard in his *The Nature and Destiny of Man* (1941), as was the psychologist Rollo May in his *The Meaning of Anxiety* (1950). Also reading Kierkegaard were the abstract expressionist painters, Mark Rothko (1903–70) and Barnett Newman (1905–70). The African American novelist Richard Wright (1908–60) also absorbed Kierkegaard extensively and incorporated Kierkegaardian themes into his novels, especially in *The Outsider* (1953).

Insofar as their existentialist aspect is concerned, Nietzsche and Heidegger did not fare significantly better than Kierkegaard as influential thinkers in America during the 1930s and 1940s. This was partially due to their association with the Nazis, who appropriated Nietzsche's work after his death, and whose party Heidegger found attractive enough to join in 1933. In Nietzsche's case, his writings were available in English since 1913 in a full set of his collected works, edited by Oscar Levy (1867–1946). Only many years later, though, mainly from a breakthrough book published in 1950 by Walter Kaufmann (1921–80), *Nietzsche: Philosopher, Psychologist, Antichrist*, in conjunction with his many translations of Nietzsche's works into English, did a more objective and intellectually compelling picture of Nietzsche emerge to render his thought more acceptable in the American intellectual scene.

Heidegger's *Being and Time* was not translated into English until 1962, so the knowledge of his seminal work was not widespread when existentialism became influential in America during the 1940s and 1950s. Heidegger's student Hannah Arendt (1906–75) did, however, publish two essays in fashionable intellectual venues during the 1940s that helped introduce both German and French existentialist thought into the mainstream. These were "What Is Existenz Philosophy?" published in the *Partisan Review* (Winter 1946), and "French Existentialism," published in *The Nation* (February 1946). The former was a lengthy essay that contained informative expositions of Kierkegaard,

Heidegger, and Jaspers that she set within a rich historical context that included Kant, Hegel, and Schelling; the latter was a shorter piece that focused on Sartre and Camus. Arendt's article on French existentialism was followed in the very same issue of the *Partisan Review* by a memorable, now often-quoted section from Sartre's novel, *Nausea*, entitled "The Root of the Chestnut Tree." Also important here is the William Barrett (1913–92), a philosophy professor at New York University from 1950 to 1979, who also wrote for the *Partisan Review* during the 1940s and whose later book *Irrational Man—A Study in Existential Philosophy* (1958) helped bring existentialism into greater popularity during the 1960s.

## Sartre, Beauvoir, and Camus

After the Second World War, French thought and French fashion were among the more pervading cultural influences that came to the United States from Europe, and part of this influx was the existentialist thought as expressed by Sartre, Beauvoir, and Camus. In 1945, Sartre visited the United States, and in 1946, Camus followed. Beauvoir came in 1947, traveling and giving numerous public talks. An immediate, if superficial, way to perceive the French existentialist influence is through the cartoon image of the "beatnik" with a beret, black turtleneck sweater, mustache, and cigarette, drinking espresso in a café. The beatnik bongo drums were an Afro-Caribbean influence, indicating that the French component of existentialism's entrance into America was not monolithic, but was part of a complex array of influences. The word "beatnik" (c. 1958), it should be added, underscored the "outsider" quality of the group to which it referred, resonating with "Sputnik"—the name of earth's first artificial satellite put into orbit by the Russians in competition with the Americans—subconsciously associating beatniks in the popular mind with communist subversives.

When imagining people wearing berets and turtlenecks and smoking cigarettes in cafés, the New York abstract expressionist painters of the 1940s and 1950s come to mind. Like René Descartes in the 1600s, who, facing the contradiction during his era between the recent advances in natural science and his religious faith, set aside all of his previous beliefs to start philosophy afresh, the New York abstract expressionists in the wake of the depression and the Second World War, finding their previously traditional subjects for painting untenable, aimed to start painting afresh. Barnett Newman describes the situation, writing in 1969:

> You must realize that twenty years ago we felt the moral crisis of a world in shambles, a world devastated by a great depression and a fierce world war, and it was impossible at that time to paint the kind of paintings that we were doing—flowers, reclining nudes, and people playing the cello. At the same time we could not move into the situation of a pure world of unorganized shapes and forms, or color relations, a world of sensation. And I would say that for some of us, this was our moral crisis in relation to what to paint. So what we actually began, so to speak, from scratch, as if painting were not only dead but had never existed. (Newman 1992: 287)

The emergence of abstract expressionism involved a number of influences, among which were the artists' previous training in representational painting that they were trying to surpass, their early exposure to surrealist art and psychological theories of the unconscious, the coincident politics of American anti-communism that negatively associated realism and representation in painting with Soviet socialist realism, not to mention investments in modern art by financially powerful individuals who had an interest in culturally sustaining that artistic style. The abstract expressionists' idea of completely starting afresh is particularly Sartrean, though, inspired by his theory of freedom, for Sartre spoke inspiringly and modernistically as if one could set aside entirely one's past and choose whatever one wants, if only one could realize for a moment consciousness' inherent and absolute freedom. Via Sartre, the ideas of freedom, the associated Kierkegaardian anxiety in the face of freedom, and the positive quest for authenticity entered influentially into the abstract expressionist movement of the 1940s and 1950s.

An American art movement that embodied yet another aspect of Sartre's existentialist philosophy emerged a few years later, namely, the Pop Art of the 1960s. Contra Freud and the surrealists, Sartre denied the existence of unconscious depths to the human mind and maintained a more surface-oriented conception of consciousness awareness. In this respect, the superficiality of Pop Art in its depictions of soup cans, comics, and such is apt. Also present is the general existentialist idea of being down to earth in one's outlook, as displayed in the artistic effort to create art that is about art itself. In painting, for example, one paints "paint," as in Roy Lichtenstein's works where the subject depicted is a large brushstroke, for example, *Brushstroke* (1965) and *Brushstroke with Spatter* (1966).

Most appropriately, Sartre's account of the superficiality of consciousness and perceptual objects is coincidentally expressed well by Andy Warhol's remark in 1967 that "if you want to know all about Andy Warhol just look at the surface of my paintings and films and me, and there I am. There is nothing behind it" (Berg 1967: 3). Compare how Sartre stated over twenty years earlier that "the Other-as-object is on principle a whole co-extensive with subjective totality; nothing is hidden." (Sartre 1956: 389).

With respect to the American postwar receptivity to existentialism, a kindred and more upbeat outlook was entering simultaneously from Japan in the form of Zen Buddhism. Zen is among the most extreme down-to-earth outlooks, and with its freedom-conducive lack of scriptures and doctrines, inherently rebellious rejection of rationality, fundamental attunement to nature, and lightheartedness, all accompanied by the possibility of immediate enlightenment, it became popular during the 1950s and 1960s, significantly from the writings of D. T. Suzuki (1870–1966) and Alan Watts (1915–73). Among the Beat Generation poets in particular, Zen Buddhism deeply influenced the work of Gary Snyder (b. 1930). Zen and French existentialism historically overlapped within the American context, where Zen, moreover, was inherently more compatible with the positive atmosphere in America.

Camus's *The Myth of Sisyphus* was published in 1942, with an excerpt in English appearing in the spring 1946 issue of the *Partisan Review*. His novel *The Stranger* appeared in English in 1946. Camus himself arrived in the United States in March 1946 and gave a memorable address at Columbia University on March 28 entitled "The Human Crisis." As his lecture title leads one to expect, Camus spoke about his experiences during the war and his consequent impressions of Western society. He did not emphasize the absurd nature of the human condition, but rather highlighted the need for people to respect and sympathize with each other, as he stood concerned with how easy it is for people to disregard the humanity of others. Camus's sincerity, sense of justice, compassion, and social responsibility showed through, and the social consciousness he displayed became the more influential aspect of his American reception, as opposed to his absurdism.

Complementing the lectures that Beauvoir gave at various universities during her visit to the United States, she summarized her opinion of America in an article entitled "An Existentialist Looks at Americans," published in the *New York Times* magazine, May 25, 1947. This was before the appearance of *The Second Sex* in 1949 and its subsequent translation into English in 1953—a book from which stems her genuine influence in America as a monumental contributor to feminist thought.

Beauvoir's article about Americans was noticeably critical and it is tempting to speculate about the reasons for her—and also Sartre's, which was comparable—attitude toward America. To a great extent, they felt alienated: both had lived through a war that had torn their country apart, with experiences punctuated with death, betrayal, danger, confusion, food shortages, and general hardship, and found themselves immersed in a culture marked by affluence, confidence, and progress, where many people appeared not to have realized that there had been a war going on. Beauvoir's reactions were not unique when she asserted that America was characterized by a cult of money and that "the young American . . . does not perceive any other objective criterion of value besides money" (de Beauvoir 2004: 311). *The Dialectic of Enlightenment* published in 1944 by Theodor Adorno and Max Horkheimer—two German intellectuals who fled Europe to settle in California—maintains similarly that the American motion picture industry at the time was motivated mainly by capitalistic gain. Heidegger also criticized America in his 1946 essay "What Are Poets For?," citing a 1925 remark by Rilke that America was importing into Europe "empty indifferent things, sham things, dummies of life" (Heidegger 1971: 113), that is, mere commodities drained of life. Beauvoir's article echoes these views, reiterating Hegel's warning about the dangers of "abstract thinking": contrary to ordinary practice, Hegel advocates that one should try to understand any product, item, object, or thing in a historically complete way, in conjunction with the processes that engender it, rather than as an isolated, bare result, in abstraction and detachment from those processes. Beauvoir writes the following:

> The fact is that the world "abstraction" constantly comes to mind when I try to define my vision of America. This may seem paradoxical since this country is so completely bent on concrete results. But to cut the result from the human movement which engendered it, to deny it the dimension of time, is also to empty it of every sort of quality: only dry bones remain. With

quality lacking, the only measure that remains with which to estimate the work and achievement of man is a quantitative one—money. (de Beauvoir 2004: 311)

When Sartre was in the United States, he was saddened to see the kinds of social relationships that racial segregation was precipitating. Beauvoir felt the same, as we can read in her travelogue *America Day by Day* (1948)—a book that documents her four-month trip to the United States in 1947. During her visit, she spent time with Richard Wright (to whom she dedicated her book, along with his wife, Ellen), who, in February, brought her to a service at the Abyssinian Baptist Church in New York, led by the Reverend Adam Clayton Powell Sr. (1865–1953), which impressed Beauvoir as being "less of a religious gathering than a political meeting." She conveys Wright's views on the style and assumptions behind the meeting in the following passage:

> The political, lay aspect of the service impressed me: one must understand, Wright said, that there is not a single minute in the life of a coloured man that is not penetrated by a social conscience: from the cradle to the grave, whether working, eating, loving, walking, dancing or praying, never can he forget that he is black, and this makes him conscious at every minute of the day of the white man whence the word black derives its meaning. Whatever he does, a negro remains in "bondage." And there is not a single coloured writer who remains unaware of this problem of "bondage." (de Beauvoir 1952: 50)

Having affinities toward the kind of existentialist outlook that Sartre and Beauvoir expressed, even before he had ever heard of "existentialism," Wright had traveled to Paris in 1946 before Beauvoir's visit to America, and decided in 1947 to leave the United States to remain in France for the longer term, adopting it as his official residence until his death in 1960. His novels written both before and after his departure from the United States such as *Native Son* (1940), *Black Boy* (1945), and *The Outsider* (1953) speak directly to the injustice and brutality that racial prejudice and oppression generate, and accentuate themes such as poverty, dread, anger, injustice, desperation, loneliness, and alienation.

Wright's characterization of the African-American consciousness is telling: there are circumstances where the external factors that contribute to the constitution of one's personal identity are so overwhelming that it is difficult to conceive of oneself in terms other than how society—whether this happens to take the form of values imposed from a prevailing national mentality, religion, subculture, or one's immediate family—has defined "who" one is.

Sartre's and Beauvoir's respective existentialist views have slightly different reactions in this respect. Sartre emphasizes that we are still essentially free to choose who we will be. Beauvoir observes that this is easier said than done, especially when it concerns the imposition of racist and sexist values upon an individual that starts from the day the person is born. The situation is particularly acute in the African-American setting, for this involves a group of people who did not need two world wars to feel a sense of alienation and disillusionment from the prevailing culture in which they were situated, but who, with a history of slavery, constituted an alienated and subordinated population in America from the very start. For centuries, women have had a similar history worldwide of being defined as people of secondary status, as Beauvoir also appreciated. As a woman without a dowry and prospects for a socially acceptable marriage, who struggled to succeed in a French, male-dominated society, she could understand Wright's perspective.

During Wright's and Beauvoir's times in the 1940s and 1950s, the effects of war exacerbated the prevalence of prejudicial thinking insofar as wartime itself inevitably injects stereotype-centered verbiage into the warring factions and the population at large. One group demonizes and dehumanizes the other as a matter of psychological necessity for waging an effective war, as people refer to each other as "communists," "Nazis," "collaborators," and so on. In 1957, Roland Barthes noted how this kind of categorizing, "abstractive" (as Hegel would refer to it) mentality permeated travel guidebooks, using the very phrasing Sartre employed to characterize the disposition that is involved in essentializing and objectifying oneself and others. Barthes furthermore called it a "disease":

> For the *Blue Guide*, men exist only as "types." In Spain, for instance, the Basque is an adventurous sailor, the Levantine a light hearted gardener, the Catalan a clever tradesman and the Cantabrian a sentimental highlander. We find again here this disease of thinking in essences, which is at the bottom of every bourgeois mythology of man. (Barthes 1972: 75)

As an indication of how permeating this style of thought was in the 1940s and 1950s, we can reflect on Beauvoir's 1947 essay itself "An Existentialist Looks at Americans," where at the outset, the title defines her essentialistically as an "existentialist," and where she states on the very first page that "I Am an Existentialist," writing as if she were a devout and fixed advocate of a doctrine. Even Beauvoir, who knew better, fell into the verbiage of bad faith.

The close association between Richard Wright and Simone de Beauvoir, in addition to Wright's own residence in France in company with French existentialist writers, can lead one to consider some sources of the interest and assumptions that the French thinkers had in view of America, particularly in connection with their perceptions of African-American culture. A significant antecedent factor in France was the notoriety of Josephine Baker (1906–75), who, during the times of the Lost Generation, left the United States in 1925 to become one of the most well-known African-American dancers and entertainers in Paris:

> At the height of her career, Baker performed at the Folies Bergère, appearing onstage wearing next to nothing but a little skirt of plush bananas. It is the outfit with which she would be identified for the rest of her life. (Cheng 2011: 42)

It is probably no coincidence that Sartre's 1947 essay in *The Saturday Review* (November 29, 1947) entitled "I Discovered Jazz in America" begins with the words "Jazz is like bananas—it must be consumed on the spot." Sartre associates jazz, and implicitly, African Americans, with bananas. In *Nausea* (1938), he displays a similar style of stereotypical thinking in his reference to a song, "One of These Days," that he describes as having been written in New York by a "Jew with black eyebrows" and sung by legendary "Negress." One cannot help observing furthermore that during her visit to America, Beauvoir befriended two outstanding authors—Richard Wright and Nelson Algren (1909–81, author of *The Man with the Golden Arm* [1949])—who were respectively African American and Jewish. Both Sartre and Beauvoir were great contributors to our sense of individual freedom and social liberation, and were good friends with individuals from oppressed groups, but their writing was often infected by superficial stereotypes.

James Baldwin (1924–87) was another African-American author who, leaving the United States in 1948, settled in France during the postwar era. Like Richard Wright, Baldwin lived in Paris and associated for a time with French existentialist thinkers. He was not a disciple of Sartre, Beauvoir, or Camus, however, but his incorporation of existentialist principles into his thought was more penetrating and potentially more liberating than Wright's. With a social perception that compares to that of Michel Foucault (1926–84), and more on the Sartrean end of things, Baldwin appreciated, like Barthes as well, that the categories society imposes upon people are not fixed in stone, that one need not accept them, and that one is more free to define oneself than in usually realized. Through the simple slogan, "Black is beautiful," popular in the 1960s' counterculture, one can see this more fundamentally rebellious awareness in action as it later entered into the mainstream media.

The assimilation and, one can say, "acceptance-as-valid" of society's definitions into one's sense of personal identity was the critical point that Baldwin leveled at "protest novels." This he expressed in an article entitled "Everybody's Protest Novel," published in the *Partisan Review* (June 16, 1949), where he compared Wright's novel *Native Son* (1940) to *Uncle Tom's Cabin* (1852). Baldwin did not rest content with the attitude of the main character in *Native Son*, Bigger Thomas, who assimilated, was overwhelmed with, and was finally destroyed by the categories imposed upon him by the prevailing white society in America:

> For Bigger's tragedy is not that he is cold or black or hungry, not even that he is American, black; but that he has accepted a theology that denies him life, that he admits the possibility of his being sub-human and feels constrained, therefore, to battle for his humanity according to those brutal criteria, bequeathed to him at birth. But our humanity is our burden, our life; we need not battle for it; we need only to do what is infinitely more difficult—that is, accept it. The failure of the protest novel lies in its rejection of life, the human being, the denial of his beauty, dread, power, in its insistence that it is his categorization alone which is real and which cannot be transcended. (Baldwin 1949: 585)

Along lines that are similarly more consistent with the existentialist idea of authenticity, one can conceive of the linkage between jazz and existentialism, not in stereotypical terms, but in reference to their actual contents. Jazz music and existentialism have a common denominator and compatibility in their mutual foundation in freedom and creativity. In jazz, the musician is spontaneously and constantly creative; in the existentialist quest for authenticity, there is an ever-persistent atmosphere of self-questioning, as one realizes that one's very existence is an "issue" for oneself. There is also a shared emphasis upon individuality: in jazz music, the player with a noticeably personal, imaginative, groundbreaking, and musically sound style receives the highest respect; in existential thought as inspired by Kierkegaard, Heidegger, and Sartre, the ideal of authenticity is embodied by the individual who self-creatively stands against the world and the weight of tradition.

## 10.2  Existentialism in 1960s' America

As we have seen so far, Europe's experience during the Second World War led to a social situation involving disillusionment and the need for reevaluation and reconstruction that made it receptive to existentialist thought. The postwar society in the United States, with its victorious position and affluence, at least for the mainstream population, was less needful of existentialist ideas. One needs to wait until the 1960s to see social divisions in America that threatened to break the society apart: there was a war in Vietnam and a corresponding war "at home." The latter involved a tension between the values of the mainstream society and a confluence of the interests involving the African-American civil rights movement, those who were campaigning for greater women's rights, and those who were protesting for an end to the Vietnam War, many of whom were returning African-American soldiers who had been drafted into service precisely because they had come from disadvantaged backgrounds.

One of the monologues in the movie, *Platoon* (1986), describes this situation well. The main character, Chris Taylor, an army volunteer and middle-class white American from a patriotic family, mentions in a letter to his grandmother from a battle-zone in Vietnam, how so many of the soldiers came from small towns, often without having graduated high school, and often without any future job prospects—poor and unwanted people, as he described them. What bothered Chris was that they were fighting and dying bravely for their country, fiercely and tough-mindedly, without adequate public recognition and gratitude from the people back home.

Not only was there a growing disillusionment during the 1960s with the United States' government decision to engage in a war in Vietnam, there was a disillusionment with the basic trust people had in the elected government, particularly in view of the assassinations of political leaders who stood for peace such as President John F. Kennedy (1917–63), his brother, Senator Robert F. Kennedy (1925–68), and the civil rights activist, Dr. Martin Luther King Jr. (1929–68). Although existentialism in its French variety, as well as its original expression in Kierkegaard, had a strong individualistic tone, emphasizing the solitude and freedom of the individual, Sartre, Beauvoir, and Camus, as we have seen, also had a social consciousness implicit in both their views and public presence. Camus worked for the resistance newspaper, *Combat*, during the 1940s, Beauvoir published her landmark book in the history of feminism, *The Second Sex*, in 1949, and in 1967, Sartre served as the executive president of the International War Crimes Tribunal that was organized to investigate United States' war crimes in Vietnam. In practice, they were social activists, and to that extent, their views fit well into the revolutionary atmosphere of 1960s' America.

As mentioned within the contexts of describing the American culture in general after the Second World War as optimistic and relatively affluent, there were factors that tempered the reception of existentialist thought in its entirety. The peace movement emphasized social unity rather than the alienation of the individual against society at large. The Asian philosophies that entered into the American culture—varieties of Hinduism and Zen Buddhism especially—emphasized a sense of oneness, either with the cosmos or with the nature as a whole, which had the effect of defusing feelings of anxiety in the face of death—feelings that are the hallmarks of Kierkegaard's and Heidegger's existentialism. The psychedelic movement in the counterculture contained as well an implicit philosophy of universal oneness and peace. Not all of the key components of existentialism defined the spirit of the times during the 1960s in America, but Sartrean freedom permeated the atmosphere throughout it all, as can be seen in the popular poster, hung in the rooms of countless numbers of high school and university students, "Today is the first day of the rest of your life."

# 11

# Existentialist Psychology

Among other subjects, a medical doctor must understand the structure of the human body, the rudimentary academic knowledge of which is communicated by textbooks. As we know, anatomy textbooks contain diagrams, images, photographs, and other representations of human organs and body parts, shown typically in their normalized, idealized forms, that serve as a measure against which to compare and contrast the actual bodily structures of individuals, healthy and unhealthy. The textbook diagrams provide the "map" of the "terrain," which is the set of actual human bodies, where no two bodies are exactly alike. A map is an abstraction and idealization; the terrain is the existing, fully detailed reality. The development of anatomy as a science has taken centuries and great sacrifice, and our present-day knowledge of that map, namely, how the body's muscles, bones, and organs work together ideally as a mechanism, despite its abstractive quality, remains impressive, useful, and essential for sound medical practice.

If we turn from the structure of the human body to the structure of the human mind, it stands that Sigmund Freud's psychoanalytic theory made an enormous breakthrough at the beginning of the twentieth century in its description of the mind as a mechanism—a mechanism driven fundamentally by survival instincts, both at the individualistic level of self-preservation and at the reproductive, that is, sexual, level of species-preservation. Freud was a scientist at heart, who, as a medical doctor, conceived of human beings in primarily physiological terms, despite how his theory of dream interpretation had its literary and poetic aspects.

Advances in neuroscience have been dramatic since Freud's time, and have reinforced a conception of the human mind as a function of brain activity, and accordingly, an approach to treating psychological disturbances as conditions that predominantly concern brain structure and chemistry.

Instead of being restricted exclusively to talking to a patient, watching the patient's behavior, and reviewing the patient's history as the basis of making a diagnosis, therapy can begin with a brain scan to discern which sectors of the brain are not functioning normally, or are not functioning at all. Prescribing pharmaceutically induced modifications to brain chemistry can follow as an important aspect of therapy.

Understanding the mind as a mechanism, whether neurologically as a brain function or psychoanalytically as a complex interaction of drives nonetheless, has its limits. Neither approach has at the *forefront*, although it is certainly taken into account, "what it is like" to be the person who is the object of therapy, where the quality of the person's experience is understood as issuing specifically from fundamentally *human* concerns. It can seem reasonable that this aspect of the person should not be central to the therapeutic situation, if one assumes that brain chemistry is at the basis of consciousness and behavior, or if one has available a usable, mechanical model of the mind that can categorize and explain nonstandard behaviors.

Here, though, a crucial difference between humans and other animals comes into play. As Heidegger expressed it, a distinguishing feature of human beings is that, as we live, our being is an issue for us. We wonder why we exist and engage in establishing meanings for our lives—meanings that give us stability, hope, and a sense of purpose. Unlike other animals, we are also reflective beings with a sense of time that renders us aware that we will die, saddled with anxieties that accompany that fact.

Certain kinds of psychological disturbances accordingly issue from our being human per se, where, upon those occasions when there are corresponding neurological expressions, those expressions are present as the physical consequence of our reflections rather than as the foundation of our condition. In such cases, it would seem to be psychotherapeutically one sided, if not misguided, to believe that one is merely treating a "diseased brain" or malfunctioning mechanism, as opposed to treating "a fellow human being." Appreciating this, Rollo May (1909–94), a leading American existential psychologist, wrote the following:

> The existentialist emphasis in psychology does not, therefore, deny the validity of conditioning, the formulation of drives, the study of discrete mechanisms, and so on. It only holds that we can never explain or understand

> any *living* human being on that basis.... *The more absolutely and completely we formulate the forces or drives, the more we are talking about abstractions and not about the living human being.* (May 1960: 14)

Making a similar point in his book, *The Divided Self* (1960), the existential psychiatrist, R. D. Laing (1927–89) noted that the very vocabulary of scientifically oriented psychiatry interferes with the perception of the human being as a unified being, for it disposes us to regard people disjointedly as composed of discrete parts, like, as one could say, the segments of a marionette.

Such observations about the limits of the scientific perspective are not new, and they trace back to the beginnings of the industrial age and the perceived danger to people's psychological integrity that the mechanization of the workforce was believed to involve. Over two centuries ago, in his *Letters on the Aesthetic Education of Man* (1795), Friedrich Schiller maintained that unlike ancient Greek society, which he believed was constituted by people who were healthier and more psychologically "whole," modern society was breaking up the human psyche through narrowly defined divisions of labor, and in the course of this, stifling human potential. Schiller believed that modern industry was transforming people dehumanizingly into the equivalent of specialized factory instruments, as did Karl Marx some years later.

Laing writes in the same historical spirit, as he discerns the divisive forces inherent in the contemporary style of conceptualization that underlies the more physiologically grounded and mechanically minded varieties of psychiatry:

> The most serious objection to the technical vocabulary currently used to describe psychiatric patients is that it consists of words which split man up verbally in a way which is analogous to the existential splits we have to describe here. But we cannot give an adequate account of the existential splits unless we can begin from the concept of a unitary whole, and no such concept exists, nor can any such concept be expressed within the current language system of psychiatry or psycho-analysis. (Laing 1960: 19)

The idea that certain methods, ways of speaking, and cultural conditions have a tendency to partition people misrepresentatively and distortively into separate and opposing segments—ones reminiscent of the construction of a stained-glass window, robot, motor, or marionette—invokes an alternative way of understanding people and society where the guiding values include "wholeness," "harmony," "balance," "integration," and "organic unity." Within the social and linguistic register, L. L. Zamenhof (1859–1917) represents this attitude as well when he described as a quest for unity his motivation for developing Esperanto—an artificial language that he hoped would serve as an international language:

> The place where I was born and spent my childhood gave direction to all my future struggles. In Bialystok (in northeast Poland) the inhabitants were divided into four distinct elements: Russians, Poles, Germans and Jews; each of these spoke their own language and looked on all the others as enemies. In such a town a sensitive nature feels more acutely than elsewhere the misery caused by language division and sees at every step that the diversity of languages is the first, or at least the most influential, basis for the separation of the human family into groups of enemies. I was brought up as an idealist; I was taught that all people were brothers, while outside in the street at every step I felt that there were no people, only Russians, Poles, Germans, Jews and so on. This was always a great torment to my infant mind . . . so I often said to myself that when I grew up I would certainly destroy this evil. (Janton 1993: 24)

As we have seen, "existentialism" is understandable as an outlook characterized by a cluster of variously definable concepts that include "authenticity," "freedom," "anxiety," "individuality," "being-down-to-earth," "death," "meaningfulness," "responsibility," "absurdity," and "existence," where different existentialist philosophies prioritize certain concepts in the cluster over others. One of the dividing points among existentialist theorists resides in whether the individual person should be conceived of as an entity that is set off against the world as an absolutely free, yet isolated, self-contained being, as we find expressed in Kierkegaard and Sartre, or whether the individual should be conceived of as being more enmeshed in the world from the very start, as implied by Heidegger's view that a sense of "being-with" other people—our core sense of sociality, in other words—is a universal feature of human being itself. The former theorists recognize a hard barrier between "subject" and "object," or between "subjectivity" and "objectivity"; the latter acknowledge a blend between subject and object, or between the individual person and society at large. A person may feel disconnected from the world and terribly lonely, but the latter theorists recognize that the fundamental sociality that constitutes our "being human" provides a ground to mitigate such feelings.

Unlike the reception of existentialism in America, where Jean-Paul Sartre's influence was salient, existentialist psychology has a strong Heideggerian foundation, although Sartrean and Kierkegaardian influences are also present. Ludwig Binswanger (1881–1966), one of the initial leaders of existentialist psychology, wrote the following, influenced by his reading of Heidegger's *Being and Time*:

> Heidegger, in his concept of being-in-the-world as transcendence, has not only returned to a point prior to the subject-object dichotomy of knowledge and eliminated the gap between self and world, but has also elucidated the structure of subjectivity as transcendence. Thus he has opened a new horizon of understanding for, and given a new impulse to, the scientific exploration of human existence and its specific modes of being. The split of Being into subject (man, person) and object (thing, environment) is now replaced by the unity of existence and "world," secured by transcendence. (Binswanger 1958a: 193–94)

As a matter of historical background to understanding the relationship between subject and object as being blended or organically unified, it helps to recall how the concepts of "organic unity" and "life" became pronounced in the nineteenth century theorizing in response to the mechanistic outlook of the seventeenth and eighteenth centuries, significantly as a reaction against the advance of natural science in its apparent threat to freedom and traditional religious belief. This reaction, however, assumed two different forms, depending upon the conception of "life" that was advanced.

One conception of life—more popular earlier in the century and present in philosophies such as Hegel's—associates life with balance, integration, organic unity, growth, development, and ultimate fulfillment. A harsher conception—one that took root later in the century, as in Nietzsche's outlook, although it was foreshadowed by Schopenhauer's—regards life as essentially "red in tooth and claw," violent, predatory, selfish, willful, filled with suffering, and driven by instinct as a nonrational force. The more anti-rational and alienation-emphasizing versions of existentialism issue from the latter; the more reconciliatory and integrative forms, from the former. The spirit of existential psychology is in the more integrative vein, as noted, with a history that extends back to Hegel and his emphasis upon organic unity, the identity of "subject and substance" as he described it, and development toward conditions of increased self-consciousness and freedom, although some central aspects of Kierkegaard's existentialism (viz., anxiety) and Sartre's (viz., freedom of the individual) also enter into the movement.

A way to appreciate the concerns and approach of existentialist psychology is to recall the leading question of Albert Camus's existentialism:

> There is but one truly serious philosophical problem, and that is suicide. Judging whether life is or is not worth living amounts to answering the fundamental question of philosophy. All the rest—whether or not the world has three dimensions, whether the mind has nine or twelve categories—comes afterwards. These are games; one must first answer. (Camus 1955: 3)

Suicide is not merely a central philosophical problem; if Camus is correct, it is a psychological problem when it involves debilitating experiences of emptiness and worthlessness. Such experiences can be characterized variously as the loss of meaning in one's life, a dissolution of hope, the feeling that life has nothing more to offer, or a sense that one has reached a dead end. In philosophical terms, it is coming face to face with nihilism. The occurrences can range from periods in ordinary life such as a midlife crisis where one's career has lost its meaning and no other options are visible on the horizon to extreme contexts, as in wartime, when one has lost virtually everything and everyone one has cared about. Existential psychology, significantly due to its philosophically centered grounding in view of what is fundamentally human, is particularly effective in treating mental conditions that involve a loss of personal meaning and the consequent will to live.

We have seen how some of the leading existentialist philosophies prescribe ways to render one's life meaningful in the face of a universe that, objectively speaking, appears itself to be utterly meaningless. Camus, realizing that everything will eventually be forgotten, prescribes that we extract value from the present moment as effectively as we can, and live life as if one were playing a grand and exciting game. Nietzsche, realizing that there is no otherworld, peaceful heaven, or God to provide respite from life's frustrations and sufferings, prescribes that we live each moment as if we had to live it over again and again, striving to experience growth and a continual sense of getting better than we were before. Sartre, realizing that we are utterly free as individuals in a thoroughly absurd and uncaring material world, prescribes that we appreciate our potentialities more creatively, assume full responsibility for ourselves, and resist accepting in an escapist manner, convenient and constricting social labels and titles. Kierkegaard, similarly appreciating that there is a sense in which we are absolutely free, prescribes that we maximally exercise our freedom in making ungrounded leaps of faith that bring our individuality into full consciousness. All of these are prescriptions for people living in an ordinary context, who are not, or are not necessarily, in terribly extreme circumstances, and who are reflective about their place in the cosmos and the nature of life in general.

## 11.1 Viktor Frankl (1905–97)

With regard to the theme of suicide and the meaning of life, the existential psychology developed by Viktor Frankl is noteworthy in having its inspirational source not in ordinary circumstances or in general philosophical reflection, but in extreme situations where a sense of meaning for one's life has come under devastating attack from without. In Frankl's case, these were the circumstances that surrounded him during his incarceration in Nazi concentration camps during the Second World War. As a psychiatrist, and experiencing suffering and injustice of an extraordinarily disturbing kind on a daily basis, he was able to understand the dynamics involved in both losing and constructing human meaning—an understanding that later informed his development of a therapeutic method to treat individuals who had experienced a debilitating loss of personal meaning.

The following excerpt describes how some individuals in the camps were able to resist the temptation to commit suicide within a context defined by dehumanization and degradation:

> I remember two cases of would-be suicide, which bore a striking similarity to each other. Both men had talked of their intentions to commit suicide. Both used the typical argument—they had nothing more to expect from life. In both cases it was a question of getting them to realize that life was still expecting something from them; something in the future was expected of them. We found, in fact, that for the one it was his child whom he adored and who was waiting for him in a foreign country. For the other it was a thing, not a person. This man was a scientist and had written a series of books which still needed to be finished. His work could not be done by anyone else, any more than another person could ever take the place of the father in his child's affections. (Frankl 1959: 79)

Important here is the implicit diversity of ways in which a person can find meaning in life and consequently a strong reason to live. The scientist's reason did not concern the love of another person on the face of things, but a sense of his scientific work's importance. Not knowing the topic of his research, it is difficult to say what kind of love, if any, was involved. Someone could be a professional antique collector, for example, who, knowing the hidden whereabouts of one of the most desirable and collectable pieces of furniture in the world, could find a reason to live for the sake of later retrieving it. Someone, perhaps an experienced lawyer, filled with unquenchable moral indignation as a result of witnessing continual abuse and injustice, could find a powerful reason to live for the sake of later bringing the criminals to legal judgment. Many of the reasons that people find to live under extreme circumstances can be personal, may or may not involve love, and may or may not involve a universal theme. Nonetheless, it was clear to Frankl that having a determinate, well-defined, future goal toward which to look forward can have an effective survival and therapeutic value.

The variability in ways to find meaning is consistent with Frankl's view that the general philosophical question about "the" meaning of life is not effectively to the point. The question needs to be approached more concretely, for each person has a special, personally defined way of finding meaning:

> One should not search for an abstract meaning of life. Everyone has his own specific vocation or mission in life to carry out a concrete assignment which demands fulfillment. Therein he cannot be replaced, nor can his life be repeated. Thus, everyone's task is as unique as his specific opportunity to implement it. (Frankl 1959: 110)

Frankl's existential psychology—he refers to it as "logotherapy" ("meaning-therapy" as he understands the term)—is concerned with treating people who suffer from mental disorders that are related especially to finding a meaning for one's life, where it is assumed that "striving to find a meaning in one's life is the primary motivational force in man" (Frankl 1959: 99). Even if the specific mental disorder has other causes, Frankl believes that the disorder can be helped if the person's sense of purpose is strengthened. There is obvious value in this project, in particular during times when a sense of meaninglessness becomes a common attitudinal quality, as happens as a consequence of war.

At the same time, the therapeutic idea of having a person find a meaning for life requires vigilance, precisely because purposes can differ. Someone in a hopeless, desperate, suicidal condition could find meaning in an ideology, or "ism"—some of which are morally questionable—in which to adhere wholeheartedly, and subsequently derive personal strength from that kind of self-definition. Sartre would refer to this as bad faith. To be in bad faith, though, would not imply that the person's identification with the label, or "ism," would not supply the therapeutically positive psychological meaning that alleviates feelings of emptiness.

Within the social-political sphere the situation is particularly filled with risk. It is a known technique of effective leaders to provide a sense of purpose to a general population by defining a great "task"—a task defined and presented as being so important, that those who adopt it can become willing to work hard and sacrifice themselves for it. A country in the midst of a shattering economic depression where hopelessness is the pervasive social feeling can become receptive to a talented "meaning-giver" who arouses hope and consolidates the people under a single ideology.

In such cases, the population can acquire strong sense of meaning that reinforces a powerful purpose to continue and prevail, as the meaning itself and the people's collective will thereafter stands susceptible to being directed in a questionable way, for example, toward war. It is consequently one thing to be able to alleviate meaninglessness and to provide a sense of purpose and strength to people who suffer from severe depression—and this is a general benefit of existential psychology, particularly of the logotherapeutic kind—but it is another matter that some of the purposes through which people derive strength for themselves can be potentially harmful, either to themselves or to others.

## 11.2 R. D. Laing (1927–89)

Another theorist in the field of existential psychology is R. D. Laing, who takes a further step in grasping the limits of the prevailing psychiatric conceptions of people, conceived of as mechanisms, brains, objective scientific objects of study, and such. He perceived that the behavior of people with mental illness varies with the context within which they are situated: if, for instance, a mentally troubled person is brought in front of a class of medical students to be observed like an object, referred to publicly with an objectifying and subordinating academic vocabulary that is itself describable as a "vocabulary of denigration," the person will act differently—perhaps angrily, resentfully, and wildly—than when situated in a friendly, homelike environment.

Laing noted the tension in working with a psychiatric vocabulary that conceives of and describes with perfect sanity, a mentally ill person as a kind of mechanism, and moreover, that fosters social interactions with the person as if he or she were an impersonal object of scientific study (as in the above class of medical students), while judging at the same time, that anyone who regards himself or herself as a mechanism or robot must be insane. There is a sense in which Laing can be understood as having the project of subjecting to therapy, the very vocabulary and attitude of contemporary scientific psychiatry.

Laing's appreciation of the dehumanizing and objectifying tendencies that the standard practices of scientifically grounded psychiatry were reinforcing led him to a therapeutic alternative at the other end of the spectrum: he brought people with mental illness to live together in a homelike, non-judgmental, non-oppressive environment, where they could be free to express themselves in a more natural way. This was the therapeutic principle that governed his residence for people with psychoses at Kingsley Hall, a community center in London, which he managed from 1965 to 1970.

By regarding the mentally ill person as a "human being" per se, one of the valuable upshots of Laing's outlook is to question the absolute subordination of the mentally ill person to the so-called normal or sane person, as if the mentally ill person were akin to a diseased organ or malfunctioning motor standing in need of repair, with no redeeming value. To the contrary, Laing observed that there are moments when the mentally ill person sees more truth than the normal or sane person:

> I am aware that the man who is said to be deluded may be in his delusion telling me the truth, and this in no equivocal or metaphorical sense, but quite literally, and that the cracked mind of the schizophrenic may *let in* light which does not enter the intact minds of many sane people whose minds are closed. (Laing 1960: 27)

The idea that some mentally ill people can see more truth than normal people inevitably stimulates the question of the degree to which "ordinary" or "normal" society is itself "sane." Laing was able to perceive—as did Sartre—that the common practices, values, and expectations to which a person is ordinary exposed can close a person's mind as much as open it:

> Our civilization represses not only "the instincts," not only sexuality, but any form of transcendence. Among one-dimensional men, it is not surprising that someone with an insistent experience of other dimensions, that he cannot entirely deny or forget, will run the risk either of being destroyed by the others, or of betraying what he knows. (Laing 1960: 11)

Laing developed a conception of mental illness that underscores how people can find themselves in toxic social circumstances where "no-win" situations are imposed, where whatever choice the person makes, the person will be in the wrong, will be punished, or will otherwise suffer. To survive in such oppressive, mind-snapping contexts, a person can develop behaviors that, if understood as such, are nothing more than rational reactions to the crushing circumstances, but that also immediately appear within the context of ordinary social norms to be strange, bizarre, absurd, or straightforwardly dysfunctional, and hence, insane. From an existentialistically influenced psychiatric standpoint where the mentally ill person is respected fully as a person, and where the causes of mental illness can be traced to the nature of the social context itself, such as the immediate family, but even to society at large, it is a short step to arrive at a critique of family units or larger social groups that are responsible for causing people to go insane.

One of the upshots of Laing's version of existential psychology is consequently how it leads us to question the values that our "normal" or "ordinary" society embodies insofar as those values can drive certain types of people into neurosis or into more severe mental conditions. A society, for example, implicitly prescribes a set of respectable professions with which each member must decide to engage or not. It is easy to imagine certain people landing in a double-bind position where frustration and disappointment follow if either none of the accepted professions turn out to be well suited to the person, and the person nonetheless feels compelled to develop a career in one of them, or if the person refuses to enter one of the accepted professions, and is socially denigrated as a consequence.

Another example is when the prevailing ideals of attractive physical appearance draw certain kinds of sensitive people into comparable double-binds and generate feelings of hopelessness. This can happen when, in view of the ideal, disappointment follows either when a person judges that his or her natural looks do not measure up to the social norm or when subsequent to extended efforts to modify his or her bodily appearance, for example, through clothing, dieting, exercise, or surgery, the efforts are judged to be unsuccessful. To make matters worse, even if one achieves success at the latter, the problems do not end, for as one gets older, appearances cannot but degrade. Ludwig Binswanger describes an extreme case where the frustration becomes severe enough to drive a person to suicide:

> Every day she feels herself fatter, which according to her own statement means getting both older and uglier. Here too we find the all-or-nothing principle at work: "If I cannot remain young, beautiful, and thin," we have in her words, "then rather—Nothingness." (Binswanger 1958b: 282)

One of the general results of reflecting upon the philosophical inspirations that underlie existential psychology is to reiterate the sharp difference between various kinds of existential philosophy. In the prevailing, nonprofessional, understanding of existentialism typically encountered, "existentialism" is associated almost immediately with Jean-Paul Sartre's philosophy. What we have seen, however, not only in connection with existentialist psychology, but also in the religiously oriented existentialisms of figures such as Paul Tillich and Martin Buber, a distinctively anti-Sartrean outlook that regards as essential to our being human, our "being-in-the-world-with-other-people," if one were speak in Heidegger's style. In this respect, Heidegger's influence as a leading existentialist thinker is equal to that of Sartre's.

Sartre's existentialism has its appeal and value, especially in how it urges us to realize our freedom, assume responsibility, and resist conventional roles and labels that objectify and constrict our self-awareness. At the same time, though, there are aspects of Sartre's outlook of which one should be cautious, in particular his sharp and unbridgeable distinction between consciousness (being-in-itself) and the physical world (being-for-itself), its view that genuine human community and fusion is unattainable in loving relationships, and its view that when people look at each other, they are always in a mutually objectifying relationship. Revealing in this respect, and not intended to refer to Sartre's philosophy when it was written, but rather to a psychological condition that carries the potential for mental illness, is R. D. Laing's characterization of the schizoid mentality:

> The term schizoid refers to an individual the totality of whose experience is split in two main ways: in the first place, there is a rent in his relation with his world and, in the second, there is a disruption of his relation with himself. Such a person is not able to experience himself "together with" others or "at home in" the world, but, on the contrary, he experiences himself in despairing aloneness and isolation; moreover, he does not experience himself as a complete person but rather as "split" in various ways, perhaps as a mind more or less tenuously linked to a body, as two or more selves, and so on. (Laing 1960: 19)

This characterization applies to the general atmosphere of Jean-Paul Sartre's existentialism, and it implicitly constitutes a critique of his outlook from the standpoint of existentialist psychology. If so, then we might consider whether it would beneficial to revalue the celebratory position of Sartre's philosophy in the history of existentialism. There is a complication involved, however, in suggesting that Sartre's outlook is less healthy than Heidegger's: it requires us to consider how Heidegger himself, in his political affiliations, did not display the humanism and care for fellow human beings that his philosophy appears mainly to profess. Given this tension, understanding the position of Heidegger's philosophy in view of his Nazism is perhaps the greatest paradox and contradiction in the history of existentialist thought.

12

# Existentialism in the Cinema

Although, as we have seen, "existentialism" refers to a variety of outlooks and attitudes toward the world and our presence in it, we can identify a cluster of themes that in various intensities characterize the existentialist outlook. There is an interest in being down to earth, individualism, alienation, personal responsibility, authenticity, anxiety in the face of freedom and death, and within this context, an overriding concern with either finding or establishing meaning in an apparently meaningless world.

There are thousands of motion pictures, so any extended list of "existentialist" films will vary inevitably with the tastes of the compiler. We will consequently attend initially to two movies that have been cited repeatedly and non-controversially as paradigm examples of existentialist cinema—*The Seventh Seal* (1957) and *Ikiru* (1952)—produced during the time when existentialism was popular. We will complement these with two recent examples from a filmmaker, Woody Allen, whose work has been influenced by philosophical reflections throughout his career and often incorporates existentialist themes, namely *Irrational Man* (2015) and *Midnight in Paris* (2011). We will then put these four films into perspective though some reflections on a groundbreaking film from the 1960s, *The Pawnbroker* (1964). The chapter will conclude by considering how aesthetic considerations that govern the composition of a film can interfere with the portrayal of existentialist themes.

## 12.1 *Ikiru* (1952)

The main character of *Ikiru* (to live)—a film directed by Akira Kurusawa—is Kanji Watanabe, a bureaucrat and aging widower who lives in postwar Tokyo with his unappreciative son and daughter-in-law. Watanabe's wife, who he loved dearly, had died decades before, leaving him to raise his son in what has turned out to be an empty, perfunctory existence. When we meet Watanabe, he has been working for years as a section chief in a public affairs office, processing endless piles of complaints and achieving little in actual assistance to people, surrounded by a like-minded group of uncaring public servants, all of whom are immersed in an ineffective, slow-moving administrative system. Not having missed a day at the office in almost three decades, Watanabe's subordinates refer to him secretly as "the mummy," for he works quietly at his desk, emotionless, unsmiling, and unoffending. When the film begins, we learn that he has been troubled by a stomach ailment that has led him to see a doctor.

The doctors do not reveal the truth of Watanabe's condition, but from their roundabout communications he infers correctly and devastatingly that he has terminal stomach cancer and only six months to live. Despondent, he takes some time off from work and prepares to die, saying nothing to his son and daughter-in-law about the fatal diagnosis, who he accidentally overhears talking one evening about how, since they are tired of living with him, they might convince him to use his pension to buy a house for themselves. Experiencing meaninglessness at home, meaninglessness at work, and death closing in, Watanabe gravitates into sadness and self-pity, crying himself to sleep next to the photograph of his wife and the certificates of twenty-five years of appreciation that have lost their significance.

While walking the city streets one evening, Watanabe meets a novelist, into whose confidence Watanabe shares his story, and who, taking pity on him, invites Watanabe for a wild night on the town. They meet women, dance, drink, laugh, sing, and have experiences that Watanabe had not enjoyed in decades. The evening concludes with Watanabe riding home in a taxi with the novelist and two women, where at one point he asks the taxi driver to stop. Unable to handle the excess of liquor, he steps into the shadows to vomit. The women, familiar with such scenes, watch from the taxi repulsed, but mostly annoyed with the disruption to their otherwise pleasant evening.

Ending the night wearing a new, rakish hat, Watanabe is starting to feel alive again. Much like Camus and Kierkegaard's aesthete, the novelist had explained to him during the evening that one should be greedy about life and live it sensuously to the fullest at every moment. Watanabe's sudden immersion into the aesthetic lifestyle has the effect of shaking him out of his sadness, and opening the way for him to discover an even more satisfying way to achieve a meaningful life.

As he is walking his home in the early morning daylight, Watanabe coincidentally meets one of his subordinates from work, Toyo Odagiri—a young woman who, tired of the office, has been seeking Watanabe's official stamp for the paperwork that will allow her successfully to find a new job. Having his stamp at home, they return together to Watanabe's house where he signs and authorizes her papers. With his new hat and morning arrival with an attractive young woman, Watanabe's son and daughter-in-law misread the situation and scold him for his shameful display.

Toyo's lighthearted liveliness attracts Watanabe, and he asks Toyo if he can see her again, simply as friends. When they later meet and discuss her new job, Toyo explains that she has found happiness and meaningfulness by making playthings for children, for she imagines through her work that she is playing with every baby in Japan. This inspires Watanabe to wonder with such little time left, what he could possibly make himself. It soon strikes him that at his office, he could proceed to rectify a previously ignored complaint that had been lodged by a set of women who were living next to a putrefying cesspool—a cesspool which, with some work, could be transformed into a children's playground. This playground's construction becomes Watanabe's single-minded administrative task to which he devotes the remaining months of his life.

Setting aside the aesthetic lifestyle, Watanabe shifts into a "great-task" style of rendering life meaningful, and his dedication is relentless: he humbles himself to the deputy mayor and humiliates himself to administrators of other departments whose cooperation he needs to complete the project. A meek man by nature, he courageously defies thugs who threaten his life, sent by restaurant owners who were trying to take over the playground area to install their own businesses.

Watanabe succeeds in constructing the playground, although after he dies, we see in a flash-forward how high-ranking administrators steal the credit for Watanabe's successful playground construction. He nonetheless dies content in the playground one evening, alone, rocking slowly back and forth upon one of the swings, singing a wistful song "Gondola no Uta" ("The Gondola Song"), a popular romantic ballad from 1915 that carries a Buddhist flavor. Its haunting lyrics remind us to fall in love and enjoy life before one's passions cool with age; it advises us to live right now, when we have today, for today will never return.

Casting a different light on Watanabe's efforts to secure meaning for his life, some revealing moments in *Ikiru* display the difficulties people can face in trying to free themselves from the momentum of daily routine, or *das Man*. During Watanabe's funeral, a question surfaces among his colleagues about why no one else took the initiative to develop the playground project, since the existential point was made that, like Watanabe, any one of them could die at any moment. Motivated by this reflection, Watanabe's coworkers vow enthusiastically—at that point thoroughly intoxicated—to continue his example of fighting the foot-dragging system. Upon returning to work the next day, however, they quickly repeat their old ways and ignore the kinds of petitions upon which Watanabe had so conscientiously acted.

Although his coworkers' lack of fortitude confirms the exceptional nature of Watanabe's achievement, we can ask how Watanabe's own attitudes might have changed had the doctors' stated diagnosis, namely, that he was suffering from a mere stomach ulcer that would clear up with time, had been genuine, and if Watanabe had learned after his successful effort in having the playground built that he probably had a couple of decades, rather than months, to live.

Perhaps within that context, the single achievement of having constructed a children's playground would not have been sufficient to sustain the enlivening transformation in his outlook on life, and perhaps, like his colleagues, he would have become lost once again in administrative routine and average everydayness. Watanabe's impending death introduced a sense of adventure into his life and at the end, he was fortunate to die at the perfect moment. Without such closure, though, the question persists of how, or whether, one can live a meaningful life without an organizing and purpose-instilling principle such as, at least as it was for Watanabe, knowing that one has only a few months left to live.

If, in the midst of working once more within the bureaucracy and encountering fierce resistance and possible failure in a second attempt to shake the system, Watanabe were to become more expansively philosophical, he might reflect on the playground's existence, contemplating the long-term passing of time, the relatively few people involved in the project relative to the world's population, and how from a large spatial distance, the earth itself, along with the playground, appears to be a speck of dust.

From this perspective, Watanabe's perfect and concluding moments on the swing could be regarded as fleeting and meaningless in the more objective scheme of things. Nonetheless, from the standpoint of his feelings and sense of place in his society, he felt satisfied and at peace with himself during his final moments. Within his circumscribed world, Watanabe took advantage of a last chance to live life to its fullest, seeming also to realize that that very world and achievement would eventually dissolve, just as his consciousness was doing on the swing.

Despite everything, the immediacy of Watanabe's achievement remained powerful enough to overshadow any feelings of meaninglessness that might have eroded his satisfaction. Had there been any such feelings, they added at most a wistful tone to his contentment in the playground within which he passed away, like some clouds passing before a beautiful evening moon.

## 12.2 *The Seventh Seal* (1957)

To express its existential theme of how death is constantly beside us, *The Seventh Seal*—a film by the great Swedish director Ingmar Bergmann—situates its narrative during the population-devastating Black Plague of the 1300s. The story concerns Antonius Block, a knight who is returning home from a long crusade, hoping to find his wife still alive and waiting for him in his castle. He is accompanied by his lively and earthy squire, Jöns, whose war-hardened nihilism contrasts with Block's ineradicable puzzling about God's existence, notwithstanding the deep skepticism that war has bred in him.

The film traces Block's journey back to his castle, where he passes by corpses, a church artist who paints themes of death, a family of traveling players who happily dance, sing, and juggle, a group of fanatical penitents who whip themselves in the belief that the plague is a punishment for sin, a group of soldiers who burn a woman at the stake for having consorted with the devil, and a former theologian who has degenerated into a ghoulish thief and rapist.

At the outset of his carnivalesque journey, Block meets Death himself, who states that he has come to take Block away.

With the hope of postponing his death long enough to return to his castle, Block comes to an agreement with Death: they will play a game of chess, where as long as the game continues without Block's being defeated, Block will live. The game begins with a few moves and continues throughout the film as Death and Block resume their play periodically over the span of a few days.

Death, however, is a cheat. While inside a church, Block hears a presence in a confessional booth and enters to confess to a priestlike figure within. Revealing his existential worries, Block admits how life can be terrible, but worse yet, he adds that if there were no God and only nothingness that awaits us all, then life, and the death that follows, would be an outrageous and unlivable horror that he could hardly face. Block mentions in passing that he is playing a game of chess with Death, and that with the short time he has left, he would like to perform one truly meaningful act in a life that, so far, has been like most people's lives, relatively futile and filled with empty talk. The figure then asks Block innocently how he plans to defeat Death, and Block confides that he will use a combination of a bishop and knight that Death has not yet seen. Turning toward Block, we see that it is Death himself with whom Block had been speaking, posing as a priest.

The film highlights a juggler named Jof as an especially gifted, visionary figure, who is accompanied by his wife, Mia, and young son, Mikael. Although Death is everywhere in the countryside, Jof remains happy, pure in heart, and loving toward his wife and son. One afternoon, he sees the Virgin Mary with the infant Jesus walking peacefully in the distance. Later in the movie, he sees Block playing chess with Death, suggesting to the viewers that the Death figure is not a figment of Block's imagination, but is a genuine, albeit predominantly invisible, reality. To everyone else, Block appears to be playing chess by himself.

Block, knowing Death's plan to take him along with everyone traveling in his group, realizes that the good juggler, wife, and baby son do not deserve to die. Near the film's end, Jof himself, observing from a distance that Block is playing chess with Death, and sensing the danger to his family, quickly gathers his wife and son to flee. Block, noticing over Death's shoulder that Jof and his family are making their escape, tips over the chess pieces to distract Death, and gives the innocent family the few extra moments they need to slip away.

This is the one meaningful act Block was hoping to perform, and it liberates him to face his own death peacefully. He cheats at the chess game by tipping the pieces, and with this, he cheats Death of his intention to kill Jof and his family. As soon becomes evident, the film's action grounds itself upon a battle between Death and Block, two cheaters, but of different kinds: Death is the evil cheater who takes lives; Block is the good cheater who saves them.

Upon arriving at his castle soon thereafter, traveling with a blacksmith and his wife, along with Jöns, who had in the meantime found a young woman companion, Block reunites with his wife, now much older, greatly relieved to see her once more. It is not long, however, before Death knocks at the castle's door to take the three couples away. The saving grace is that no one in the group dies sadly alone. Each departs with their beloved partners, and no one suffers by watching their partner die before them. The couples might surely have led longer lives together, but dying together at this appointed time involves no tragedy, and the film concludes satisfyingly and idyllically. The next day, Jof sees the three couples silhouetted upon a distant hill, led by Death, holding their hands together in a dance of death.

*The Seventh Seal* is distinctive in how it conveys the presence of death so thoroughly in virtually every scene. In addition to skulls and death symbols that appear repeatedly in the background, the sharp black-and-white photography creates a cool and objective foundation for the action, as do long-distance shots of the individuals, which make the film's viewers feel as if they are looking down on the actors in a detached way. As we watch Jof and his family laugh and play, and watch one of the other actors frolicking sexually in the woods with a female friend, we know how Death, who is always observing and waiting around the corner, will eventually be turning their sensuous enjoyment into nothing. Few movies provide as effectively and permeatingly this distanced and reflective perspective upon sensuous experience in view of death.

From an existential standpoint, we can ask about the exact nature of Block's one meaningful act, which can be interpreted in various ways. Its meaningfulness can be understood as his having saved some other human lives in general (as when, for instance, one finds meaning in helping persecuted people who live in a murderous regime find refuge in another country), or, more specifically, as his having saved a young and happy family from death, or even more specifically, as his having saved an innocent infant from death, along with his caretakers for support. The film emphasizes the value of the innocent Mikael, as one sees how much his parents love him, as one hears how his father would like to raise him to continue the family tradition, and as one sees in Jof's vision a similar infant Jesus guided by the Virgin Mary.

The latter imagery suggests that *The Seventh Seal's* existential message is that life becomes meaningful when one protects, nurtures, and raises young children, regarded as innocent, pure, beings. From a wider perspective, it suggests that meaning in life can be obtained by fostering the continuance of the species: when people become absorbed in raising their children, or in raising the children of others, as in the role of a teacher, or in supporting the happiness of children, as when building a playground, as did Watanabe, or as someone who sustains health, such as a medical practitioner or psychological counselor, or someone who delivers or produces food or provides shelter, this gives a sense of life's meaningfulness. That the children themselves will one day die, and perhaps that all humans will someday die, either does not enter as a factor that undermines this way of living meaningfully, or it enters mildly without being overwhelming, as in *Ikiru*.

We should note that *The Seventh Seal* is less directly representative of twentieth-century atheistic existentialism, as we find it expressed by Jean-Paul Sartre, as much as it conveys the spirit of the nineteenth-century crisis of faith from which existentialism grew, where doubts about God's existence emerged within the context of Christian institutions that were no longer providing religious inspiration. Insofar as Block wants desperately to believe in God, continues to speak with priests, and continues to pray until the very end, the film is more Kierkegaardian than Sartrean.

God is mostly silent throughout *The Seventh Seal*, but the story is not particularly tragic. Alongside Death, as mentioned, a redeeming vision of the Virgin Mary and infant Jesus appears; at the film's conclusion, fate, or God, or chance, allows Jof, Mia, and Mikael to escape death. Everyone in Block's circle dies fortunately with their beloved. Although the film shows the horrible burning of a woman at the stake, the tortured writhing of a plague victim, along with frightening faces of corpses, its satisfying moral closure does not, as later existentialist thought tends to emphasize, convey the idea that ordinary life is inevitably a miserable, debilitating, and absurd enterprise—for even

Death, personified as an intelligent character in the film, appears to have his own reasons to take people.

## 12.3 *Irrational Man* (2015)

Woody Allen's *Irrational Man* is inspired by Dostoevsky's novel *Crime and Punishment* (1866), wherein the respective main characters cross paths with morally repugnant individuals and decide to murder them for the sake of cleaning up society. They believe that for the sake of justice, laws must sometimes be broken. In the case of *Irrational Man*, the murder victim is a judge who is guilty of having unjustly reduced a woman and her children to misery in a divorce case, in addition to other implied abuses of his role and responsibility as a judge; in *Crime and Punishment*, the victim is a cruel pawnbroker who never hesitates to offer a mere pittance for cherished items that penniless individuals bring to her in desperation. In *Crime and Punishment*, the murderer is a twenty-three-year-old, impoverished student named Rodion Raskolnikov. His counterpart in *Irrational Man* is a successful, middle-aged philosophy professor named Abe Lucas. A sense of moral indignation drives them both, as they observe people hurt others selfishly, profit thereby, and then go unpunished.

Abe Lucas's story begins with his arrival to teach a summer session course in existentialist philosophy at Braylin College, a small (fictional) institution in Newport, Rhode Island. Abe has a reputation for brilliance, for social activism, for having faced danger in foreign countries, for being attractive to young women and students, and for having taken sexual advantage of those attractions. He is perceived as a magnetically stylish, academically regarded professor with a dodgy social reputation.

Behind this appearance, Abe is depressed, alcoholic, tired of life, and disrespectful toward expected professorial behavior in the world of small colleges. With a bloated stomach protruding from his otherwise thin frame, he sips from a flask of hard liquor as he walks around campus, soon to become involved in an affair with one of his married colleagues, a chemistry professor. Abe is hopeless, marking time in the wake of a personal judgment that his years of writing, teaching, and activism have been worthless.

After settling in, Abe attends a house party hosted by a student named April, where he sits alone on a couch despondently while the festivities go on around him. When April daringly removes her father's handgun from a cabinet to display it to her friends, Abe observes the students' naivete as they mimic a game of Russian roulette, spinning the chamber and laughing. Taking the gun himself and inserting a live round, he spins the chamber, holds it to his head and pulls the trigger as everyone watches aghast. He displays his fearlessness to the students, and to the film's audience, his feelings of worthlessness. One of the students shouts foreshadowingly that if he really wants to kill himself, then he should go to the chemistry lab and swallow cyanide, but not do it in front of them.

On a later day, while having meal in a diner with Jill Pollard, one of his students, with whom he is developing a friendship and budding romance, they overhear in the booth immediately behind them a disturbing story of a corrupt judge named Thomas Spangler, whose corrupt rulings are breaking up a family and causing an innocent mother and children heartrending distress. The episode recalls a scene in *Crime and Punishment* when Raskolnikov overhears some men talking in a café about a despicable pawnbroker woman, where the men conclude that the world would be a better place without her.

Abe's romantic relationship with Jill eventually becomes his downfall. Jill begins the film with a loving, faithful, and patient boyfriend named Roy, another student, but as her infatuation with Abe intensifies, she loses interest in Roy and sets him aside as unimportant. One evening, as her relationship with Abe is transforming from a friendship into a love affair, Jill takes Abe to an amusement park where he plays a game and wins her a prize. With a choice ranging from large teddy bears to trinkets, Jill decides pragmatically upon a small cylindrical flashlight, a token of their relationship, which she keeps warmly thereafter in her handbag.

Realizing that he could get away with murdering Spangler, who he describes as "vermin," a "cancer," and a "roach who would be better stamped out," Abe decides to take Spangler's life for the sake of justice, conceiving of himself as superior to the law, and feeling now as if his own life will finally have some meaning. The murder plot and its accompanying risk give him the great purpose and excitement he was seeking, and with a surge of enthusiasm, his attitude toward everyone at Braylin makes a turnaround. Most notably, his affair with the chemistry professor, Rita Richards, after having begun depressingly with Abe's inability to function sexually, becomes steamy, excitingly athletic, and lustfully energetic. The surge inspires Rita, who is bored and frustrated at Braylin, to consider leaving her husband to run away with Abe to Europe.

Taking advantage of how Rita coincidentally kept the keys to the college's chemistry lab in her pocketbook, Abe steals Rita's keys, removes some cyanide from the lab, observes Spangler's daily routine, follows him to the park where he exercises each morning, and poisons him with a cyanide-laced drink. The murder appears to have been perfectly executed, and Abe returns to the Braylin campus enthused.

After learning that Spangler is dead, Abe's excitement increases exponentially. Unlike Raskolnikov, who was tormented by guilt after murdering the pawnbroker along with the pawnbroker's innocent half-sister who happened innocently to have to entered the room during the murder, Abe shows no remorse. He feels liberated, "authentic," and happy to have done something meaningful. Whereas Watanabe in *Ikiru* creates a children's playground, and whereas Block in *The Seventh Seal* saves a young family from death, Abe Lucas's meaningful act is to murder a corrupt judge. Guilt does not enter Abe's feelings, at least not at first.

This is partly because Abe conceived of himself as someone beyond the law and akin to characters in Dostoevsky's novels, given how he wrote Spangler's name in the margins of his copy of *Crime and Punishment* on the very page where Raskolnikov admits to his deed—"It was I who killed the old pawnbroker woman and her sister Lizaveta with an axe and robbed them"—along with a notation to see Hannah Arendt's discussion of the banality of evil (*Eichmann in Jerusalem: A Report on the Banality of Evil* [1963]), invoking thereby an association between Judge Spangler and the notorious Adolf Eichmann, the Second World War conspirator and accomplice to mass murder. Below the notation for Arendt, Abe inscribed a list of Dostoevsky's characters, which included his own name: "Raskolnikov, Stavrogin, Kirilov, Verkhovensky, Lucas."

Abe's perfect murder starts to unravel when it surfaces that Spangler did not die from a heart attack, as the newspapers reported initially, but was in fact a homicide, and when Jill, in later conversation with Rita Richards, subsequently begins to suspect that Abe himself was the murderer. Unsure, Jill confronts

Abe, and when Abe admits to the deed, she is stunned, frightened, and morally outraged. Now terrified to the bone, she tells Abe that she can no longer see him. Complicating the situation—an event that also occurs in *Crime and Punishment*—another person is arrested for Spangler's murder, undermining the moral purity of how Abe was conceiving of his murderous act.

The situation is ironic, for while lecturing earlier to his undergraduate class on Immanuel Kant's moral theory, Abe criticized Kant for being unrealistic in his adoption of a morally pure standpoint. Abe himself, however, based his own meaning-giving action upon the same lofty assumption. With Spangler's murder, he expected to perform a morally pure act, but the messy, imperfect, existential, world he invoked in his philosophy class to criticize Kant—a world of "real, nasty, ugly life, which contains greed, and hate, and genocide"—tangled and fouled his expectations.

Somewhat unluckily, while Abe is stealing the cyanide from the chemistry lab after hours, April, the student who hosted the party where Abe played Russian roulette and survived, entered the lab. Although surprised to see him, April seized upon the opportunity to ask him for help with a philosophy paper she is writing on Kant, saying that she did not understand Kant's moral principles, punctuating the irony. April later told Jill that she saw Abe in the lab, confirming Jill's suspicions.

The problem with Abe's decision to murder Spangler, however, goes beyond the mismatch between perfect conceptions and imperfect spatiotemporal existence. Abe's conception of justice was distorted to begin with. Spangler may well have been a corrupt man who betrayed his position as a judge, but he was not to anyone's knowledge, responsible for anyone's death. Abe nonetheless decided to impose upon Spangler the death penalty, comparing Spangler to Eichmann, as well as to murderous mafia men. If we reflect upon the latter, though, even Don Corleone—the mafia godfather in the well-known movie of the same name—displayed a more balanced conception of justice. He refused to kill a pair of vicious men who had terribly beaten up a young woman, when asked by her father to do so for the sake of justice. When the young woman's father, an undertaker, implored to Don Corleone, "I ask you for justice," he immediately replied, "that is not justice; your daughter is still alive."

When Jill learns that an innocent person is being held in police custody for Spangler's murder, she revisits Abe and threatens him adamantly that if he does not turn himself in, she will do it herself. Cornered by Jill and realizing that he is facing life imprisonment that he knows he could not endure, Abe decides that his only option is to murder Jill to keep her quiet.

Arranging an elevator door to open deceivingly into an empty shaft, Abe meets Jill near the elevator and tries to push her down into the elevator shaft as the door opens. During the struggle, the flashlight that Abe won as a prize for Jill at the amusement park—a symbol of the sexual relationship between the older professor and younger student—falls from Jill's handbag to the floor. Stepping on the flashlight, Abe slips backward and falls to his death down the elevator shaft, hitting the bottom with a grisly thud to wrap up the film's moral and social tensions.

The flashlight occurrence recalls one of Aristotle's observations in his *Poetics* about how to construct a good tragedy, namely, that coincidences are more powerful when they seem to have an air of design. Aristotle himself used the example of how a statue of Mitys, a charioteer who had been murdered, later fell upon Mitys's murderer and killed him. Such events, Aristotle observed, do not appear to be due to mere chance, and are the best to use to develop a tragic narrative.

*Irrational Man* ends abruptly with Abe's death, with the flashlight providing the Aristotelian instrument to achieve moral closure: Abe murders Spangler for the sake of justice; Abe disregards how an innocent person would be imprisoned in his place; Abe tries to murder Jill to save himself; Jill's flashlight kills Abe to punish him for his transgressions; Jill returns happily to Roy and lives happily ever after.

As the story stands, Abe chooses to be Spangler's judge, jury, and executioner, he chooses to murder Jill to save himself from prison, and justice is done. Had the script allowed Abe to succeed in murdering Jill, though, we might have had a more complexly existential film in closer accord with *Crime and Punishment*, incorporating greater moral ambiguity and psychological tension. After reflecting upon Jill's death, Abe may well have begun to experience the kind of unhinging remorse that infected Raskolnikov—a sense of remorse that emerged partially because he had killed the pawnbroker's innocent half-sister—for unlike Spangler, Abe cared for Jill.

In this respect and limitation, *Irrational Man* portrays existential themes to a substantial degree, but it does not develop as well as it might have the sense of anguish and solitude that characterizes the paradigmatic existentialist mentality. Abe begins in a condition of solitude and despair, but dies before he comes to realize Dostoevsky's lesson that committing murder is an unfulfilling, psychologically corrosive way to achieve meaning and express one's freedom.

## 12.4 *Midnight in Paris* (2011)

In 2012, *Midnight in Paris*—one of Woody Allen's more widely appreciated films—was nominated for Academy Awards in the categories of best picture, director, and art direction, and it won the Academy Award for best original screenplay. The story revolves around a wealthy and successful, but discontent, Hollywood writer named Gil Pender, who is visiting Paris with his fiancé, Inez. Dissatisfied with his achievements as a young and talented screenwriter, Gil harbors aspirations to be a successful novelist, finding himself inspired by the Parisian surroundings that captivate his imagination with their rich history, romantic atmosphere, and artistic culture. Gil walks through the streets in the rain, reminisces about how the city inspired the artists and writers of the 1920s—those of the Lost Generation who came of age during the First World War—and listens to the music of Cole Porter, wishing he had been born earlier, and to have lived in the magical Paris of the 1920s.

Appropriate to his nostalgia, Gil is working on a novel that features a character who works in a "nostalgia shop" called "Out of the Past"—a store that sells items from past generations such as dolls and old radios. The first words of Gil's novel observe that although the store ostensibly sold physical items, its truth was to sell memories—memories of times that might very well have been prosaic and ordinary when they transpired, but had assumed a magical meaning with the passing of time.

Gil realized himself, if only dimly at first, that the aura he ascribed to past times, places, and things is only an illusion that the present generates and projects upon the past as it looks upon, and aims to escape its own prosaic and vulgar quality. Were it indeed possible to return to the past times and have those times become one's new "present," a rude existential awakening would follow: since no world is perfect, dissatisfaction with the new times would set in as well, stimulating once again the dream of escaping into yet another, supposedly more satisfying time, or "golden age." *Midnight in Paris* is about how Gil comes to realize this fact more fully. His novel states the fundamental truth, but Gil needs to appreciate it through an awakening that involves the firsthand experience of being transported to the idyllic 1920s of his dreams, as well as to the Parisian Belle Époque of the 1890s.

Complicating, and possibly motivating, Gil's nostalgia is the mismatch between Gil and his fiancé, Inez. Although neither is morally extraordinary, both are well-intentioned individuals whose values simply differ. Inez is content with a comfortable Southern Californian lifestyle, which includes an anticipated residence in the exclusive Los Angeles suburb of Malibu, where she can shop for fine decorative objects and enjoy a pleasing life of material surroundings. Gil, despite his success as a screenwriter, considers his work in Hollywood to be trivial, and believes that he would lead a more authentic life as a novelist, not necessarily wealthy, but at least culturally significant, appreciated, and remembered. Inez's parents—whose materialistic values exceed those of their daughter—treat Gil condescendingly throughout.

Gil and Inez slowly drift apart as the film progresses, with their differences accentuated by an affair between Inez and Paul Bates, a professorial acquaintance who Gil and Inez meet coincidentally in a Parisian restaurant at the beginning of the film. Paul is in Paris with his wife, Carol, to give some lectures at the Sorbonne. In contrast to the reflective and philosophically thinking Gil, Paul relates to others with an impressive, but superficial, storehouse of facts. Self-centered and overly confident, he presents a friendly, engaging, but domineering know-it-all attitude. Inez, impressed with his art historical descriptions of paintings, palaces, and sculptures as they visit the Parisian sights together, falls for Paul, blind to both Paul's shallowness and Gil's depth.

Upon this basis, Gil's fantastic experience begins. One evening, after a wine-tasting event, Gil, Inez, Paul, and Carol consider going dancing together, but Gil declines, mildly intoxicated and tired, preferring to walk back alone to his hotel while Inez, Paul, and Carol continue together. Soon lost in the narrow Parisian streets, Gil sits down to rest on the roadside. As the clock strikes midnight, an old Peugeot pulls up to the curb, filled with people who call Gil over to join them for a ride to a party. It is a wonderful car, for it literally transports Gil back to his beloved 1920s.

At the party—it turns out to be one for Jean Cocteau—Gil meets F. Scott Fitzgerald and Zelda, his wife, and filled with amazement, watches Cole Porter singing at the piano. Deciding to leave, Scott, Zelda, Cole, and Gil, along with some others, drive to a café where Scott introduces Gil to Ernest Hemingway, with whom Gil takes the opportunity to discuss his novel about the nostalgia shop, hardly able to control his excitement.

For the next several nights, Gil returns to the midnight curbside and the 1920s to develop his new friendships, bringing along his novel to obtain some constructive feedback from Gertrude Stein, into whose circle Hemingway introduces Gil. At Stein's residence, Gil meets and soon falls in love with a woman named Adriana, a (fictional) mistress of Pablo Picasso, Hemingway, Georges Braque, and Amedeo Modigliani. Among all her admirers, Adriana falls most deeply in love with Gil. Nostalgic as well, Adriana is discontent with her own 1920s era and yearns to return to Paris of La Belle Époque—a perfect time, she says—to visit Maxim's, one of the most exclusive bistros of the 1890s, and the Moulin Rouge, to be among the can-can dancers and artists such as Henri Toulouse-Lautrec, Paul Gaugin, and Edgar Degas.

As their romance reaches its height, Gil and Adriana return to La Belle Époque via a magical carriage ride and fulfill Adriana's dream. While in the Moulin Rouge, at one of the film's turning points, Adriana decides firmly to remain in the 1890s, and asks Gil to remain with her. Gil, however, unexpectedly setting aside his love for Adriana, which was appearing to transcend their respective historical locations, stated sadly that such a dream can only be short-lived, perceiving that every generation tends to experience discontent with its own time period, imagining a better life at a different time. For Gil, this was Paris of the 1920s; for Adriana, it was La Belle Époque; for those of the La Belle Époque as represented by Degas, Gaugin, and Lautrec, it was the Renaissance. Gil consequently arrived at a more sober, realistic, existential reflection that the present will always seem unsatisfying because *life itself* is unsatisfying. As a writer, his job was to show that nonetheless, life is well worth living.

Gertrude Stein said much the same to Gil when commenting on his novel, advising that the artist's role is to find an antidote to the emptiness of existence, rather than succumb to despair. Hemingway, too, spoke to Gil about this, and offered his own solution, which is to experience sex in combination with great love. For the Hemingway of *Midnight in Paris*, true, beautiful, and passionate sex generates confidence and bravery, dissolves the fear of death, and provides a solution to life's imperfection by relieving the anxiety that accompanies the anticipation of one's passing.

In *Death in the Afternoon* (1932), the actual Hemingway plants a seed of despair into such advice, stating—and we can recall Watanabe's loneliness—that even true love tends to promise sadness, as it typically concludes with one of the partners dying before the other:

> There is no lonelier man in death, except the suicide, than that man who has lived many years with a good wife and then outlived her. If two people love each other there can be no happy end to it. (Hemingway 1932: 119)

Jean-Paul Sartre observes even more severely in his novel *Nausea* (1938) that deep romantic love rests upon illusions: with time, the imperfections of the physical world reveal themselves within one's beloved, putting an end to the adventures, the perfect moments, and the joy of existence once shared.

This Sartrean kind of imperfection is more disconcerting than that to which Shakespeare referred so famously in his Sonnet 130. Shakespeare's mistress's eyes may not be as bright as the sun, her lips may not be as red as coral, and her breath may not be as sweet as perfume, but as a human, Shakespeare found his mistress beautiful, if not perfectly lovely. Sartre's world is more harsh, where personal relationships are marred by character flaws, disappointments, and mismatches in values that transform once-enthusiastic romantic relationships into banality, emptiness, and disillusionment.

Sartre's own remedy for this deadening and leveling out of one's experience is to be as creative and artistic as one can. The main character of *Nausea*—a historian named Roquentin—spends his time doing research for a book, but he becomes disillusioned after discerning the banality and coarseness of the personages whose lives he was researching. Roquentin compares to Gil, whose work as a Hollywood screenwriter had also become trivial to him. Sartre's *Nausea* concludes with Roquentin transforming from a historian into a novelist. That Gil begins his quest for meaning as a novelist suggests that in Sartrean terms, from the very start Gil held the key to his release from the problem of life's emptiness, without knowing it. Instead of dreaming about the 1920s, he needed only to apply himself conscientiously to writing his novel, since creative activity is satisfying in itself. Even devoting himself fully to his screenplays might have worked to secure meaning, as a fiction writer from the start.

*Midnight in Paris* does not criticize the illusory quality of ideal romances, but it ends on an existential note nevertheless. Gil comes to realize at least that living in the past is pointless, and he returns from his visits to the 1920s with the strength to admit that he is best separating from Inez. He explains to her that he will not be returning to California, and that he will remain in Paris to write his novel. Inez is upset, but not deeply. Her parents are relieved to see Gil go, with Inez's father saying mockingly to Gil as he leaves, "Say hello to Trotsky!," confirming to himself that Gil is the fool he had always imagined him to be.

The film concludes with Gil walking off idyllically in the rain with a woman named Gabrielle—a woman who Gil met in a nostalgia shop he was visiting one afternoon. Just as the clock strikes midnight in the closing scenes, Gabrielle appears, as did the time-transporting Peugeot and carriage. As Gil's mirror image and apparent soulmate, Gabrielle enjoys Paris of the 1920s, loves nostalgia, and finds Paris most beautiful in the rain. The audience is left with the satisfying thought that Gil and Gabrielle will live happily ever after.

That Gil realizes the importance of facing the imperfect present lends *Midnight in Paris* an existential tone. That he anticipates with Gabrielle a more contemporary replay of the romantic relationship he had in 1920s' Paris with Adriana is less existentially inspired. Sadness, either in Hemingway's manner, with the death of one's partner, or in Sartre's manner, where banality and familiarity precipitate disillusionment, is where Gil and Gabrielle might end.

Although *Midnight in Paris* concludes with a replay of romanticism within a more realistic, contemporary setting, released from what Paul described as the fallacy of "Golden Age thinking"—a style of romanticism where, as a consequence of not being able to deal with the imperfection of the present, one imagines that it would have been better to have lived at an earlier time period, or "Golden Age," whether it happens to be Paris of the 1920s, La Belle Époque, the Renaissance, ancient Greece, or San Francisco of the 1960s—it does come close to realizing a more effective, Nietzschean, solution to life's meaning in the face of imperfection. This solution avoids the difficulties that Hemingway and Sartre indicate, as well as the more Buddhistic solutions that prescribe that we simply should try not to hold on at all, because change is inevitable.

Gil acknowledges that his task as a writer is to develop reasons why life is worth living in the face of its tragic and unsatisfying quality. This is also Nietzsche's concern, which he characterizes as the problem of giving a meaning for suffering in a godless world. Like Hemingway in the film, and like Gil, Nietzsche's solution is to search for the perfect romantic relationship, and upon finding it, dwelling within it as long and as effectively as one can. The difference is that Nietzsche's perfect soulmate and romantic partner—one that he describes poetically at the end of Book Three in his most famous work *Thus Spoke Zarathustra* (1883–85)—is more permanent and never-leaving, for his romantic partner is, rather extraordinarily, reality itself, regarded as a kind of cosmic femme fatale, which he aims to love with all his heart. Nietzsche expresses this with his prescription to say "yes" to life, and to love "fate" in the sense of being strong enough to embrace whatever misery life happens to throw at us.

For Nietzsche, a necessary condition for loving life and finding meaning is to have a personal character that is strong, courageous, and uncommonly superior, much like Hemingway's celebration of courage in the face of death that he recognized in his matador friend, Juan Belmonte. Although Nietzsche's love of life and the world can be regarded as equally romantic and unrealistic, it remains therapeutic in its capacity to foster a positive attitude toward suffering. Within Nietzsche's perspective, a meaningful life involves being unconditionally in love with reality, despite how dangerous, threatening, cruel, painful, and ultimately fatal as it happens to be. Insofar as the individualistically oriented solution to life's imperfection that we find in *Midnight in Paris* allows for an expansion into this more permanent Nietzschean solution of saying "yes" to life as a whole, it points the way toward a more steadfast and earthly approach to creating meaning.

## 12.5 *The Pawnbroker* (1964)

In *Crime and Punishment*, Raskolnikov murders a pawnbroker to remove from the world a cold, hurtful, and selfish human being. Much the same occurs in *Irrational Man*, where Abe Lucas murders Judge Spangler, an uncaring and corrupt judge. In Camus's novel *The Stranger*, the judicial system condemns to death an office worker named Meursault, who lives on the periphery of the underworld and who, although friendly and polite, is oddly and offensively oblivious to how other people feel.

None of these works explain why the individuals who are targeted—the pawnbroker, Spangler, Meursault—either lack, or appear to lack, warmth or sympathy for other people. *The Pawnbroker*—a film directed by Sidney Lumet, based on the novel of the same name by Edward Lewis Wallant—is distinctive in that it provides some insight on this matter through the story of Sol Nazerman, a concentration camp survivor and manager of a pawnbroker shop in New York City, whose callous treatment of his customers and social acquaintances compares to the characters mentioned above that feature in Dostoevsky's, Allen's, and Camus's works.

Dostoevsky's pawnbroker, Allen's Spangler, and Camus's Meursault do not share the same background or motives as Nazerman, but Nazerman's story reveals the moral ambiguity and superficial perceptions that surround the condemnation of the "heartless human being" in these existential works. Abe Lucas justifies his murder of Spangler in a morally clean-cut manner by denying mitigating factors—"Even if he was a good family man, that's like those mafia bosses who do horrible things and we are supposed to cut them slack because they are wonderful to their wives and children?" A more concrete, existentialist awareness, however, would acknowledge that characters who appear to be purely despicable are always complicated by positive factors that temper and confuse our moral judgments.

*The Pawnbroker* begins with a dreamlike scene of a picnic in a Polish forest that Sol is remembering many years later as he rests on a lounge chair in the 1960s, spending an afternoon in the backyard of his sister's house in suburban Long Island, New York. Sol, pictured as a young man in the scene, sees his wife smiling, his children running happily into his arms, and his children's grandparents content on the grass in an idyllic family moment.

Sol's memory is then interrupted by the noisy goings-on at his sister's house: Bertha, his sister, calls to Sol and asks whether he would like some fresh lemonade. Joan and Morton, Sol's teenage niece and nephew, run around lightheartedly and to Sol, annoyingly. The house itself stands as one in a series of modest and repetitious, middle-class homes, situated non-scenically beside a busy highway, with a man in each backyard each watering his lawn. Sol, now a significantly older man in his forties, is corpulent and balding. He is polite, but emotionally distant from those around him.

Sol's pawnbroker shop in Harlem is owned by an affluent and powerful African-American gangster named Rodriguez, who, unbeknownst to Sol, owns not only the pawnbroker shop, but bowling alleys, parking lots, and brothels from which he draws his earnings. The pawnbroker shop does not make money, but serves as one of Rodriguez's money laundering fronts. Sol operates the shop with an attitude much like the pawnbroker woman in Dostoevsky's novel and he generates frustration, anger, disappointment, and aggression in his customers.

Sol's personal history goes far in accounting for his behavior. Before the Germans invaded Poland in 1939, he was a university professor in Krakow, with a loving wife and two happy children. As we learn, the heavenly picnic scene with which the movie starts comes to a vicious end when a group of German soldiers seize Sol and his family and send them to a concentration camp. Sol's young son dies heartrendingly on the floor of the transport train. His wife is later killed after having been forced into prostitution by the camp's soldiers. His children's grandparents are presumably killed as well. At one point Sol witnesses the death of his friend, Ruben, who is attacked by guard dogs while trapped on the camp's barbed wire fence. Sol is the sole survivor at the war's end, empty and uncaring, with the unnerving personal strength of a person who, with nothing more to lose, can no longer be easily scared or intimidated. Constantly haunted by his memories of the concentration camp, Sol wants nothing more than to avoid caring or committed relationships with anyone and to be left alone in peace.

With his salary from Rodriguez's pawnbroker shop, Sol supports Bertha and her family along with Tessie, Ruben's widow, who lives with her aging and infirm father, Mendel. Sol and Tessie carry on a guilt-ridden affair to which Mendel objects, and their relationships are strained all around. At the pawnshop, Sol has working for him an energetic Hispanic assistant named Jesus. He is poor, lives with his mother, looks up to Sol as a teacher and father-figure, and aspires conscientiously to free himself from his shady underworld friends to learn the pawnbroker trade from Sol, so he can also become a legitimate businessman.

Sol coldly dismisses Jesus's aspirations, though, and when Jesus questions Sol about his attitude, Sol explains that he believes only in money, which is "what life's all about" and "is the whole thing." He professes that he cares nothing about God, art, science, newspapers, politics, or philosophy and that he treats everyone equally—equally in the sense that, implicitly including Jesus, they are all "scum" and "rejects." Once a university professor interested in intellectual matters, Sol no longer finds value in people, culture, or sensory pleasures. He turns Jesus away, and Jesus, feeling rejected and aware that Sol has five thousand dollars stashed in the safe—Rodriquez's money—decides to take Sol at his word: he returns to his underworld acquaintances and plans to rob the pawnbroker shop, aiming to obtain the seed money to start his own business.

Tensions come to a head one evening when Jesus's prostitute girlfriend, Nena, enters the shop to pawn a locket and to offer her body to Sol for some extra money. While Nena is negotiating with Sol for the locket, Sol receives an agitated phone call from Tessie, who tells him that her father, Mendel, had just died. Sol responds that he is not interested in crying with her and must tend to the shop. Sitting down with his head in his hands, Nena continues her seduction oblivious to Sol's emotional state, and as she disrobes (*The Pawnbroker* was one of the first mainstream movies to show exposed breasts, here adding to the narrative's power) her naked body triggers in Sol painful flashbacks of his wife, forcing him to remember how his wife's breasts were exposed in humiliation when he had to watch her have sex with a German soldier. During the seduction in the pawnbroker shop, Nena tells Sol that she works as a prostitute for Sol's boss, Rodriguez. Already struck by Mendel's death and filled with the painful memory of his wife and her fate, Sol is shaken by this revelation, as it casts a new and disturbing light on his place in the pawnshop.

Sol feels disgusted with himself as one of Rodriguez's employees, for Rodriguez, as a brothel owner, compares to the Germans in the concentration camp who abused Sol's wife in the camp's brothel. As one of Rodriquez's employees, Sol is in the position of working for the enemy. As one of Rodriquez's employees, Sol is also in the position of Nena, the prostitute, along with that of his wife.

Slowly falling apart, Sol's interest in the pawnbroker business wanes in the oncoming days, and he begins to behave erratically with his customers, sometimes offering generous sums for relatively worthless goods. He later defies Rodriguez by refusing to sign his money laundering documents, contrary to his previously compliant and unquestioning practice. In the meantime, Jesus carries out the pawnshop theft with his gangster associates, and during its course, one of the gang members pulls a gun on Sol. Not wanting to see Sol hurt, Jesus rushes to protect Sol, and is shot accidentally when the gun fires during the commotion. The gangsters flee, leaving Sol standing numb as Jesus stumbles out of the store fatally wounded and falling to the sidewalk. Recovering his composure, Sol rushes out to help Jesus, his student and surrogate son, but Jesus dies in his arms. Sol rises with blood all over his hands, his face twisted and frozen in emotional agony.

Presumably Sol returns to Tessie thereafter, loses his job, and is possibly killed by Rodriguez. Through Jesus's death, his emotions are released powerfully after having been bottled up for so long, but only through a set of experiences that reiterate the horrors that initially turned him to stone. The film ends with Sol alone and suffering, unredeemed, standing as an individual against the world, godless, and guilty.

In his atheism, his feelings of social alienation, and sense of utter meaninglessness, Sol is an emotionally intense existentialist figure. He does not triumphantly conquer his feelings of meaninglessness through creativity, hedonism, or engagement in a great task, but represents the depths of despair that precede such constructive existential reactions to life's meaninglessness.

## 12.6 Expressing existentialist themes under aesthetic constraints

*Crime and Punishment*, *The Stranger*, *Ikiru*, *The Seventh Seal*, *Irrational Man*, *Midnight in Paris*, and *The Pawnbroker*, as works of art, involve aesthetic constraints in their form and content—constraints that can interfere with the thorough expression of existentialist themes. We will conclude by considering this aspect of these works.

Raskolnikov is the novel's existentialist character in *Crime and Punishment*, and Dostoevsky superficially presents the pawnbroker that Raskolnikov murders. Abe Lucas is the existentialist character in *Irrational Man*, and Woody Allen presents Judge Spangler similarly as a mere sketch. In *The Stranger*, Camus's Meursault compares to Sol Nazerman insofar as their uncaring, godless attitudes define their extreme isolation and this-worldliness. The characters are all murderers in one way or another. Nazerman did not intend to harm Jesus, but his begrudging attention to Jesus's conscientiousness and aspiration to become his apprentice virtually implied his demise. The film appropriately concludes with Nazerman's hands covered with Jesus's blood.

An important difference between Meursault and Nazerman is that we never discover in *The Stranger* why Meursault is so insensitive to other people's feelings. Nazerman's story sheds a light on this, for one can imagine Meursault's personal history prior to the novel's beginning, and perhaps the histories of Dostoevsky's pawnbroker and Allen's Spangler, as having been distinctively painful ones.

Charles Dickens's account of the mean-spirited miser, Ebenezer Scrooge, in his novella *A Christmas Carol* (1843) is comparable. We learn that Scrooge's mother died during his birth and that his father consequently blamed, hated, and rejected him throughout his childhood. The only person who cared for Scrooge was his sister, whose coincidental death during childbirth devastated Scrooge. Toward his sister's son, Scrooge acted as cruelly as his father did toward him. Unlike Nazerman, though, Scrooge becomes deeply humane and after being traumatically reminded of how he was once in love, how people presently despise him, and how, if he does not change, his miserly behavior will cause the death of Tiny Tim, an innocent, impoverished, and physically crippled boy.

The works by Dostoevsky and Allen convey the message that murder precipitates unhappiness, and that the gratification it promises is false. This is a thought-provoking message in view of the existentialist celebration of total freedom, which allows murder as a possible means to express one's individuality and authenticity. Regarding Raskolnikov and Lucas, at least, one could explain their choices by acknowledging that to them, freedom, authenticity, and a higher sense of morality are more important than happiness. Unlike Meursault and Nazerman who are selfish and insensitive, Raskolnikov and Lucas are motivated to murder other people for the sake of doing good.

From a more pragmatic angle, we can appreciate that works of literature and cinema are made for audiences to appreciate aesthetically and are governed accordingly by rules of composition that aim to please. Classical aesthetic practice requires a recognizable degree of organic unity and narrative closure for the sake of understandability, which in the cases of *Crime and Punishment*, *Irrational Man*, *The Stranger*, and *The Pawnbroker* are provided in part by moral reconciliations. Raskolnikov is sent to prison; Lucas and Meursault die; Nazerman remains a tortured soul after having turned away from Jesus. The creators of these works subscribe to traditional moral values, albeit unconventionally expressed, and are less existentially committed in this regard. The aesthetic demands that govern the creation of good works of art in conjunction with basic moral sentiments can interfere with a thorough expression of existentialist thought.

Watanabe, Block, and Gil emerge morally intact while remaining existentially representative, but this combination of morality and existentiality only accentuates the artistic quality of their respective narratives. Watanabe and Block discover meaning in helping children and families to survive; Gil sets aside his nostalgia, and finds meaning in the living present. Each character comes to a satisfying ending, and although they remain down to earth and discover meaning without appealing to otherworldly realities, their romantic and perfected situations exude consoling illusion, introduced significantly to achieve the aesthetic closure typical of a satisfying work of art.

Works of literature and cinema can be excellent vehicles to portray existentialist themes, for they can present details of both a psychological and a social nature that philosophical theory usually omits. At the same time, their status as works of art introduce aesthetic demands such as rational organization and narrative closure, which tend to conflict with how concrete life is an enterprise that is less organically unified and less obviously just, filled as it is with accidents, disappointments, and absurdities that undermine comprehension and aesthetic appreciation.

As a representative and summary image of this contrast between art and actual life, we can recall how when Sartre's Roquentin became fully aware of daily life's distinct lack of organic unity, he lost the ability to discern what previously seemed to be inherent narratives and rational organization in the objective structure of passing events, and this leveling out of the world brought his sense of adventure, meaning, and life's perfection to a halt.

# 13

# Conclusion: Why Existentialism Today?— The Need for Realistic, Humane, and Responsible Leadership

Among the salient features of existentialist thought is its insistence on recognizing the spatiotemporal world as the fundamental reality. Rather than directing our thought and aspirations to spiritually located heavens, nonphysical realms, and abstract dimensions that are remote from ordinary human experience, it emphasizes our immediate awareness and everyday connection to concrete items such as the trees, rocks, tables, chairs, roadways, stars, rain, cats, dogs, birds, animals, and other people.

In relation to items of contemporary technology such as computers, telephones, and televisions, this realistic, existentially grounded orientation has some significant implications. The primary disposition toward these as physical objects is akin to how an engineer, electrician, designer, or warehouse person might regard them, namely, as items that have a certain size, weight, and internal construction. This contrasts with an attitude that overlooks their immediate physicality and treats them instrumentally as openings to virtual realities within which we can imaginatively immerse ourselves. Existentially considered, the reality of a computer screen is that it is a component of a physical device that presents an array of electronically generated bits of color. In the same way, the plain presence of a hammer is that it is a heavy object with a strong handle and a solid top.

To grab the hammer simply and start hammering some nails, despite the pragmatic disposition involved, is to overlook the hammer as purely a physical object. It is to pass over the "this-ness" of the hammer. It usually makes no difference, but when the object that we are using instrumentally is not an item such as hammer, pair of eyeglasses, spoon, or doorknob, but a computer, television, or mobile phone, the implications of overlooking the primary physical reality of these items can lead to misunderstanding and a disconnection with the physical world's immediate corporeal presence.

Our technological age makes it difficult to keep illusion and reality clearly distinguished from one other. A high-resolution photograph of a person on a computer screen can be so convincing that it can seem as if one is looking at the person as a presently happening occurrence. With a similar effect, viewing a captivating motion picture made decades ago can immerse us into the illusion that the actors, some of whom might already be deceased, are doing right now what the film is portraying. The surrounding world of technological devices is effective, if not seductive and hypnotic, in drawing people into these kinds of virtual-reality worlds that provide a diversion from and a distortion of the actual, concrete world.

Throughout such immersions into a merely virtual reality, the earth continues to travel through galactic space, rotate on its axis, revolve around the sun, as winds, clouds, and rains move across its surface. As this is happening, many people's attention is drawn to and absorbed by computer screens, televisions, and mobile phones, diverted and brought further out of touch with the physical actuality of things. When turning back to the world, the images and values that extend from the virtual worlds inevitably constitute a background upon which interpretations of the actual world are grounded, almost to the point where other people can be perceived as if they were images on a computer screen, calling for less respect than they deserve as living individuals. Moreover, instances of violence and killing on television and film are so numerous, but typically so distant from the true experiential distress of these kinds of experience, that the subsequent understanding of pain and death can become misguided. This all signals a need for a radical reorientation toward a less distortive, less superficial, more realistic style of awareness.

There are many different philosophies, but only a subset of them emphasize the importance of remaining in direct, down-to-earth contact with immediate physical realities as opposed to dwelling in more imaginative, fantasy-filled spheres of attention. It is admittedly difficult to avoid projections and imaginative constructs—anticipating a long-awaited vacation is itself filled with imagistic projections that divert our attention from what is happening here and now—but there are degrees to which we can allow such constructs to infuse into our awareness. It is one thing to travel home from work in an automatic manner, remembering little of scenes that pass before one's eyes, absorbed imaginatively in mulling over the earlier events of the day, and another to travel home intensely attentive to the roadway, the surrounding buildings, curves, landscape, weather, sounds, the bumps in the road, and condition of one's body as they present themselves from moment to moment in their full perceptual quality. The difference between these two dispositions is the same whether one happens to be riding a donkey or driving a sports car.

At the most rudimentary level, though, we are almost always functioning at a level of awareness that involves an imaginative and implicit diversion from concrete realities. When reading a word, for example, we tend not immediately to register as such, the ink on the page or poster, or the electrical bits of color on a screen, but rather the "meaning" that the ink or electrical bits embody. Purer levels of existential awareness, where one is aware primarily of the ink as ink, or the electrical bits as bits, where the meanings associated with the inscriptions appear as secondary phenomena, are rare, perhaps consistently present only to those who practice Zen Buddhism.

Slightly above this level is the orientation toward the world characteristic of traditional existential philosophy. This is where we appreciate in their detail the rocks as rocks, the trees as trees, and so on, without excessive projections and fantasy overlays. It is probably inaccurate to say that this characterizes the ordinary experience of those who lived before the age of the mechanical reproduction of images and texts, since earlier populations were themselves steeped in religious and mythological imagery that shaped their interpretation of raw nature. Nonetheless, the development of mechanical reproduction of images and texts some centuries ago, along with the more contemporary development of computer technology, has gone further than ever before in seducing people to live more substantially within virtual realities. As televisions, computers, and mobile phones have become more widespread, the blend between virtual and actual reality has only become more intensified.

Existentialist philosophy offers a corrective to this contemporary condition. It is a corrective per se, for there are practical and psychological advantages in being closely connected to the concrete here and now, as opposed to being immersed in imaginative realities, some of which are noticeably dissociated from the ordinary world. Having a realistic orientation is especially important for people in positions of social responsibility, for to have a solid sense of reality is essential for effective decision making at all levels, whether one happens to be a leader at the national level or within the local community.

Among the existentialist philosophies we have considered in this book, some are more emblematic in that they emphasize not only the theme of concrete, down-to-earth awareness, but the essential solitude, individuality, and alienation that each person experiences. We must all die individually in the end, and the anticipation of death is a worry for us all. Try as one might to overcome the separation between people, as when I take a photograph to show you the object or scene I am now experiencing, or write a sentence to communicate my thoughts, this is not the same as being "me" right now having that experience in its fullness. I can experience your experience to some extent, but such overlaps are always partial and are not literally coincident with your experience per se. In this sense we each remain alone, and existentialist philosophy importantly urges us to keep this impasse between ourselves and others in mind. Despite our inherent sociality, there is no escape from the solitude that defines the boundaries of our individual consciousnesses.

At this idea's questionable extreme, as in Jean-Paul Sartre's existentialism, interpersonal relationships are marked by alienation and dramatic non-coincidence between individuals. Sartre's analysis of "the look" describes this well: when I look at you, I turn you into an object for me; when you look at me, you turn me into an object for you. The look is objectifying and insofar as it objectifies people, it falsifies them, for each consciousness is not on object. All attempts to connect intimately with people fail frustratingly in Sartre's view, whether the efforts involve sex, love, domination over others, or submission to others.

Other versions of existentialist philosophy recognize more humanely our social reality and need for communion with others. Heidegger identifies as fundamental to human being the feeling of "being with" other people. Buber recognizes the importance of the "I-thou" relationship, which resonates with intimacy, respect, and friendliness. Marcel, as does Heidegger, accentuates our inherently caring attitude as humans. Existential psychology is steadfast about resisting the objectification of people and understands the projection of extremely objectifying attitudes toward others as unhealthy. Here, in Heidegger, Buber, Marcel, and existential psychology resides a healthier, more attractive kind of existentialism, important especially for leadership.

Within this context of leadership, retaining a human and non-objectifying attitude is valuable, given the responsibility to foster the well-being of other people within an institutional setting. Greater responsibility tends to require decisions that affect large numbers of individuals, however, and it is easy to fall into an attitude that for the sake of expedience ignores the psychological depth of each individual and regards people as faceless masses of statistics. Fostering a fundamental "I-thou" attitude in one's general disposition toward the world can counterbalance the tendency to depersonalize other people that leadership roles tend to invite.

As a commendable style of existentialism, Sartre's version falls short in this respect, since it rests upon a fundamental claim that adopting an objectifying attitude toward other people is an unavoidable fact of consciousness. Strongly in Sartre's favor, though, is another aspect of his philosophy, namely, its virtue of highlighting a person's sense of responsibility to the point of rendering it as an absolute and foundational feature of being human. *Being and Nothingness* was written during the German occupation of France during the Second World War, and it was common for soldiers to relieve themselves of personal responsibility for their actions by defining themselves as good soldiers who do not question orders, no matter how inhuman their orders might be. By contrast, true leaders assume full responsibility for their actions, despite the difficulties involved. One would hope that as a rule, a supreme sense of responsibility would in itself precipitate decisions that display a respect for the humanity of each person, as Beauvoir believed.

In a world where the avoidance of responsibility is common, where contemporary technology tends to divert our attention away from the concrete realities that surround us, where the immersion into virtual worlds tends to diminish the actual reality of violence, where many people in leadership positions have been corrupted by selfishness, it is imperative that new leaders emerge who have a more intimate and realistic connection with the concrete world, a stronger sense of responsibility and commitment to others, and perhaps most importantly, a core of personal integrity and self-respect. Existentialist philosophy is not a panacea, but it can significantly assist in developing people with good character and judgment, much as Plato envisioned centuries ago when he wrote the *Republic*. In these days, when otherworldly realities are less convincing and the distant ideals that

Plato espoused are less plausible, existentialist philosophy can serve well by providing the constructive inspiration for developing more balanced, humane, and respectable social organizations along with more responsible leaders.

Adopting an exclusively down-to-earth attitude does carry a certain danger: without an avenue for appeal to otherworldly realities, often conceived of as authoritative moral guides, we must face the world as it presently is—a world filled with war, suffering, injustice, brutality, selfishness, irrationality, and absurd accident. Nietzsche saw this clearly, and understood that wholeheartedly acknowledging this world requires an attitude that does not shy away from pain. It requires strength and willpower, so insofar as existentialism can help foster a deep sense of personal responsibility and a humane disposition, it remains that the path is difficult, for it calls for a heartrending accommodation to the world's imperfection.

# Bibliography

## References

Baldwin, James. 1949. "Everybody's Protest Novel," *Partisan Review*, 16, no. 6: 578–85.

Barthes, Roland. 1972 [1957]. *Mythologies*, trans. Annette Lavers. New York: Hill and Wang.

Berg, Gretchen. 1967. "Andy: My True Story," *Los Angeles Free Press*, March 17, 1967, p. 3.

Binswanger, Ludwig. 1958a. "The Existential Analysis School of Thought," in *Existence: A New Dimension in Psychiatry and Psychology*, ed. Rollo May, Ernest Angel, and Henri F. Ellenberger. New York: Basic Books, 191–213.

Binswanger, Ludwig. 1958b. "The Case of Ellen West," in *Existence: A New Dimension in Psychiatry and Psychology*, ed. Rollo May, Ernest Angel, and Henri F. Ellenberger. New York: Basic Books, 237–364.

Camus, Albert. 1955. *The Myth of Sisyphus & Other Essays*, trans. Justin O'Brien. New York: Vintage Books.

Camus, Albert. 1956. *The Rebel—An Essay on Man in Revolt*, trans. Anthony Bower. New York: Vintage Books.

Cheng, Anne Anlin. 2011. *Second Skin: Josephine Baker and the Modern Surface*. Oxford: Oxford University Press.

de Beauvoir, Simone. 1947. *Pour Une Morale de L'Amgiuité*, trans. Bernard Frechtman. Paris: Gallimard.

de Beauvoir, Simone. 1952 [1948]. *America Day by Day*, trans. Patrick Dudley. London: Gerald Duckworth & Co. Ltd.

de Beauvoir, Simone. 2004. "An Existentialist Looks at Americans," [1947] in *Simone de Beauvoir: Philosophical Writings*, ed. Margaret A. Simons. Urbana and Chicago: University of Illinois Press, 307–16

de Beauvoir, Simone. 2011. *The Second Sex*, trans. Constance Borde and Sheila Malovany-Chevallier. New York: Vintage Books.

Dostoevsky, Fyodor. 1956. "Notes from Underground," in *Existentialism from Dostoevsky to Sartre*, ed. Walter Kaufmann. Cleveland and New York: Meridian Books, 52–82.

Frankl, Viktor E. 1959. *Man's Search for Meaning: An Introduction to Logotherapy*, trans. Ilse Lasch. Boston: Beacon Press.

Freud, Sigmund. 1930. *Civilization and Its Discontents*, trans. Joan Riviere. London: Hogarth Press.

Hegel, Georg Wilhelm Friedrich. 1948. "The Positivity of the Christian Religion," in *Early Theological Writings*, trans. Thomas M. Knox. Philadelphia: University of Pennsylvania Press, 67–181.

Hegel, Georg Wilhelm Friedrich. 1977. *Phenomenology of Spirit*, trans. Alexander V. Miller. Oxford: Oxford University Press.

Heidegger, Martin. 1962. *Being and Time*, trans. John Macquarrie and Edward Robinson. Oxford: Blackwell Publishers Ltd.

Heidegger, Martin. 1971. "The Origin of the Work of Art," in *Poetry, Language, Thought*, trans. Albert Hofstadter. New York: Harper & Row, 17–87.

Heidegger, Martin. 1977. "Letter on Humanism," in *Martin Heidegger—Basic Writings*, ed. David Farrell Krell. New York: Harper & Row, 193–242.

Hemingway, Ernest. 1932. *Death in the Afternoon*. London: Jonathan Cape.

Janton, Pierre. 1993. *Esperanto: Language, Literature, and Community*, trans. Humphrey Tonkin, Jane Edwards, and Karen Johnson-Weiner. Albany: State University of New York Press.

Kant, Immanuel. 1956. *Critique of Practical Reason*, trans. Lewis White Beck. Indianapolis: The Bobbs-Merrill Company Inc.

Kierkegaard, Søren. 1941. *Concluding Unscientific Postscript*, trans. David F. Swenson and Walter Lowrie. Princeton: Princeton University Press.

Kierkegaard, Søren. 1944. *Either/Or*, Volume II, trans. Walter Lowrie. Princeton: Princeton University Press.

Kierkegaard, Sören. 1959. *Either/Or*, Volume I, trans. David F. Swenson and Lillian Marvin Swenson. Princeton: Princeton University Press.

Kierkegaard, Søren. 1989. *The Sickness Unto Death*, trans. Alastair Hannay. London: Penguin Books.

Laing, Ronald D. 1960. *The Divided Self*. Harmondsworth: Penguin Books.

Marcel, Gabriel. 1948. *The Philosophy of Existence*, trans. Manya Harari. London: The Harvill Press.

Maritain, Jacques. 1956. *Existence and the Existent: An Essay on Christian Existentialism* [1947], trans. Lewis Galantiere and Gerald B. Plelan. New York: Image Books.

Marx, Karl. 1978. "Theses on Feuerbach," in *The Marx-Engels Reader*, 2nd edn, ed. Robert C. Tucker. New York: W. W. Norton & Company, 143–5.

May, Rollo. 1960. "The Emergence of Existential Psychology," in *Existential Psychology*, ed. Rollo May. New York: Random House, 11–51.

Newman, Barnett. 1992. "Response to the Reverend Thomas F. Mathews," in *Barnett Newman: Selected Writings*, ed. John P. O'Neill. Berkeley: University of California Press, 286–9.

Nietzsche, Friedrich. 1954a. *Thus Spoke Zarathustra*, trans. Walter Kaufmann. New York: The Viking Press.
Nietzsche, Friedrich. 1954b. "Twilight of the Idols," in *The Portable Nietzsche*, trans. Walter Kaufmann. New York: The Viking Press, 463–563.
Nietzsche, Friedrich. 1966. *Beyond Good and Evil*, trans. Walter Kaufmann. New York: Vintage Books.
Nietzsche, Friedrich. 1967. *The Birth of Tragedy*, trans. Walter Kaufmann. New York: Vintage Books.
Nietzsche, Friedrich. 1968. *The Will to Power*, trans. Walter Kaufmann and Reginald J. Hollingdale. New York: Vintage Books.
Nietzsche, Friedrich. 1969. *On the Genealogy of Morals*, trans. Walter Kaufmann. New York: Vintage Books.
Nietzsche, Friedrich. 1974. *The Gay Science*, trans. Walter Kaufmann. New York: Vintage Books.
Nietzsche, Friedrich. 1979. "On Truth and Lies in a Nonmoral Sense," in *Philosophy and Truth: Selections from Nietzsche's Notebooks of the early 1870's*, trans. Daniel Breazeale. New Jersey: Humanities Press, 79–97.
Nietzsche, Friedrich. 1983. *Untimely Meditations*, trans. Reginald J. Hollingdale. Cambridge: Cambridge University Press.
Nietzsche, Friedrich. 1986. *Human, All Too Human: A Book for Free Spirits*, trans. Reginald J. Hollingdale. Cambridge: Cambridge University Press.
Rosenzweig, Franz. 1985. *The Star of Redemption* [1921], trans. William W. Hallo [1930]. Notre Dame and London: University of Notre Dame Press.
Sartre, Jean-Paul. 1956. *Being and Nothingness*, trans. Hazel E. Barnes. New York: Philosophical Library, Inc.
Sartre, Jean-Paul. 1964. *Nausea*, trans. Lloyd Alexander. New York: New Directions Publishing Corporation.
Tillich, Paul. 1952. *The Courage to Be*. Glasgow: William Collins Sons & Co. Ltd.
Tillich, Paul. 1956. "The Nature and the Significance of Existentialist Thought," *The Journal of Philosophy*, 53, no. 23: 739–48.
Tillich, Paul. 1957. *Systematic Theology*, vol. II. Digswell Place: James Nisbet & Co. Ltd.
Tolstoy, Leo. 1960. *The Death of Ivan Ilych and Other Stories*, trans. Aylmer Maude and James D. Duff. New York: Signet Classics.

## Books on Existentialism

Abbagnano, Nicola. 1969. *Critical Existentialism*. Garden City: Anchor Books.
Aho, Kevin. 2014. *Existentialism: An Introduction*. Cambridge: Polity Press.

Bakewell, Sarah. 2016. *At the Existentialist Café: Freedom, Being, and Apricot Cocktails*. New York: Other Press.
Barrett, William. 1958. *Irrational Man—A Study in Existential Philosophy*. New York: Doubleday Anchor Books.
Collins, James. 1952. *The Existentialists: A Critical Study*. Chicago: Henry Regnery Company.
Cooper, David. 1990. *Existentialism: A Reconstruction*. London: Blackwell.
Cotkin, George. 2003. *Existential America*. Baltimore: The Johns Hopkins Press.
Crowell, Steven (ed.). 2012. *The Cambridge Companion to Existentialism*. Cambridge: Cambridge University Press.
Dutt, K. Guru. 1960. *Existentialism and Indian Thought*. New York: Philosophical Library.
Flynn, Thomas. 2006. *Existentialism: A Very Short Introduction*. Oxford: Oxford University Press.
Friedman, Maurice (ed.). 1964. *The Worlds of Existentialism: A Critical Reader*. New York: Random House.
Golomb, Jacob. 1995. *In Search of Authenticity: Existentialism from Kierkegaard to Camus*. London: Routledge.
Gordon, Lewis. 2000. *Existentia Africana: Understanding Africana Existential Thought*. New York and London: Routledge.
Grene, Marjorie. 1948. *Dreadful Freedom: A Critique of Existentialism*. Chicago: University of Chicago Press.
Harper, Ralph. 1965. *The Seventh Solitude: Metaphysical Homelessness in Kierkegaard, Dostoevsky, and Nietzsche*. Baltimore: The Johns Hopkins Press.
Heinemann, Fritz H. 1953. *Existentialism and the Modern Predicament*. New York: Harper & Row.
Joseph, Felicity, Jack Reynolds, and Ashley Woodward (eds.). 2011. *The Bloomsbury Companion to Existentialism*. London: Bloomsbury.
Kaufmann, Walter (ed.). 1956. *Existentialism from Dostoevsky to Sartre*. Cleveland and New York: The World Publishing Company.
Kaufmann, Walter. 1976. *Existentialism, Religion, and Death: Thirteen Essays*. New York: New American Library.
Langiulli, Nino (ed.). 1971. *The Existentialist Tradition: Selected Writings*. Garden City: Anchor Books.
Macquarrie, John. 1972. *Existentialism*. Harmondsworth, England: Penguin Books.
Marino, Gordon (ed.). 2004. *Basic Writings of Existentialism*. New York: Modern Library.
Molina, Fernando. 1962. *Existentialism as Philosophy*. Englewood Cliffs: Prentice-Hall.

Olson, Robert G. 1962. *An Introduction to Existentialism.* New York: Dover Publications.
Reynolds, Jack. 2006. *Understanding Existentialism.* Chesham: Acumen Publishing.
Solomon, Robert C. 2001. *From Rationalism to Existentialism: The Existentialists and their Nineteenth-Century Backgrounds.* Lanham: Rowman and Littlefield.
Wartenberg, Thomas E. 2008. *Existentialism: A Beginner's Guide.* London: Oneworld Publications.

# Index

Abraham, *see* Kierkegaard, Søren
absolute freedom, *see* Sartre, Jean-Paul
abstract expressionists  158, 160–2
absurd ("the absurd")  17, 31, 81, 82, 86–7, 101–8, 110–14, 119, 121, 132, 135, 137, 143, 163, 174, 176, 181, 191, 208, 214
aesthetic lifestyle, *see* Kierkegaard, Søren
Adorno, Theodor  164
African-Americans  158, 160, 165–7, 169, 204
*agon*  39, 114
Algren, Nelson  167
alienation  10, 61, 71, 76, 81, 85, 87, 91–2, 95, 97, 132, 137, 140, 143, 151, 154, 158–9, 164–6, 170, 175, 184, 206, 212
Allen, Woody  184, 192, 197, 203, 206–7
anxiety  10, 22, 32–3, 56, 70–1, 74, 77, 88, 91, 101–2, 109, 131–2, 136–7, 154, 156, 159–60, 162, 170, 174, 176, 184, 200
Aquinas, St. Thomas  133
Arendt, Hannah  160–1, 194
Aristotle  46, 52, 55, 59, 61, 64–6
  Mitys (statue of)  196
  *Poetics*  196
Aron, Raymond  80
Augustine, St.  99
authenticity  8, 55–6, 67, 69–77, 88, 90–2, 95, 102, 104–5, 113, 119, 135, 143, 152–3, 162, 168–9, 174, 184, 194, 198, 207

bad faith, *see* Sartre, Jean-Paul
Baker, Josephine  167
Baldwin, James  167–8
Barrett, William  161
Barthes, Roland  166, 168
Beat Generation  157–8, 163
beatniks  161

Beauvoir, Simone de  80, 100, 115–28, 134–5, 143, 158–9, 170, 213
  ethics of ambiguity  125ff
  *Untermenschen* (subhumans; *sous-hommes*)  119–20, 124–5
  visit to America  161, 164ff
being at home  76, 86, 140
being-for-itself, *see* Sartre, Jean-Paul
being-in-itself, *see* Sartre, Jean-Paul
Bergmann, Ingmar  188
Berkeley, George  3
Binswanger, Ludwig  175, 182
broken world  140, *see also* Marcel, Gabriel
Brothers Grimm  31
Buber, Martin  123, 153–6, 182, 212
Buddhism  103, 131, 187, 201, *see also* Zen Buddhism

Camus, Albert  6, 14, 21, 73, 83, 98–114, 119–23, 132–3, 135, 158, 161, 167, 170, 176, 185, 202–3, 206
  Don Juan  106–7, 112, 119, 121
  feeling of the absurd  101ff (*see also* "the absurd")
  revolt  110ff
  Sisyphus  110–12
  visit to America  159, 161, 163
categorical imperative, *see* Kant, Immanuel
categories
  in Aristotle  64–5
  in Kant  64–6, 176
choice  8–10, 20, 28–31, 33, 77, 80–1, 86–8, 92, 114, 117, 122, 126, 181, 207
  as the essential human activity  22
  fundamental choice  20, 29, 91
Christ  139, *see also* Jesus
  his life not a tragedy  26
Christianity  3, 7, 16, 18, 25, 39, 44–5, 47, 51, 79, 93, 144–7, 150–2, 191
  Christian existentialism  131–43, 153

crypto-Christianity (Sartre)   91ff, 109
  as paganistic   150
communism   93, 99, 101, 108, 135, 158,
    161–2, 166
concentration camps   177, 203–5
courage   43, 59, 186
  in the face of death   73, 136, 202
  in the face of despair   135–7
  as a quality of a great-souled person   46
  required for freedom   29, 88
*Crime and Punishment*   192–6,
    202, 206–7
*Critique of Pure Reason*   35, 148

*Dasein, see* Heidegger, Martin
*das Man, see* the They
death, *see also* anxiety; courage; Ivan Ilych
  anxiety in the face of   102,
    132, 170, 184
  death of art   25
  death of God   37, 46
  death penalty   100, 195
  fear of death   56, 76, 149, 200
  life after death   91–2, 106
  obscured by "the They"   71ff
  in *The Seventh Seal*   188ff
Declaration of the Rights of Man and
    Citizen   108
depression (economic)   161–2, 179
depression (psychological)   48, 50,
    72, 101, 179
Descartes, René   3, 60–1, 67, 91–2, 96,
    109–10, 148, 161
  *Meditations on First Philosophy*   148
despair   3, 5–7, 33, 135–6, 154, 183,
    197, 199, 200, 206, *see also*
    depression
Dickens, Charles   207
Don Juan, *see* Camus, Albert
Dostoevsky, Fydor   4, 9, 14, 109, 117,
    123, 192, 194, 197, 203–4, 206–7,
    *see also Crime and Punishment*
double-bind   16, 30–1, 181, *see also*
    Laing, R. D.
dread   10, 40, 109, 165, 168
duty   26–7, 30–1, 107, 118, *see also*
    Kierkegaard, Søren, Judge William

either/or   7, 15, 98–9
Enlightenment   2–3, 145–6

Esperanto   174
eternal recurrence, *see* Nietzsche, Friedrich
ethical lifestyle, *see* Kierkegaard, Søren
ethics of ambiguity, *see* Beauvoir, Simone de
Euclidean geometry   48
*existentiales, see* Heidegger, Martin
*Existentialism is a Humanism, see*
    Sartre, Jean-Paul
existentialist ethics, *see* Beauvoir,
    Simone de, ethics of ambiguity

fascism   80, 100, 135
Feuerbach, Ludwig   3
Fichte, J. G.   14
fourfold ("the fourfold"), *see*
    Heidegger, Martin
Frankl, Viktor   6, 177–9
freedom   121ff, 174, 176
  as the ability to say "no"   85,
    87, 110–11
  as absolute (*see* Sartre, Jean-Paul)
  and creativity   109, 120, 168
  as disengaged from rationality   8ff,
    22, 54, 125, 127
  as an expression of
    authenticity   56, 119, 207
  Kant's understanding of   44
  poetry as a vehicle for   75
  as a quasi-divine quality   109
  as a source of anxiety   71, 74,
    77, 109, 184
  as stifled by bad faith (*see* Sartre,
    Jean-Paul)
  as stifled by "the They" (*see*
    "the They")
  as tragic   127
Freud, Sigmund   10, 43, 162, 171

gift giving (Marcel)   141–3
God   1, 18, 30, 60, 92, 101, 110, 118, 120,
    132, 133–4, 142–3, *see also* Hegel,
    G. W. F., unhappy consciousness;
    Kierkegaard, Søren, Abraham;
    Rosenzweig, Franz
  as a contradictory idea   96
  cosmological argument for the
    existence of   138
  death of   37, 46, 109
  embodied in Jesus   131
  Lessing's proposition   15

moral argument for the existence
  of   3, 35–6
personal relationship with   136ff,
  147, 153–6 (*see also* Abraham;
  Kierkegaard, Søren, truth as
  subjectivity)
role in 1600's-1700's philosophy   3
uncertainty of the existence of   188ff
unification with   4–7
Greeks   21, 25, 37, 39, 40–6, 52–3, 94,
  114, 121, 134, 136, 146, 173

Hebrew scriptures   4, 134, 152
hedonism   23, 120, 159, 206
Hegel, G. W. F.   3, 13–17, 20–1, 58,
  62–3, 111, 118, 120, 144–7,
  150–2, 161, 175
  against "abstract thinking"   14, 164, 166
  philosophical system   13, 15–17, 105
  theory of art historical stages   24–6
  master-slave relationship   97
  unhappy consciousness   4–7, 17,
    121, 134, 139
Heidegger, Martin   14, 57–78, 80, 122,
  133–5, 140, 149, 153–4, 157, 164,
  169–70, 172, 174–5, 182, 212
  his association with Nazism   183
  his conception of "Being"   58, 60–1
  *Dasein*   63ff, 71, 76–7, 93, 142
  *das Man* (*see* the They)
  *existentiales*   65, 67, 134, 142
  fourfold ("the fourfold")   74, 76–7
  language as the "house of Being"   95
  *Letter on Humanism*   74, 92ff
  reception in America   160–1
Hemingway, Ernest   199–202
Hinduism   170, *see also* Upanishads
hippies   158
Horkheimer, Max   164
Hume, David   127
Husserl, Edmund   80

individuality   87, 90, 91, 169,
  174, 177, 212
  and authenticity   70ff, 102, 207
  as intensifed by anxiety   71, 74
  as obscured by other people (*see*
    "the They")
  *vs.* sociality   69, 74–5, 122ff
  as subordinated to universal concepts
    and/or energies   27, 30, 39, 56, 137

(*see also* Kierkegaard, Søren, Judge
  William; Nietzsche, Friedrich,
  metaphysical comfort)
International War Crimes
  Tribunal   170
Irigaray, Luce   124
I-Thou relationship, *see* Buber, Martin
Ivan Ilych   72

Jaspers, Karl   104, 161
Jazz   167–9
Jesus   4, 7, 39, 52, 92, 131–2, 139–40,
  142, 150–2, 189, 191
Jews/Judaism   139, 144–52, 156, 167,
  174, *see also* star of redemption
Judge William, *see* Kierkegaard, Søren

Kant, Immanuel   3, 8, 14, 38, 55, 61–2,
  94, 148, 161, 195
  categorical imperative   30, 34
  categories of the understanding
    (*see* categories)
  *Critique of Pure Reason*   35, 148
  moral theory   8, 21, 26–7, 30, 34–7,
    44, 118, 126, 128
  views on space and time   35
Kaufmann, Walter   160
Kennedy, John F.   170
Kennedy, Robert F.   170
Kierkegaard, Søren   3–5, 7–9, 13–33,
  63, 72, 75, 92, 104, 109, 119, 131,
  133–4, 143, 145, 149, 150–5, 170,
  174–7, 185, 191
  Abraham   150–1
  Abraham and Isaac story   21, 30–3
  aesthetic lifestyle   18, 21ff, 119, 186
  criticism of Hegel   13–14
  ethical lifestyle   20–2, 26ff,
    30–2, 119–20
  Judge William   21–2, 26–9, 120
  knight of faith   31
  leap of faith   131, 154
  pseudonyms   20
  reception in America   159ff
  religious lifestyle   20–2, 29ff, 119
  teleological suspension of the
    ethical   32
  truth as subjectivity   16, 62, 155
  view of Socrates   15–16
King, Martin Luther, Jr.   170
Kingsley Hall   180

knightly values, *see* Nietzsche, Friedrich
knight of faith, *see* Kierkegaard, Søren
Kuki, Shūzō   80
Kurusawa, Akira   184

La Belle Époque   199, 201
Laing, R. D.   173, 179-83
leap of faith, *see* Kierkegaard, Søren
Leibniz, G. W.   3, 105, 115
Lessing, G. E.   15
Levinas, Emmanuel   80
Levy, Oscar   160
Lichtenstein, Roy   162
logotherapy   178
the look, *see* Sartre, Jean-Paul
Lost Generation   157, 159, 167, 197
Lowrie, Walter   160
Luther, Martin   137

Marcel, Gabriel   133, 138, 140-3, 153, 212, *see also* gift giving
Maritain, Jacques   133
Marx, Karl   13, 173
marxism   80, 96-7, 109
master and slave morality, *see* Nietzsche, Friedrich
May, Rollo   6, 160, 172
meaninglessness   4, 9, 19, 38-9, 73, 102, 105, 110, 112, 114, 117, 121, 132, 136-7, 142, 155, 176, 178-9, 184-5, 188, 206
meaning of life   132, 157, 177-8
  in a "great task"   19, 45, 48, 51, 179, 186, 206
mechanistic explanation   44
  mechanistic view of nature   44, 49, 50, 55, 95, 175
  mechanistic view of the mind   171-3, 179-80
Mitys (statue of), *see* Aristotle
modernism   96
monasticism   91
morality   28-9, 37, 44-5, 107, 113, 207-8, *see also* Beauvoir, Simone de, ethics of ambiguity; Nietzsche, Friedrich, master and slave morality
  rationality as the basis of   21
  utilitarian   46

nausea, *see* Sartre, Jean-Paul
Nazis   99, 125, 160, 166, 177, 183
New Being (Tillich)   139-40
Newman, Barnett   160, 162
Niebuhr, Reinhold   160
Nietzsche, Friedrich   3-4, 7-8, 14, 19-20, 34-56, 59, 73, 102, 108, 114, 120-2, 126, 132-3, 135, 140, 201-2
  *The Birth of Tragedy*   36ff, 53
  eternal recurrence   41, 47, 49-54, 56, 73, 176
  hierarchy of types of people   119, 135
  knightly values   46
  master morality   46, 52
  metaphysical comfort   40, 136-7
  reception in America   159ff
  slave morality   45, 46
  *Übermensch* (superhuman)   44, 46-8, 51-3, 56, 119, 135
  violent conception of life   175, 214
  will-to-power   39
nihilism   3, 39, 42, 50, 55, 73-4, 120, 121, 124, 176, 188
Nobel Prize   79, 101
nothingness   155, 182
  *Being and Nothingness*   80-1, 88, 91, 109, 115, 117, 122, 149, 153, 213
  consciousness as   84, 90, 141
  death as   54, 73, 87, 101, 110, 189

Old Testament, *see* Hebrew scriptures
optimism   158
original sin   92
otherworldliness   1, 6, 15, 23, 26-7, 36, 41, 44, 47, 55-6, 59, 76, 78, 81, 101, 107, 121, 131-2, 138-40, 151-2, 176, 208, 213-14

paganism   150, 152
phenomenology   63, 65-6, 80-2, 84, 86, 93, 96-7, 141-2
Plato   2, 15-16, 22, 135, 150, 213-14
Platonic ideas   36
Plotinus   99
poetry/poets   7-8, 14, 74-7, 94, 124, 163-4, 171, 202
Pop Art   162
Powell, Adam Clayton, Sr.   165

quietism   133

Raskolnikov   192–4, 196, 202, 206–7
rationality/reason   17, 20–2, 25, 27, 39,
    43, 46, 49, 54–5, 65, 95, 104–5,
    125–7, 133, 145, 148, 151, 163,
    181, 208, *see also* categories; Kant,
    Immanuel, moral theory
  *Critique of Pure Reason* (*see*
    Kant, Immanuel)
  God as a rational being   132
  humans as rational animals   8–9, 118
  as the slave of the passions   127
*The Razor's Edge*   159
religious lifestyle, *see* Kierkegaard, Søren
responsibility   9–10, 29–30, 71, 104, 121,
    163, 174, 182, 184, 192
  absolute   87, 110, 176
  and anxiety   22, 77, 88, 91 (*see also*
    Sartre, Jean-Paul, bad faith)
  as a feature of good leadership   211ff
  as foreign to the aesthete   28
revolt, *see* Camus, Albert
Rilke, Rainer Maria   164
romanticism   201
Rosenzweig, Franz   144–52
Rothko, Mark   160

Sartre, Jean-Paul   14, 17–18, 29, 56,
    74, 79–97, 98–101, 104, 109–10,
    114–15, 117, 119, 122–4, 128,
    132–3, 135, 137, 140–3, 149, 153–4,
    158–9, 174–6, 179, 181–3, 191,
    200–1, 208, 212–13
  absolute freedom   85, 94, 96, 110,
    115, 120, 123, 128, 131, 135–6, 154,
    162
  bad faith   81, 86–8, 95–6, 104, 119,
    124, 167, 179
  *Being and Nothingness* (*see*
    nothingness)
  being-for-itself   81ff, 124, 154, 182
  being-in-itself   81ff, 124, 137,
    141, 154, 182
  as crypto-Christian   91ff
  *Existentialism is a Humanism*   93,
    115, 123, 140 (*see also* Heidegger,
    Martin, *Letter on Humanism*)
  the look   212
  as a modernist thinker   96

nausea (existential)   39, 83, 87–8, 91
*Nausea* (novel)   17, 80, 99, 167, 200
  visit to America   161ff
Schelling, F. W. J.   14, 161
Schiller, Friedrich   173
schizoid mentality   183
Schopenhauer, Arthur   4, 9–10, 37–41,
    51, 55, 62–3, 101, 120, 175
science   35, 43, 59, 62, 95, 100, 161,
    171, 175, 204, *see also* mechanistic
    explanation
Shakespeare, William   103, 200
Shestov, Lev   104
Sisyphus, *see* Camus, Albert
slave morality, *see* Nietzsche, Friedrich
slaves/slavery   32, 45–6, 97, 111, 119, 166
Snyder, Gary   163
social labels   1, 68–71, 88, 90, 119, 124,
    176, 179, 182, *see also* Heidegger,
    Martin, "the They"; Sartre,
    Jean-Paul, bad faith
Socrates   2, 19
  Kierkegaard's view of   15–16
  Nietzsche's view of   39, 42–3, 52
*sous-hommes* (subhumans), *see*
    Beauvoir, Simone de
Spinoza, Baruch   3, 60–1
star of redemption   149
Stein, Gertrude   199
Stoddard, Lothrop   125
subhumans, *see* Beauvoir, Simone de
substance-oriented style of
    thinking   59ff, 82, 155
suffering   33, 72, 103, 113, 132,
    175, 206, 214
  finding a meaning for   3, 37ff, 121,
    149, 176–7, 187, 202
suicide   33, 86, 101, 104–5, 110, 120,
    124, 177, 182
  no one is lonelier in death than   200
  as the one truly serious philosophical
    problem   176
superhuman (*Übermensch*), *see*
    Nietzsche, Friedrich
Suzuki, D. T.   163

technology   59, 76, 95–6, 209–11, 213
Ten Commandments   22, 44, *see also*
    Hebrew scriptures
theism   138, 143, 156

the They (*das Man*)   67–76, 95, 102
Tillich, Paul   132–40, 153, 182,
    *see also* New Being
Tolstoy, Leo   4, 14, 72, 123, *see also*
    Ivan Ilych
tragedy   26, 168, 190, 196
    Aristotle's theory of   196
    Nietzsche's theory of   36–42, 47,
        52–3
truth as subjectivity, *see* Kierkegaard

*Übermensch*, *see* Nietzsche, Friedrich
unhappy consciousness, *see* Hegel
*Untermenschen* (subhumans), *see*
    Beauvoir, Simone de
Upanishads   159
utilitarianism   45–6

van Gogh, Vincent   108
Vietnam War   158, 169–70
Virgin Mary   189, 191

Wagner, Richard   42
Warhol, Andy   163
Watts, Alan   163
Whitehead, Alfred North   105
will to power, *see* Nietzsche, Friedrich
Wittgenstein, Ludwig   144
World War I   98, 155, 144, 157, 159, 197
World War II   80, 88, 92, 99, 157–62,
        166, 169–70, 177, 194, 213
Wright, Richard   123, 160, 165–8

Zamenhof, L. L.   174
Zen Buddhism   163, 170, 211

www.ingramcontent.com/pod-product-compliance
Lightning Source LLC
Chambersburg PA
CBHW050138240426
43673CB00043B/1713